THE BELL OF SHANGRI-LA

香格里拉之鐘

Sam Chau was born in Hong Kong. He came to the UK in 1973, and now lives in Glasgow with his wife and two children. He has long been associated with voluntary community work and in 2004 was awarded an MBE in recognition of his service to the Chinese community and race relations in Glasgow. Sam Chau is now working in a Chinese Elderly Centre and he is also the head teacher of the Glasgow Chinese School, Stow College.

THE BELL OF SHANGRI-LA

An Adventure to the Lost Horizon

SAM CHAU

Order this book online at www.trafford.com/08-1305
or email orders@trafford.com

Most Trafford titles are also available at major online book retailers.

Illustrated: Sam Chau
Edited by: Holly and Callum
Cover design by: Callum Chau
Photography by Sam Chau
Translation work by Tom Mitford and Sam Chau

Note for Librarians: A cataloguing record for this book is available from Library and Archives Canada at www.collectionscanada.ca/amicus/index-e.html

ISBN: 978-1-4251-7477-4

We at Trafford believe that it is the responsibility of us all, as both individuals and corporations, to make choices that are environmentally and socially sound. You, in turn, are supporting this responsible conduct each time you purchase a Trafford book, or make use of our publishing services. To find out how you are helping, please visit www.trafford.com/responsiblepublishing.html

Our mission is to efficiently provide the world's finest, most comprehensive book publishing service, enabling every author to experience success. To find out how to publish your book, your way, and have it available worldwide, visit us online at www.trafford.com/10510

www.trafford.com

North America & international
toll-free: 1 888 232 4444 (USA & Canada)
phone: 250 383 6864 ♦ fax: 250 383 6804
email: info@trafford.com

The United Kingdom & Europe
phone: +44 (0)1865 487 395 ♦ local rate: 0845 230 9601
facsimile: +44 (0)1865 481 507 ♦ email: info.uk@trafford.com

10 9 8 7 6 5 4 3 2 1

ACKNOWLEDGEMENTS

I thank The Glasgow Mitchell Library staff who have been most patient and generous in making available old materials from its collections.

I am grateful to colleagues at the Glasgow Chinese School who have given me advice, especially Violette Zhu for advising how to publish a book; Lin Fan and Di Xing for helping me to obtain reference books in China. Also, I thank my colleagues at Wing Hong Centre, Mei Foong and Alistair Bell for advice.

I must give a special thanks to Tom Mitford who has devoted his time and effort to help with the translation, and also for sending me books while he was working in China.

Finally, I thank my family, my wife Lin for giving me lots of inspiration and endless support; Holly for proof-reading and researching materials; and Callum for proof-reading and design and editing of this book.

CONTENTS

Prologue   1

1   Dreams of North-West Yunnan   5

2   The Last …   39

3   Pursuing …   61

4   Mysterious Journey   88

5   A Place Beyond   121

6   The Lamasery   146

7   The Valley without a Name   176

8   References   220

9   In Search of the Bell   240

Epilogue   259

A NOTE ON THE DEMOGRAPHICS OF THE CHINESE ETHNIC MINORITIES

China officially recognises 56 distinct ethnic groups, the largest of which are Han Chinese, which constituted over 90% of the total population of 1.28 billion in the year 2000. The largest ethnic groups in terms of population include the:

Han:	1159.40 million
Zhuang:	16.17 million
Manchu:	10.68 million
Hui:	9.81 million
Miao:	8.94 million
Uyghur:	8.39 million
Tujia:	8.02 million
Yi:	7.76 million
Mongols:	5.81 million
Tibetans:	5.41 million
Buyei:	2.97 million
Yao:	2.63 million
Koreans:	1.92 million
Others …	

These ethnic minority groups, together with the Han majority, make up the greater Chinese nationality known as Zhonghua Minzu, literally Chinese ethnic group or Chinese nation.

Putonghua, the standard form of Chinese, is the common language of all Han people. In Hong Kong and Taiwan, it is called Mandarin or 'Guoyu', literally meaning 'national language'.

PROLOGUE

"I have often observed that no matter how much I read about a foreign land before visiting it, yet I find by experience that it differs widely from what I expected; it is always fresh, though I had read of it a score of times before."

Frank Kingdon-Ward 1926

There is an old Chinese saying: "To read ten thousand books is not as good as to walk ten thousand miles." Experience can never be fully expressed in writing.

Often, when I was little, I would hear the song on the radio : *"Beautiful Shangri-La, its mighty mountains and rushing torrents, red walls and green tiles, willow trees and flowers in profusion, balmy spring breezes, a wonderful picture, it's my dream home…"* Everyone knew this song in Hong Kong in the 1960s, and sometimes I would hum along as I listened. I just knew then that Shangri-La was a wonderful place.

Just before I left Hong Kong at the beginning of 1973, there was a Hollywood film adapted from a book called *The Lost Horizon*. In the movie, the lovely princess, played by Olivia Hussey, was running away from Shangri-La. When she stumbled in the snowstorm, Michael York went to her rescue and he found that the princess had turned into an old ugly woman. That was all I could recall from the film, and I did not hear anymore about 'Shangri-La' for a long time.

Time flies when you're busy. All of a sudden, I was in my mid-forties. The pace of life was slowing down. I decided to take some time off, as means would allow, to do some of the things I enjoyed, or even to follow a dream.

It was through reading an article about 'Shangri-La' in 1998 that memories came flooding back to me. I began to notice that there were many reports and television documentaries on finding Shangri-La; travel agencies had organised tours of Shangri-La; the bookshops had a wide selection of similar topics. I chose to read the original story *The Lost Horizon*, and became more and more drawn to it. My own journey in search of Shangri-La had begun.

The Lost Horizon was published in 1933. James Hilton, the author, made up the name 'Shangri-La,' about a remote, mysterious place where people led a self-sufficient life without war or crime, and where different religions provoked no conflict. The setting of the story was vague; James Hilton did not disclose where Shangri-la was. People have always wanted to find out where it may be, but no one has been able to find a place that quite matches the description in the book.

'Shangri-La' has since become a popular commercial name, for big hotels and small cafés. A friend of mine opened a restaurant in Glasgow and named it 'Shangri-La'. I asked him the meaning of it. He said, "I'm not sure. It's probably a paradise. It sounds beautiful. It's the name of a five star hotel. It must be good." Nowadays, people normally associate the name with a beautiful and harmonious place.

In September 1997, the Yunnan Provincial Government announced that Shangri-La was located in Diqing on the Tibetan Plateau. There was integration of the Chinese and Tibetan cultures, lamaseries, snow mountains, grassy plains, all consistent with the descriptions in *The Lost Horizon*. After the breaking of the news, people from near and far began rushing to Diqing to see this wonderful place. Articles and books followed. I could no longer resist the lure and planned to see it myself.

Home is in Scotland. Tibet has not been an easy destination. It has involved much planning, with time taken off work, and I have had to travel as inexpensively as possible. On my first visit to north-west Yunnan, on a snowy pass at 4,300 metres, I felt exhilarated, with no ill effects in the rarefied air at high altitude From then on I felt confident in exploring the high plateau.

I have since visited Lhasa three times, and each time, as soon as I stepped out of the plane, I felt miserable, but only for about half a day, and after that I happily acclimatized. The worst occasion was at Daocheng in Sichuan Province, with nausea and headache for two days. I find by experience that a cheerful outlook helps in adapting to high altitudes.

A local friend of mine has just come back from Lhasa, Tibet. He told me that he passed the first three days lying in bed, suffering with high altitude sickness. I asked if he wanted to go again. He said, "Certainly, I have seen the real Tibet. I have found that many people have a misperception about the place. I would love to go again." More than a million visitors travel to Tibet every year. Why do they want to go there despite the long journey and the risk of high altitude?

In these last five years, I have been travelling to the cold wastes of Everest, over long and precipitous roads between Yunnan, Sichuan and Tibet. I have left the big cities for the remote places, enjoying the natural beauty and searching for traces of Shangri-La. I hope that I can share this pleasure with readers of this book.

When a friend asked what my book was about, I said, "I've found Shangri-La." He said, "What is so amazing about that? I've just come back from there!" Another said, "Have you proof?" Others laughed, probably thinking that I was not sober.

When my wife knew that I was writing about Tibet, she was quite worried and said, "It's a sensitive topic. Beware!" Her words are always in my mind. Whenever I am working on my laptop, I keep away from any political elements or in-depth discussion of Tibetan Buddhism. When I told my family that I had discovered the secret of Shangri-La, my daughter asked at once, "How do you know that nobody else knows the secret?" Though I felt a bit upset at this, she was quite right. For over half a century, many people have tried to solve the riddle.

This is a story of my travels and the ideas that have come from the books that I have studied. These are mainly books written by early travellers to Tibet. I have quoted from their writings in several places to provide stronger evidence to support my findings. Over the years, the range of literature on the subject has increased. I hope that this book may provide a new approach, and that it will bring joy and interest to the readers and especially the lovers of Shangri-La.

Sam Chau, September 2008

North-western Yunnan

CHAPTER 1

DREAMS OF NORTH-WEST YUNNAN

One day I told my wife that I was off to Yunnan.

"Good idea!" Lin said, "It's spring all year round in Yunnan. There are many ethnic minorities in Yunnan, it's a splendid place for a holiday. I've a friend in Kunming who can go with you to Dali. It's beautiful there."

"It's not Kunming or Dali that I have in mind. I want to go to the north-west, to Lijiang and Zhongdian. It takes an hour from Kunming by air," I replied.

"It's so remote. Why do you want to go there?"

"I want to find Shangri-La!"

"Shangri-la?" Lin seemed surprised, "Do you need to go that far to look for a hotel?"

"No, it's a place, not a hotel."

"What sort of place is it?"

"It's said to be a heaven on earth, people are content and self-sufficient."

"What is there to see?"

"There are lamaseries, churches, different ethnic minorities with their own cultures; also beautiful mountains and rivers, and there is gold everywhere ..."

"A place like that!" she exclaimed, "And how do you know it's in Yunnan?"

"The Yunnan Government announced that Shangri-La is in Zhongdian County in the north-west, as it's so like the Shangri-la in James Hilton's book. I want to go to see!"

"Who's James Hilton?"

"He wrote 'The Lost Horizon', the book about Shangri-La."

Lin thought for a while. "Aren't you happy at home?" she said, "Off all that way to find your heaven?"

"Everyone has their own dreams," I said, "Especially around my age!"

She paused. "Very well. While you can still cope, go and see more of the world!"

When Holly heard these plans, she said, "You're crazy, Dad! Mum, you can't let him go!"

Callum went further: "Dad, you can't go, you're not fit enough and it's too risky!"

My children did not approve at all, but my wife encouraged me, though she was worried too. I was going to somewhere far from the cities, where there were bandits; it was high too, and perhaps I could not adjust to the thin air with the risk of altitude sickness. Actually, I was worried myself, and thought of not going at all. But whenever I thought of Shangri-La, it was like a call to me drawing me on. I made my decision, put on my rucksack and set off for north-west Yunnan to search for my dream.

LIJIANG

In May 2002, I flew from Glasgow to Hong Kong. Due to the 9/11 terrorist attack, airport security had become much tougher. Heavily armed police were patrolling on high alert. Travellers feeling distressed and worried were waiting for security checks. All schedules had been delayed. I finally got to Hong Kong and travelled to Shenzhen by train, and then by an internal flight to Lijiang in Yunnan Province. After about forty-eight hours, I arrived at a guesthouse in the old quarter of the town. It was already after ten o'clock at night. I was exhausted. After having some biscuits and a cup of green tea, I went straight to bed, and slept till morning.

The 'Big Stone Bridge' guesthouse was named after the bridge beside it. It was transformed from an old village house, and it retained its wooden carving and its original colours. My room had a small balcony with a string of red lanterns and along the eaves hung rows of corncobs. Sitting by the railing, I could look over a stream about three metres wide to a little Naxi restaurant opposite. It was already full of customers, and they all waved when they saw me. There were swallows flying over the water. Coming from a city, I found this place enchanting.

Heshi

At the reception, a short, dark middle-aged man approached me. "Would you like a guide?" he asked, and offered me his business card. The card read, "Heshi, driver guide."

It was my first visit to Lijiang, and I had ten days to travel in north-west Yunnan. I thought that hiring a guide would help me save time, and would be safer for me. We discussed his fee and our route, and reached an agreement.

"Heshi, your name is a rare name. I've heard of the renowned corrupt official, Heshen, in the Qing Dynasty. His wealth could match the Emperor's. Are you related to him?" I asked my guide.

"'He' and 'Mu' are common names among the indigenous people of Lijiang. We have been here for more than two thousand years. I don't know if the 'Heshen' you mentioned was anything to do with us. He certainly didn't leave us anything, or I wouldn't be driving a car for a living." He smiled.

"'Mu' is an unusual name too."

"It was a king's name. Have you noticed that there is no city wall round the old town here? It's because the name 'Mu' means 'wood' (木) in Chinese. With an enclosure round it that would make the Chinese character 'Kun' (困) which means 'besieged' or 'cornered'. Do you understand?"

"And was the King besieged?" I asked.

"How odd, you are the first person that has asked me that, and I don't know!" We both laughed. "Mr Chau, is there anywhere here that you specially want me to show you?"

"Shangri-La! I've come to the north-west of Yunnan to look for Shangri-La."

Heshi looked puzzled at first and then he said, "Okay! No problem!"

"Do you know where it is?" I asked, surprised.

"Yes, certainly. Shangri-La covers the whole of north-west Yunnan which includes Lijiang, Zhongdian and Deqin. Let me show you around. It will be an unforgettable holiday." He sounded confident and business-like.

"Very well, you decide where to go, and I'll follow you!"

"We'll start with Lijiang."

Many people think that Lijiang is Shangri-La. This is because of the Austrian botanist, Joseph Rock, who lived in Lijiang for twenty-seven years. He was associated with many places in Yunnan, Sichuan and Tibet. He contributed several articles to the National Geographic Magazine, and it is said that James Hilton drew on his diaries for his own story. I intended to explore the paths that Rock had visited, and to see if I could find my dream.

Joseph Rock's house

Heshi drove a Volkswagen saloon. I sat behind in comfort. The weather was not very good. It was drizzly, and even in May it felt very cold. Heshi was attentive. He reminded me to dress warmly. It was easy to catch a cold in this weather, he said, and I would be in trouble if I became ill.

After about thirty minutes, we came to Xuesong village, some fifteen kilometres north of Lijiang. This was where Joseph Rock used to live. As soon as I got out of the car, a woman, with a little boy behind her, carrying a baby on her back and with an umbrella in her hand hurried across to sell me some kind of fungus. She was determined and a little pitiful. As my journey was just starting, and it was awkward to carry anything extra, I looked at her and asked her a question to divert her attention. "Where is Jade Dragon Mountain?" I asked. She pointed beyond the village. "Over there!" she said. I looked, but all that I could see was swirling grey clouds and mist. "Thank you!" I said, and walked into the courtyard of Rock's house. She did not follow.

The courtyard was desolate, cold and silent, with no sound except for the rain dripping off the eaves and the click of my camera. I was alone, imagining the busy scenes that took place here in earlier times. An attendant was waiting at the door of the exhibition room. She tore a ticket out from her book and handed it to me. I paid six yuan for my ticket and went in to see the exhibition. The lighting was dim, and there was not very much to see. In the old glass cupboard were instruments that Rock had used to extract teeth, a chisel and a file, and there were some books for sale. On the wall were many black and white photographs that he had taken, many faded and indistinct. They appeared to be photocopies rather than his original work. There were no other visitors. The attendant hovered closely behind me. Heshi told me later that he was making sure that I wasn't using my camera.

Upstairs was Rock's bedroom, where he worked and had meals. There was not much to see here, his wooden furniture, a bed,

chairs, a table, and two oil lamps on the bookcase There was a hanging scroll on the wall, but it looked more recent than Rock's time. In the centre of the room was a large metal basin to provide a fire for warmth. Rays of light came through cracks in the wall. It was a lonely place for a man to spend many years of his life, and all that is left today is an excellent name that the people of Lijiang are happy to talk about.

Joseph Rock and Lijiang

Joseph Rock came from Burma to Yunnan in April 1922. In Dali, he met the Scottish botanist George Forrest who told him that Lijiang was a most beautiful place with a moderate climate and a botanical treasure house. He recommended that Joseph Rock should settle in Nguluko village, now called Xuesong, at the foot of the Lijiang snow range, and it had been his own base in the area. Joseph Rock took Forrest's advice. He arranged for the equipment that he needed, and arrived with a big caravan of porters and horses in Lijiang. He rented a house in Nguluko village where he stayed for twenty-seven years, and the house is now a museum commemorating him.

Joseph Rock was sponsored by the American Department of Agriculture. He had plentiful resources, and promptly hired the Naxi men who had been working for George Forrest. He also took over the Naxi employees of Francis Kingdon-Ward by offering them better pay. To avoid competing with Rock, Kingdon-Ward left for the west of Yunnan, leaving Lijiang to Rock. The first impression that Rock made in Lijiang was a swashbuckling one, as he was always accompanied by armed guards, and crowds of porters and packhorses. He said himself that if someone wanted to set up in a remote place, he should show that he was a person of consequence.

After he had established himself in Nguluko Village, he straightaway began his botanical work, and for many years he was traversing wide areas of south-west China. His forays lasted weeks, and sometimes months, and whenever he returned he had quantities of finds that filled his courtyard. The people of the village would crowd in for the occasion, sitting on the steps and against the pillars, helping to arrange the seeds and animal specimens. For years he kept sending these back to America.

Joseph Rock's other interest was to study the language and culture of the Naxi. He had spent some thirty years in compiling an *'English - Naxi Encyclopedia'*. Unfortunately, he did not live to see this work published. It is of great value as it describes the picture writing, the history and the religion of the Naxi people.

Joseph Rock used to treat illness among the villagers and won their respect. Though he is often said to have been a reclusive man, he tried to identify with the local people. He taught his Naxi cook western dishes, and paid for two of his assistants to visit America. Between 1924 and 1935, the National Geographic Magazine published nine articles of his travels together with many photographs. In this way, he introduced south-west China to readers worldwide. When he wrote about the lovely landscape and the amazing forests and flowers, it would always remind him of the honest Naxi people who had accompanied him for years and became his dear friends.

When I came out of the exhibition, Heshi and the attendant were drinking tea on the steps. He asked me to sit down.

"Well, what did you think of it?" he asked me.

"To tell the truth, the exhibits are all so old," I said.

"Of course they are. It's a museum!"

"No, I mean they could all do with a good clean."

The attendant gave me a look.

"Have you read Joseph Rock's journals?" Heshi asked.

"Yes, I've read them. They are splendid. I'm sure James Hilton would not have missed them."

"That's right. It's commonly believed that Hilton must have

based Shangri-La on his journals." He continued, "Lijiang has Jade Dragon Mountain, it has a lamasery, the mix of Chinese and Tibetan life and culture, these are all features of Shangri-La; and further, a stone tablet was found beside an old well in Xionggu village by Lijiang with an inscription from the Qing Dynasty, namely 'Shanggeli village'. The name is close to 'Shangri-La' in pronunciation."

Heshi was eloquent, but I still was not convinced, though I didn't say so. I totally disagree that there is any link at all between the two names. 'Shangri-La' was named by James Hilton, an English name without any special meaning.

Old Town of Lijiang

Lijiang is renowned for its distinctive culture and history; the old town was the first in China to be listed as the World Cultural Heritage Cities by UNESCO in 1997. It was an important town along the ancient tea and horse trail between Yunnan and Tibet.

With ceaseless supply of water from the snow mountain to the north, the town is nourished by many streams running side by side along the streets, through the courtyards and along the front of the houses. Various sizes of stone and wooden bridges are seen with weeping willows everywhere.

In the centre of the old town is a public square. The streets run out from the centre, lined with shops, handicrafts, snacks, restaurants and coffee shops. It is very busy, with many tourists coming and going. Among them, one could see Naxi women walking slowly along the streets, wearing their 'moon and stars' costume, a symbol of their hard work through day and night, retaining their traditional poise.

A visit to Lijiang must include a Naxi concert. When I arrived for a seven o'clock performance, there were hardly any tickets left. Inside, there was confusion, and it was some time before I could find my seat. There were a lot of westerners in the audience. In came the musicians one by one, elderly folk, and sat down with their instruments, waiting quietly with their eyes closed for the evening to begin.

The master of ceremonies, Mr Xuan, stood at the front of the stage and introduced each item with humour. He told a Lijiang joke: a foreigner who came to Lijiang wondered why the Naxi people walked so slowly. He asked an old lady. She explained. "Since we were born, we're all walking in one direction, to the grave. The faster you go, the closer you get. So why hurry?" The foreigners laughed with gusto. It is said that Mr Xuan tells this joke every night. With his skill in Naxi music, Mr. Xuan has composed 'The Sound of Shangri-La' which draws many people in, including government leaders and many important foreign visitors.

After the concert, around nine o'clock, the streets were still very busy. The cafes and restaurants were full of tourists, with voices raised, music and singing and people stopping to watch, like an open air show.

I left the busy centre square and went to quiet streets. The roads had just been washed, and the moonlight gleamed like mercury on the damp cobbled paving and flashed on the many rapid streams. Here the shops were closing their doors and the lights quickly went out. There were a few old Naxi men squatting at the verge, their eyes on the road, looking up from time to time at passers-by, and talking intermittently in low voices. They smoked tranquilly, and seemed to have noticed that I was observing them. They nodded and I took the chance and sat down. One old man looked at me, nodded and smiled, tweaked his moustache and slowly enquired, "What do you think of Lijiang?"

"I like it. It's full of character, and feels comfortable." I looked at him and tried to start up a conversation. "What's your name?"

"Li."

"I thought people here were all Mu's and He's," I ventured.

"Not at all! There are also many Li's and Chau's in Lijiang!"

"Is that so? How old are you?"

"I'll soon be eighty-five! The old town hasn't changed much, but it's become much busier, there are more and more tourists and a lot of foreigners."

"Did you grow up in the old town?"

"No, I was born in Nguluko village and grew up there."

"Oh, then did you see Dr Rock?" I teased.

"Certainly! Many times my father took me to his house to see them sorting plants and seeds, and later I learnt to do this myself." He paused a little, "He often gave me chocolates which they called '…burys'."

"Cadbury! I guess."

"That's it." He smiled, "The children were all very fond of them. He often used to take our photos. At first, we didn't know what the camera was and we were scared and ran away. Once, when I had toothache, my father took me to see him and he pulled my tooth out with a pair of pliers, and gave me some ointment to relieve the pain. I was fine in a few days."

The old man sounded excited talking about Joseph Rock. Most of the time, he kept his head down as he tried to recall his past. "He did a lot for Lijiang. As well as medical work, he studied the Dongba language and wrote a book about it. He brought us the name 'Shangri-La', and this attracted many people here."

Then he looked at me. "No need to look further, Shangri-La's here in Lijiang." He smiled as he spoke. He seemed to have read my thoughts.

In 1941, a Russian traveller Peter Goullart (1901–1975) came to Lijiang and was much taken with this peaceful place. The scenery, the simple, kind people and their mysterious culture deeply attracted him, and he decided to settle down here. And yet it is a pity that sixty years later Lijiang has become a noisy tourist destination and an investment opportunity.

Goodbye to Lijiang

Early on the morning that I was leaving Lijiang, I went up to Wangulou tower on Lion Mountain to enjoy the view. The Jade Dragon Mountain to the north was still hidden in clouds, and the foreground was filled with rooftops, as though the whole of Lijiang was covered in a mass of heavy tiles. The morning mist mixed with the smoke from cooking stoves gave an ethereal effect. This reminded me of the two photographs, published by Joseph Rock in 1924, which were probably taken from where I stood. He described that the houses were made of sun dried mud-bricks and a wooden superstructure covered with heavy tiles without chimneys. The Naxi kept their grains, cured pork and other supplies in the loft, while the family lived on the ground floor. Eighty years later, the heavy tiled roofs still remain, but most of the houses have been turned into shops and guesthouses, and most of the people in the streets are tourists from all quarters.

One morning, Rock looked out over the Lijiang plain from the north and wrote: "Long before sunrise, I stood on the platform before the temple gate to watch the snow peaks turn from gray to pink. Soon the range was blood-red, while the blue smoke which rose from the houses at our feet lay over the valley like a veil, pierced here and there by the dark tops of the fir trees."

Could the old town of Lijiang be James Hilton's Shangri-La?

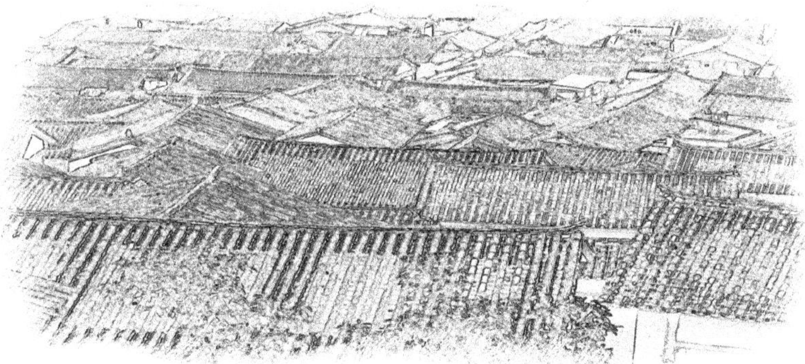

TIGER LEAPING GORGE

We carried on up the road in the footsteps of Joseph Rock, going north to Zhongdian in Diqing Tibetan Autonomous Region. The first stop was the First Bend of the River Yangtze. It was still early, and traders were busy setting up their stalls, hammering and fitting together the metal frames, laying wooden planks on them, and spreading old plastic sheeting over the top. In no time, they were open for business, each selling the same variety of souvenirs. It was a rather messy spot, with plastic bags blown around in the wind and rubbish everywhere.

The Yangtze was a magnificent sight, sweeping down from the north-west and, at Siku, turning abruptly north again in a great bend, flowing broad and smooth. Sightseers were arriving all the time, and after I had taken a photograph, we hurried on our way. We soon came downriver to Tiger Leaping Gorge.

Tiger Leaping Gorge is between Jade Dragon Snow Mountain and Haba Snow Mountain. There are three parts to the gorge, and it is around 17 kilometres long with a drop of some 210 metres. The gorge is about 3,600 metres deep. I had heard that the middle part of the gorge was much wilder than the upper part, and less visited, and I suggested that we drove straight there.

Joseph Rock described the Tiger Leaping Gorge as the finest of all the gorges in Yunnan: "It slashed through the mighty snow range as with a giant's sword. The cliffs rose steeply on both sides. In many places the river is only 20 yards in width and the rapids are compressed into a narrow ribbon of white foam."

Heshi and I followed a local guide down a tiny path into the gorge. The river there was about fifteen metres wide. By the stony shore was a great boulder some five metres high, jutting out over the river, flat on top with room for about ten people to stand. A rope had been fixed for adventurous people to scramble up. The river crashed against the side of the boulder with a tumultuous roar. You could feel the vibrations as you stood on top, and I preferred to lie flat and listen to the guide's stories.

Once, it is said, the two walls of the gorge were only about ten feet apart. A hungry tiger used to leap across to prey on sheep and cattle. Later, an earthquake brought down the cliff face, and the great boulder fell into the river. After that, the tiger used to leap from the boulder to the other side of the river. Hence the names 'Tiger Leaping Gorge' and 'Tiger Leaping Boulder.'

The guide then told me the story of the fairy escaping through the gorge. I began drifting off, rather like the characters in the story, and with the mild breeze and the roar of the river, might easily have fallen fast asleep.

"You stay awake!" the guide laughed, "Otherwise I'll have to go down to the Three Gorges Dam to fish you out!"

I gave her a smile, but she was right. I took the advice and left in a hurry.

That evening, we stayed in a guesthouse under the cliffs, a tranquil place facing Jade Dragon Mountain. The mountain was only the breadth of the river away from us, as though one could almost have reached out and touched it. But the vertical face went up into infinity, and the peaks were beyond.

In February 1996, Lijiang was struck by a powerful earthquake. Many houses in the old town collapsed and there was great damage. The owner of our guesthouse recalled the ground moving and a noise like thunder rumbling through the mountains. He had seen rocks falling off the mountain, ricocheting from one wall of the gorge to the other, pulverising as they impacted and leaving white streaks on the cliff face. These could still be seen. I felt a bit worried when I heard about the earthquake, as there would be no escape if the mountain tumbled over.

But this was too beautiful a place for negative feelings. There was a delicious dinner of stewed chicken with mushrooms and rice. Heshi advised me to go to bed early, and prepare for a tough hike the next day. The sound of wind and rain in the night blended with the noise of the river. I slept well, and was up early. The air was damp, with Jade Dragon Mountain above and the river below hidden in streaming mist. I was delighted with such a tranquil environment. It was so poetically picturesque, and it impelled me to compose a poem:

Clouds wreathe the great cliffs a hundred chiang high,*
The Jade Dragon spits over the precipice one thousand feet down.
Violent rains at midnight form flying torrents,
Morning's floods resound like musical strings.

** 1 chiang=10 foot*

In the morning, Heshi had arranged a long hike. The local guide took me along under Haba Snow Mountain. We climbed some 500 metres up and then followed a narrow path, twice crossing small rivers by waterfalls. The rocks were wet and quite dangerous. There were several places on the edge of cliffs where I felt weak at the knees, one slip and I would have fallen into the abyss. Joseph Rock was here in 1925. He described the trail as exceedingly dangerous, as rock slides occurred continuously in this place.

There was no habitation in sight. After perhaps two hours on the path, we met a western couple. We exchanged a few words and discovered that they were from Britain too. They were going down to the lower part of Tiger Leaping Gorge, and were planning to cross the Jinsha Jiang (Gold Sand River) to the town of Daju and then make their way back to Lijiang. My guide was concerned, and he asked me to tell them to be careful, as some years before brigands had killed a foreigner walking that stretch of the path alone. The men had been arrested. The couple thanked us. There was not time for introductions; we just said 'Good luck!' and went on our ways. I stopped for a while and saw them disappearing along the trail.

Another thirty minutes and we arrived at Pentiwan village. Every household was growing potatoes in its fields, and this was the staple diet of the villagers. There were apple trees laden with fruit, and many peppers and walnut trees, the villagers' livelihood. It was an animated scene, this village among the mountains, with its bamboo groves and the hubbub of its dogs and poultry.

We rested at the Halfway Guesthouse. The owner was very friendly, and gave us free cups of tea. He told us about Pentiwan, his village. All the visitors were backpackers, and more and more were coming. There were some thirty households and only two places for tourists to stay. He said that he was hoping to attract more guests by installing a karaoke machine. I felt a great shock when I heard this. I was worrying that this tranquil and lovely place would be ruined by a set of modern musical equipment. The owner here did not appreciate that backpackers who made it to Pentiwan would want to experience its calm and simplicity. I did not wish to be dismissive and made no comment on these plans but very much hoped that nothing would come of them.

Before leaving, I visited the guesthouse toilet. It was a remarkable one, the best in days: fresh and clean, it enjoyed natural air conditioning, with instant provision of fertilizer to the fields, apple branches for decoration and a fine view over to Jade Dragon Mountain.

It was drizzly and the going was difficult on a wet, slippery path. My guide moved fast and effortlessly in smooth soled plastic shoes. I was well kitted out, smart in my anorak and hiking boots, but however hard I tried to keep up, she was always ahead, often stopping far in front to wait for me. I was rather embarrassed.

Altogether, we had walked about twenty kilometres along the mountain path, five hours or more including rests. For the first time, I felt stiff and worn out. Heshi was waiting by the car. I was too tired to talk and just climbed straight into the car and lay down to rest. After a short while, he started up the car, and we were on our way to Zhongdian.

ZHONGDIAN

When we passed the township of Tiger Leaping Gorge, we were now in Diqing Tibetan Autonomous Region. I was intent on seeing this remote and beautiful place that went by the name of 'Shangri-La'. We were heading north, and the country was becoming higher and road narrower as it ran up a gorge, among forests of conifers. The slopes were brilliant with purple rhododendrons. In several places there had been excessive felling and tree trunks were strewn about, some of the ridges were denuded and frequently there were scars left by land slips.

After crossing a pass, the road began to level out with extensive views, and the landscape was more Tibetan in character. Here and there were the square flat-roofed Tibetan houses, the colour of the earth. They were all flying bright colourful flags from the roof tops, fluttering at the end of long poles. Below a bright sky with white clouds, everywhere was brilliant with flowers. In the damper ground small red and yellow flowers bloomed, and the meadows were richer still, with sheets of crimson and a profusion of other colours. Tibetans wearing purple scarves were working in the fields. Sometimes there were snatches of high pitched song, the words coming across clearly to me though I could not understand them. Barley was drying in the sun on tall racks. Cattle and sheep were grazing. Sometimes a solitary monk in red robes walked along the road. It was an enchanting place.

We were now making good progress on a broad surfaced road. Many people waved as we passed, some sitting at the side of the road dangerously exposed. When I looked back, they were still waving.

"Heshi, are they waving for help?" I asked.

"They'd like a lift."

We had driven for four hours, and arrived in Zhongdian at dusk. In 1930, a government official, Liu Manqing had travelled from Lijiang to Zhongdian taking many days. Her book *Kangzang Yaozheng* includes a meticulous account of Zhongdian at that time: As they travelled on west from Lijiang, the road was made up of rocky steps ascending steeply like a ladder to heaven. There were old juniper and coniferous trees. The mountains were shrouded in mist and cloud all day long. They seemed to be heading towards a hidden world. Then suddenly they entered a vast grassland, stretching to the horizon, filled with yellow flowers; herds of cattle and sheep were grazing and there were many tents. Further on, they found themselves in a place with neat rows of houses with their cooking smoke spiralling into the air. This was actually the county town of Zhongdian, near the border of Yunnan and Tibet.

At that time, there were no wells in the town, and only the one spring. At dawn and in the evening, the women all congregated there for water, singing sweetly. Soon a thudding noise started up in every home of milk being pounded in wooden pails. That was how the Kham people extracted the butter oil and the curd and yogurt were made, and these were their staple food. After this task was done, cooking smoke rose on all sides into the morning sunshine.

Liu described the houses in Zhongdian as built of earth with wooden roofs, the roofs weighted down with large round stones to hold them firm in strong winds. Each roof had a pole flying colourful flags, fluttering all over the town. The Kham people were devout followers of Tibetan Buddhism. Sanskrit inscriptions on the flags spread its teaching in the wind.

Zhongdian is called 'Jiantang' in Tibetan, meaning 'great plain'. At a height of 3,200 metres, the air was thin, and although it was June, I felt the cold. Zhongdian is an important town on the ancient Tea and Horse Trail. Every year, on the fifth day of the fifth lunar month, there is a big horse racing festival with the whole town celebrating, and with dancing and singing. Today, Zhongdian is already being called 'Shangri-La' and the airport opened in 2006 is named 'Diqing Shangri-La Airport.'

"Is Zhongdian 'Shangri-La', then?" I asked Heshi.

"Of course, Zhongdian is the heart of Shangri-La, and Shangri-La covers all the Diqing Tibetan Autonomous District. We've got the Songzanlin Monastery, we've got Meili Snow Mountain, and the Chinese-Tibetan ….."

"Where's the monastery?" I cut in deliberately as his assertions were always the same.

"I'll take you there right now," he said at once.

Songzanlin Monastery

Songzanlin Monastery is outside Zhongdian to the north. It is the largest Tibetan Buddhist temple in Yunnan. From far off it stands out brilliant and imposing against the mountain, with its ochre perimeter wall, the great temple in the centre, and its golden roofs. It is known as the 'Little Potala', and was completed in 1681 in the reign of the Qing Dynasty Emperor Kangxi. The Chinese name is 'Guihua' Monastery. It is said to have more than seven hundred monks.

At the main gates, there was a stream of tourist traffic filling the air with dust and sand. Many stalls were selling all kinds of Tibetan herbal medicines and handicrafts. Inside the gates, a long flight of steps led up to the temples and the monks' quarters. At the heart of the complex was the principal temple. Inside, it was the rows of huge square columns supporting the roof that drew my attention, covered in bright paintings. The interior was dim, solemn and impressive with its sumptuous frescoes and Buddhist statues in their different poses, with the constant low murmur of the chanting of scriptures and the suffocating smell of butter oil.

Could this be the monastery that James Hilton describes in 'Shangri-La'? It seemed unlikely to me as I could not recall any mention of Songzanlin Monastery in Joseph Rock's writing. Where else could James Hilton have learned about it if it wasn't from Rock?

A Little Lama

Nearby, I saw a little boy of about twelve or thirteen sitting on a step. He wore a red gown, and had a prayer wheel in his hand. His mouth was moving as though reciting scriptures. I walked over slowly and sat down beside him. There were many visitors, and he thought nothing of it. A smile was the best way to introduce myself. I asked what he was doing.

"I am praying for the world and for peace," he replied.

So I asked him, "Do you know how big the world is?"

He paused, and then he drew a great circle in the air with his arms, as far as he could reach, and, when that was done, said, "It's very, very big! Where are you from?" He went on, "Are you from the South?"

Perhaps it was my accent! I shook my head. "No, I'm from a place far away in the west. I flew here, by plane." I didn't think he would know where Scotland was.

"A country in the west, and you came in a plane!" He pointed at the sky, and he made a flying gesture with his hand. He hesitated a while, and suddenly asked, "Are there many zoos in countries in the west?"

"Quite a lot."

"Do they keep dragons in the zoos?"

"I've not seen any yet," I didn't want to say 'no' outright. "Who told you about that?"

"My old master told me," he said firmly. "Do you know that thunder is caused by the wind being churned up by the scales of flying dragons? He also told me that in the west there are people with dogs' and cows' heads. Have you seen them?"

"No, I've not seen them either." I saw the little boy's certainty, and did not want to patronize him. From the gesture he had just made, he seemed to realize that the world was round.

"Did the old master tell you about Shangri-La?" I asked lightly.

"Shang … what?" he said doubtfully.

"Oh, never mind!"

As we chatted, the innocence of his mental world was apparent. Yet the lamas are gradually becoming sophisticated. Some of the larger monasteries now have modern communications, and computers, mobile phones and four-wheel drive vehicles are all familiar to these lamas, some of whom speak good English.

As the sun set, the golden temple roofs were more dazzling than ever. We stayed in a Tibetan hostel for backpackers. All the furnishings were in traditional Tibetan style. It was very inexpensive, at just twenty yuan (£1.50) for a bed. The washing facilities were good. There were a lot of westerners staying there.

A young French tourist asked me if this was Shangri-La. I did not give a direct answer: "It's beautiful here, and the folk traditions are rich. But you will enjoy it best if you haven't come here to find Shangri-La."

"Okay, I'm with you!" he replied.

NORTH TO DEQIN

Since Zhongdian was confirmed as Shangri-La, there has been a continuous programme of bridge building and road improvement to accommodate the growth of tourism. It is about two hundred kilometres from Zhongdian to Deqin, and there were road works for most of the way. We often heard explosions. Vehicles were moving forward over miles of rough unfinished road, often held up behind slow trucks working on the site. The sun was hot and the air full of dust. It was an unpleasant ride in a car without air conditioning. The road ran along the mountain sides, with great precipices. Everything depended on the driver's skill. One little mistake could send us thousands of feet down into the chasm.

After a couple of hours, we reached Benzilan. One long street ran through the town, carrying all the traffic. Along both sides were dozens of little restaurants, especially Sichuan cuisine, it seemed. Most tourists have a halfway stop here. Not far beyond, we reached Baimang Snow Mountain pass, and stopped to stretch our legs. "Have you brought an oxygen bottle?" Heshi asked.

"No, I haven't."

"We're now at 4,300 metres and must watch out for altitude sickness. On the high plateau, the sun is very hot, but out of the sun you'll at once feel the cold. Don't catch a cold, wear plenty of clothes, take your time and don't rush."

This made me nervous. I slowly opened the door. Pure, cool air filled my lungs. Slowly, I walked up the slope, and all felt well. Then I tried going faster, and immediately felt the effects: my heart was pounding and I panted for breath. Heshi motioned to me to slow down, take deep breaths, and regulate my breathing gradually, and then I would be fine.

"Have I got altitude sickness?"

"No! This reaction is quite normal. Mountain sickness is unpleasant. You would feel nausea, dizziness and severe headache. Bad cases need to be hospitalized. Your health seems excellent!" he said. This praise made me feel grand.

Worshipping the Mountain God

It was the first time that I had seen a Mani cairn, a great pile of stones two metres high. In the centre was a wooden post, with myriad flags of every colour tied on at every angle, fluttering in the strong wind and covered in Sanskrit and Tibetan texts, a wonderful sight for any photographer.

Suddenly, a four-wheel drive vehicle braked hard, three Tibetans leapt out and came over to the cairn. They put their hands together above their heads and shouted "Lha sol-lo! Lha gyal lo! Kei-Kei-ho, hooo!" Then they picked up a stone each to place on the cairn, jumped back into the car and tore off.

Heshi told me that it was the Tibetan custom, when they passed a cairn on the top of a mountain pass, for everyone to get out of the car and chant, "The gods are victorious, may they grant us peace!" Heshi and I did this too. We put our hands together and shouted "Lha sol-lo! Lha gyal lo! Kei-Kei-ho, hooo!"

It was another twenty kilometres to Deqin. The petrol pipe under the car had shaken loose, and petrol had been leaking for some time. Luckily, Heshi noticed, and surprisingly he managed to fix it with a pair of pliers, and we pressed on. We finally made it to Deqin at dusk.

Stories of Deqin

The old name for Deqin was Atunzi. It is a county town with one main street through which all the Yunnan Tibet traffic passes. The houses are built against the sides of a steep valley, many of them newly built and single storey. It is a cold place, with deep snow in winter and spring, and it was known as 'Snow Mountain Market'. It is often misty here, even inside the houses. It was also called the 'House of the Natural Fragrance'.

According to Liu Manqing, pilgrims coming from Eastern Tibet and as far away as Lhasa to the sacred mountains must all pass through Atunzi. They travelled over great distances in large groups which included children and elders, bustling along in unending procession. The Atunzi people called them 'Arjopas'.

At that time, most of the Atunzi women did not work in the fields. They traded instead with the Arjopas who usually stayed out on the grassy plains. The women went to the shops and used their ornaments as security for bolts of cloth, needles and thread, copper pots and other goods, exchanging these with the Arjopas for such things as musk, medicines, skins and wool. There was a curious custom that women would observe the skies to predict the numbers of Arjopas coming, like farmers predicting the weather for harvest.

Today, the Arjopas are gone, and in their place are pilgrims and tourists heading for Mt Meili. The celebrated Kaakerpu, 'the sunlit golden mountain' has become the lure of the frenzied photographer and the tourist's dream.

Sunlit Golden Mountain

I was up at five o'clock. It was completely dark, but the sky was clear. Heshi, well-informed as ever, had recommended an early start as the opportunity was too good to miss. We packed and had a little breakfast and soon were away, off to Feilai Temple about fifteen kilometres outside the town.

We were climbing all the time on a winding road, over several passes. All at once, a dazzling peak appeared and vanished beyond the forests. I was transfixed. I had never seen a mountain so beautiful. Though it was behind the woods, I could still feel the grandeur of it, a golden mountain suspended mid-air. Suddenly, there it was to the left, suddenly ahead, then it was gone again. I held my breath, and kept watching for it.

"That's Mt Miyetzimu on the right." Heshi was excited too. "We're almost there."

The golden light in the darkness was compelling. I gazed ahead. "Hurry! Hurry!" I said.

When we reached the slope in front of Feilai Temple, I already had the car door open before we had stopped. My camera and video were all ready to catch this view, unlike anything I had ever seen. Heshi understood. He quietly reached for my jacket in the boot and put it over my shoulders. "Don't catch cold!" he said. I was grateful for his consideration.

The sun had not yet risen, but daylight was slowly spreading from the east, turning the fringes of the grey clouds to gold. The sunlight first struck the summit of Mt Kaakerpu and gradually came down the slopes, till the whole mountain shone out golden against the dark blue sky. Confronted by this, I experienced feelings that I could not express in words. I gazed at the dazzling snow range, the highest summit, 6740 metres high, and the glacier streaming down to the Mekong River. The weather was always changing. Mists and cloud appeared and all was obscured, then they parted and the peaks stood out sublime.

Very quickly, the sun broke through the clouds, and everywhere was bathed in light. All the golden peaks turned to silver, and the view changed. The glistening ranges stretched to the horizon in pristine majesty, the loveliest mountains that I had ever seen. It was a unique opportunity and I scampered about the slopes with my camera and video.

Circumambulating the mountain

As day arrived, more and more tourists were coming to see the Meili snow range. By now, smoke from the nearby incense stoves was rising, filling the air with the smell of pine resin. Mt Meili is one of the most sacred mountains for the Tibetan people, and they all pay homage to it as they pass. A pilgrimage to it secures outstanding merit in the eyes of the Tibetans, and if one circumambulates the mountain three times there is complete expiation for evil deeds, and if a hundred times full enlightenment. Each year, many pilgrims come from far when the busy harvest time in autumn is over, whole families of adults and children, carrying what they need, making for the sacred mountain.

"I would like to see what it's like, going round the mountain," I said to Heshi.

"Fine, then I'll be back in a fortnight to collect you!" He laughed.

"Two weeks?"

"Yes! And it's dangerous too."

Among the circumambulators, I saw a ragged elderly couple. They were wrapped with thick, heavy clothing and not carrying

Mt Meili (Kaakerpu range)

much. They were walking far behind the others, with sticks for support. I went over and gave them something to eat. They nodded, and went limping on their way.

"How can they manage a two week walk round the mountain?"

Heshi hesitated. "Indeed; their plan is that this walk should be their last."

A constant stream of pilgrims trod the narrow trail with the sacred prayer 'Om Mani Padme Hum' ever on their lips as they whirled prayer wheels in their hands. Heshi told me that many would commit suicide by throwing themselves down the Dokerla, for to die on that sacred spot means emancipation and deliverance from rebirth. Some would prostrate themselves, measuring with their own bodies the whole distance up and down the rocky path over the pass.

Often, the pilgrims suffer terrible hardships. Running out of food, they may resort to theft or murder other pilgrims. Alexandra David-Neel gave an account of a party of pilgrims who had been robbed of all their belongings by some of their travelling companions. She saw some women, who had been wounded, unable to continue their journey, having to shelter themselves in a mountain cave, waiting to die.

I watched the groups of pilgrims, like a great dragon stretching into the distance along the foot of the mountain. All the time others were joining them. Sometimes the peaks were clear, sometimes in clouds. I listened to the colourful prayer flags fluttering in the sharp wind. It was a moving sight. I sat on the bank, gazing at the ever changing views of Mt Meili, questions building up inside me.

Tibetans spend their whole lives in pilgrimage, despite the arduousness and the risk of death. Are they superstitious or devout? Are they stubborn or determined?

Why is mankind on this earth? Mankind is constantly generating pollution and destroying nature, to an extent that is almost beyond solution; people take advantage of each other and everyone out for himself; countries threaten other countries with their endlessly upgraded weapons so that an error could start a great war, which once begun could not be stopped, with life reduced to ashes. Do we have responsibilities? Have we obligations to our future generations?

Life is short and soon passes: what is its significance? My brain went blank. Then I remembered the words of John Lennon's song: "Imagine there's no heaven, … no hell, … no religion, … no greed, … no hunger, … all the people living life in peace."

"Mr Chau! Time's getting on!"

"Oh!" I was miles away.

"You've been lucky, you know. There are people who come here many times and have never yet managed to see this mountain," Heshi said.

"Maybe I won't see it again!" I said.

"Off we go!" Heshi had started the engine and slowly reversed his car near to where I sat, and was wanting to be on the way.

I got in with reluctance, and we hurtled off. As we sped along, the view outside seemed a blur. I was thinking of the golden mountain, the pilgrims in long file, and these images were for long to remain in my heart.

Lige Village

LAKE LUGU

After a night in Zhongdian, we returned to Lijiang. Then we continued towards the north-east making for Lake Lugu and what is said to be the last surviving matrilinear society in China – Ladies Kingdom.

From Lijiang to Lake Lugu was about seven hours, through Ninglang County, over a high pass, and into the Lake Lugu region. Here were great shimmering forests of pine trees, and beyond them the famous high plateau lake, Lugu. The setting, the clear water hemmed in by green mountains, was exhilarating.

Lake Lugu was not any longer a mysterious place. With road improvements and the development of tourism, travel companies were all sending groups here. It had become a popular destination. Ladies Kingdom, Mosuo girls, the walking marriage and pig trough boats were what they were now coming to see. Luoshui Village at the lake side is a popular tourist spot, with many attractive new Mosuo houses built in wood. The pig trough boats were lined up along the shore, and Mosuo girls in colourful traditional costume were waiting to take visitors out on the lake. Many houses had been converted into shops, guesthouses, internet cafes and karaoke bars. Heshi probably understood how I felt. We soon left after I had taken some photographs.

Drashi's home

About ten kilometres along the shore, we came to a quiet village called Lige by the lake and at the foot of Lion Mountain. The village was close to the water and did not seem to have much protection from it. I supposed a gale would blow water into the houses. Heshi took me to a Mosuo friend's home. Drashi came out smiling to welcome us.

This was a typical Mosuo house. The front door was open all day long. Inside on the left was a stable, and beside the door were piles of straw and firewood. Dogs, hens and pigs wandered round the yard looking for food. At the back was a large field full of potatoes and vegetables. There was an open air lavatory providing fertilizer, but it was not sanitary.

Drashi took me upstairs to unpack. Wherever I walked, the floorboards creaked and I could feel the room shake. Partitions were very thin, and every movement next door could be heard. There was a small wooden frame window in my room looking out onto the still lake, a splendid sight reaching out to the horizon where the sky and the water met.

After I had rested a little, Drashi invited me in to his grandmother's room. I stooped and lifted my foot high, under the low lintel and over the high doorstep. The room was only lit by one light bulb. It was dim and had a strong smell of damp. The old lady had already passed away, but the family still called it her room. In the centre was a bright fire burning, and we all sat round it. I don't know where all the flies came from, buzzing everywhere in the half dark. They were dreadful, and I kept swatting them off. Drashi didn't seem to bother at all. His wife gave us green tea and a bowl of melon seeds. We drank the tea, cracked open the seeds, swatted the flies, and listened to Drashi recounting the stories of Lake Lugu, as though bringing out family treasures to show me.

Ladies Kingdom

"Many people, especially men, think 'Ladies Kingdom' sounds a bit strange, and 'walking marriage' over the top. But outsiders misunderstand the Mosuo," Drashi told me earnestly. "The Mosuo families honour the women, and we have a unique walking marriage tradition. Men do not take a bride, women do not marry a husband, they do not live together, there is no marriage bond, no formalities or ceremony. When a couple have a child, the responsibility for its rearing belongs to the mother and to her brother. Hence the name, 'Ladies Kingdom'. "

"That means, then, that the Mosuo men have no status," I said.

"No, it's not like that. The men have their responsibilities too. Much of the heavy work is done by them," He said.

"How do the children relate to their fathers?"

"Many people suppose that Mosuo children do not know who their fathers are, but that is a misunderstanding. It's not so complicated. Usually they know. They are brought up by their mothers and uncles, and relations with their fathers are certainly not very close. When children reach thirteen, there is a coming of age ceremony. The fathers come with presents and congratulate their children on becoming adults, with adult freedom and responsibilities. That doesn't mean, though, that they are then ready for the walking marriage. No, no!" he said firmly, "a girl is only ready for walking marriage after she has matured socially.

"A mature girl will have her own 'flower room'. Boys are not so privileged. They must find walking marriage companions, otherwise they have no definite place to sleep. Walking marriage means that the boy goes to the girl's house in the evening to spend the night, but he must leave before the sun is up.

"Please do understand that walking marriage is not promiscuity," Drashi stressed. "Normally, lovers have only one partner. Having several or frequently changing partners will draw contempt and ridicule."

From what Drashi described, the Mosuo walking marriage seemed very reasonable. There was no compulsion, and it only operated when there was a mutual wish for it. If they did not get on, then they separated, without the constraint of a marriage contract. This was much like conventional marriage, divorce and remarriage, apart from the wedding ceremony and marriage certificate.

We were cracking open melon seeds, drinking tea and talking. I kept yawning from time to time. Drashi saw this and suggested that we continued our conversation next day.

All the lights were extinguished, and it was completely still. Outside the window, the moon shone high above the lake. A slight breeze disturbed its bright surface. I listened contentedly to the lapping of the waves, and went to sleep.

At about six o'clock, cockerels began crowing, a noise that I had not heard for a long time, first in the distance and then nearer and nearer. Lige Village was waking up. Sitting by the window, I saw Drashi standing beside the lake with a blanket over his shoulders talking. Women were taking pails to the lake for water, and villagers were washing their faces by the lake. The village was slowly becoming busy again. Young men and women were off to work. I could not see any trace of a walking marriage. Children in small groups were going to school, firing at birds in the trees with catapults. I had heard that they had a two hour walk to reach their school.

There were three pig trough boats out on the lake. Fishermen were standing precariously in these long thin boats casting nets. The boats are dugout canoes with a rim attached. They are the only boats on the lake. It is said that once there was a great flood, the village was submerged and many of the villagers drowned. One woman was fortunately feeding pigs. Seeing the floods approaching, she jumped into the pigs' trough and floated to safety. Ever since, the Mosuo have used these boats for fishing and gathering water plants, and today they are very popular with visitors who go for rides.

After breakfast, Drashi arranged for a boatman to row me across to the island in the middle of the lake. I was told that Joseph Rock had been stranded in the island for two months because riots broke out in Yongning region. I saw the little house where he had lived and a Tibetan temple. It took us an hour or more to tour round the island, then we hurried back to Lige village.

Yongning Hot Spring

After lunch, Drashi suggested a visit to Yongning hot springs which were about fifteen kilometres away. I was glad to have a chance for my first bath in five days. Drashi's family all came along.

Yongning hot springs used to be open to the sky and bathing was mixed. With better roads, and more and more tourists now coming, the local people decided to build a modern bathhouse with separate pools for men and for women.

I was looking forward to a good soak, but when I saw the bath, I changed my mind. Most people at the bath were local, and they seemed to treat the pool like a bath at home. It was full of soap suds and looked rather messy. The piping was rusty and leaking, and green moss was growing along the edge of the pool. I saw that many other tourists went in and came out as I had done, returning disappointed to their coach. Nevertheless, Drashi's family all enjoyed themselves so much.

Yongning mountain district is home to minority peoples. On the road, we passed a wedding procession of Yi people. They were all dressed in traditional costume, and the horses and carriages were decorated in bright colours. We also saw a mule train of about thirty animals, their bells ringing all the way, carrying goods in large and small bundles, and seven or eight drivers, off to a mountain village thirty kilometres away.

That evening, Drashi took me to a bonfire party. Villagers were wearing splendid costumes, singing and dancing around the fire. The bonfire parties are a traditional way in which the young Mosuo find partners. If a girl is fond of a man, she prods the palm of his hand as a sign that he can come at night to her flower room for a walking marriage. The bonfire parties are now an important source of income, and something that tourists at Lake Lugu are keen to see.

The Man of Mother Lake

Tourism has brought prosperity to Lake Lugu, but it has taken away some of the quietness and simplicity of the Mosuo way of life. The Mosuo are gradually adopting conventional marriage. Except in remote mountain villages, walking marriage is becoming just a memory. The young people are being slowly urbanized, and the transmission of Mosuo culture is problematic.

"Have you heard of a Mosuo girl called Yang Erche Namu?" Drashi asked me.

"Yes, indeed. She's very well known. She left Lake Lugu many years ago and went to the States. Didn't she write a book?"

"Yes, 'Leaving Mother Lake'!" Drashi exclaimed.

"That was it! She was probably the first person to introduce the mysterious Ladies Kingdom to the West, and it became famous. I saw her interviewed recently on a television programme, and she was stylish, with high heels, a short dress, talking and laughing and not at all like a Mosuo."

"The world is changing, and people are changing with it," Drashi said with a laugh. He seemed animated when we spoke about Yang Erche Namu. He was born at Lake Lugu and grew up in the Zhamei Temple in Yongning. He spoke Tibetan, and couldn't read Chinese though he spoke it well.

"Have you ever left Lake Lugu?" I asked him.

"Yes, I have! Some years ago, I lived for a while in Shanghai and Shenzhen, but I couldn't adapt to the pace of life there." He laughed. "If I had a ghost writer, I would publish a book called 'Returning to Mother Lake'."

"I'm no good at writing, otherwise..." and we both laughed.

Drashi was the first person in Lige village to have a conventional marriage, and he lives with his wife and his little boy and girl. He extended his house to include accommodation for visitors. When I asked about his son's future, he said at once that it was for his children to make their own decisions; he would not impose his wishes.

"Even though we have departed from the walking marriage, we have still retained most of the Mosuo traditional culture." Drashi was hoping to build a temple in Lige village to house materials relating to his people's history and way of life, so that the villagers would honour Tibetan Buddhism and so that later generations could know these unique traditions and their memory would not be lost.

After talking together for several days, I now had a better understanding of Ladies Kingdom. On the last day I asked Drashi what I owed him for meals and accommodation.

"Forget it!" he said. The friendliness and kindness of his answer took me aback. In all the places I have been to I had never been treated like this. Most of the time, people seem grasping, hoping to clean all the money out of your pocket. In the end I did give him something I thought reasonable, and through him made a donation to the local school. He gladly accepted.

As we said goodbye, I said jokingly, "This seems to be the 'Shangri-La' in the novel."

Drashi laughed. "Shangri-La isn't here and it isn't there; it's in your heart!" Many people must have asked him about Shangri-La. He gave the answer without a thought. But my curiosity was not satisfied, and I just smiled.

With this ended the first phase of my search for Shangri-La.

Mosuo

CHAPTER 2

THE LAST …

Travel brings joy and happiness. It broadens our horizons with new perspectives and allows us to challenge and to appreciate our abilities and courage. Many people think that it is the experience that counts rather than the destination, but I feel that both are important. Life itself is like this! If one doesn't achieve one's goals, one feels regret.

I do not know when I became fond of travel. Living in the West for many years, I am so drawn to the beautiful landscapes of China, and I try to find time to visit there each year. In the past ten years, I have been travelling from the great cities to quiet country towns, from poor villages to desolate mountain quarters. Sometimes I have felt lonely and at other times have been in the company of good friends. After a long and tiring journey, I return once again to my home in Scotland and resume my routine life. Very soon though, I begin to dream of my next trip.

One day, Lin printed out an article from the Internet. "Shangri-La has been found. You can stop dreaming now."

"Where?"

"Bingzhongluo, on the River Salween in Yunnan Province."

"Bing…zhongluo? What makes you think that?" I asked.

"It says that there is a church, gold in the river, Chinese and Tibetan culture. It all fits Shangri-La."

"That's how they always talk, but it's not as simple as that!" I said. "This is the first time that I've heard of Bingzhongluo, and I doubt James Hilton had heard of this place either." When I said this, Lin seemed to lose her interest and went off.

"You know!" I raised my voice a little, "India, Nepal, Kashmir have all claimed that Shangri-La has been found in their countries. They have one purpose in common. They all want to promote their tourist industry."

"Fine! Dream on!" she exclaimed, and continued with her own work.

A few days later, I was sitting on the sofa reading a book on Tibetan history when Lin handed me another printout.

"This time it's for real," she said, "and it's the last time too, it's 'the Last Shangri-La'."

I looked at her suspiciously; was she beginning to feel the charisma of Shangri-La? The article was headed, 'The Last Shangri-La – Daocheng Yading'.

"What?" I replied in some surprise, "so there's a first and a last Shangri-La, is there?"

I reached for the article. It was simply promoting the scenery of Daocheng Yading, with its snow mountains, Tibetan temple, and the gold in the river, all features of Shangri-La. I find it interesting that Joseph Rock had published an account of travels to Konkaling with a vivid description of the three sacred mountains there, and it was this that had attracted people's attention.

"Where is Daocheng Yading?" she asked.

"In the southwest of Sichuan Province. It's a long way from Chengdu, two days by road, and there is no direct transport."

"Two days! Is it inhabited?"

"It's a Tibetan area."

"Are there brigands?" she asked.

"Brigands?"

"I mean the robbers in the mountains!" Anxiety was setting in.

"Oh! It's hard to say," I replied. "I heard there were a lot in the past."

Daocheng Yading is within the southeast of the Qinghai-Tibet plateau, among the great gorges that cut through the mountains there. The area is distinctive in its geology and its scenery is remarkable. A travel advert said, "The last unspoilt place, with awe-inspiring peaks, still lakes, virgin forests, grassy meadows, Tibetan temples and the simple way of life. It's the destination of the explorer Joseph Rock and James Hilton's Shangri-La - Daocheng Yading!"

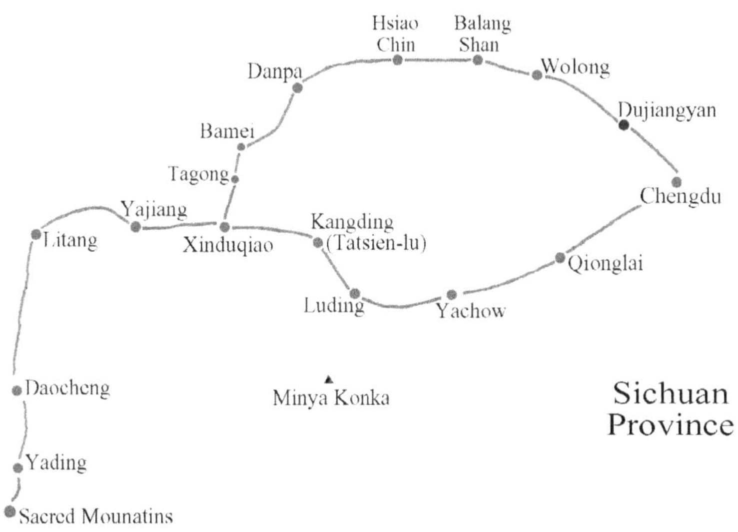

ON THE ROAD AGAIN

Once again, I shouldered my kit and left for my dream. There was the usual unrest at home. On September 15, 2005, Callum drove me to the airport. Once more, I quickly felt a sense of loneliness at heart, and this was only aggravated by the irritation of all the mobiles ringing and interminable conversations in the crowded waiting lounge. Little children were running around and babies screaming. Airport security was as tight as usual. When boarding was announced, anxious passengers rushed here and there for the departure gates. No wonder city life seems to get more and more stressed.

As soon as I reached Hong Kong, I took a bus to Shenzhen for the flight on to Chengdu where I checked in at a youth hostel. It only cost thirty yuan a night in a room for eight. Most of the lodgers were young backpackers from many countries, all with a love of travel in common. We sat sharing information and quickly became good friends. If we were going to the same places, we would team up and travel together. To save time, I chose to join a tour to 'The Last Shangri-La' with a local travel agency.

The Tour Group

There were twenty-nine in our group. To my surprise, more than half were from Guangzhou. This meant that Cantonese was more widely spoken on the coach than Putonghua (Mandarin). Our young guide was talking from the outset about Shangri-La. "Shangri-La is 'Shambhala' of Tibetan Buddhism," she told us, "a paradise, full of flowers and birdsong, where immortals dwell; and we're on our way now to the last Shangri-La."

Everyone listened with fascination as she told us about the immortal story, and followed up with a round of applause. It was clear how eager they all were to go to Shangri-La. The young couple in the seat in front were listening to the guide and burying their heads in a book called *Searching for the Last Shangri-La*, and then passing the book round for the others to see. I felt like the only man sober with everyone else addicted to the 'Last Shangri-La'. I spent most of the time looking out of the window at the scenery. Though I had not confirmed the location of Shangri-La, I took the guide's commentary with a pinch of salt.

The guide impressed upon us to watch our health and not to catch cold. Almost the whole of our tour would be on the Qinghai-Tibet plateau at an average height of at least 4,000 metres; it would be cold and altitude sickness was a risk. She told us not to be alarmed because every person responded differently to altitude. Altitude sickness usually occurs following a rapid ascent and can be prevented by ascending slowly. But 'altitude sickness' sent the whole coach into alarm, and people were discreetly checking their bags to see if they had brought the right medicines and wondering how they were going to fare.

We were heading north-west, and it was foggy with no distant views. After about an hour, we began to climb up the valley of the River Min. We soon came to the well known water control project, Dujiangyan. This was a hydraulic engineering feat constructed two thousand years ago, and it is still managing the flow of the river and irrigating the crops. The guide introduced it briefly, as we needed to press on.

The Balang Mountain Pass

At noon, we entered the Wolong Nature Reserve Area where most of the mountain sides were covered with dense bamboo thickets. We stopped for lunch in a restaurant which seemed to be the only building in the valley, purpose-built for the tourists. Afterwards we went to visit the Panda Centre. Adults and baby pandas enthralled us with their cute antics, especially one just born which everyone was keen to photograph.

Beyond Wolong, the road climbed steadily, winding steeper up the mountain slopes. In some places the road was too narrow for another vehicle to pass, and the driver hooted constantly at the corners. One side was cliff, and the other an abyss. If we had gone over the edge, the salvage operation would have been a challenge. Fortunately the road was said to have been recently tarred, and this reduced the danger of skidding.

Suddenly, the temperature in the coach dropped and everyone reached for extra clothing. I was looking out of the window all the way though mist obscured the views both downwards and above and I was constantly aware that we were climbing all the time. The inside of the coach fell quiet. After about thirty minutes, it grew bright, the mist cleared, and blue sky appeared ahead with the strong light of the high plateau bringing warmth once again. At the top of the pass, we pulled into a lay-by for a rest.

The guide took the microphone. "This is Balang Mountain Pass, 4,500 metres. Please take it gently." When we heard this, we all asked each other how we were feeling. Some were confident and stretching themselves. Others were quiet, wondering whether they had altitude sickness symptoms. The Balang road is well-known as a dangerous place, and frequently there are accidents. Drivers themselves are nervous, and our guide had not spoken about the pass in advance so as not to worry us. There were many coaches and tourists at the viewpoint, and one looked over to the splendid Four Maidens Mountain, at 6,250 metres the second highest in Sichuan Province.

A little girl of about five called Zhuoma was sitting on a rock at the pass, wearing a lovely Tibetan costume. She happily answered our questions, and without any shyness she posed for photographs. The daylight was fading, and we got back onto the coach. Zhuoma waved and said goodbye to everyone, and she was left on her own. No one seemed to be worrying about her, the guide said that her home was a farm nearby, and that she would be fine.

On the other side of the pass, the road was fairly level and the scenery began to open out. There was rich pasture with Tibetan houses, cattle and sheep. We reached the town of Rilong at eight o'clock, at a height of 3,220 metres. We were staying at a family-run Tibetan hostel and the facilities were satisfactory.

On the Roads of Kham

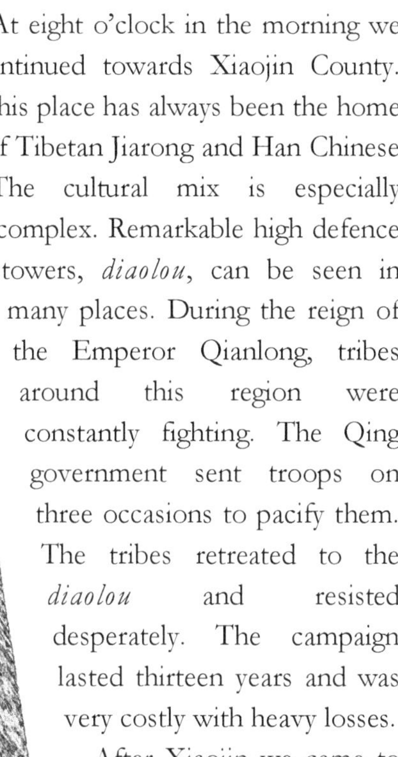

At eight o'clock in the morning we continued towards Xiaojin County. This place has always been the home of Tibetan Jiarong and Han Chinese. The cultural mix is especially complex. Remarkable high defence towers, *diaolou*, can be seen in many places. During the reign of the Emperor Qianlong, tribes around this region were constantly fighting. The Qing government sent troops on three occasions to pacify them. The tribes retreated to the *diaolou* and resisted desperately. The campaign lasted thirteen years and was very costly with heavy losses.

After Xiaojin we came to Danpa where we had lunch in a Tibetan home. Every household here was growing apples, peaches, pomegranates and pears. The fields abounded in millet and barley, chilli, peppers, aubergines and many other vegetables.

After lunch, two girls in the party decided to leave us as they found the altitude too difficult to cope with. Everyone expressed their sympathy as they forewent seeing the 'Last Shangri-la' and returned by bus to Chengdu.

The guide said, "We need to get to Xinduqiao today. It's quite a long way. Please would you all keep good time."

Everyone seemed cooperative. We were on the coach all afternoon. Sometimes the guide took the microphone to speak about some of the places we were passing: "This is Tunggu scenic spot, it's called a 'natural miniature landscape' … this is Tagong Meadows where Princess Wen Cheng of the Tang Dynasty passed on her way to Tibet … there's Tagong Temple." It was after eight o'clock at night when we reached Xinduqiao, and most people were asleep.

Xinduqiao is a very Tibetan town and is known as a photographer's paradise for its beautiful landscape and scenery. We spent the night in a Tibetan hostel near an army service station, its car park filled with transport vehicles. Our driver suggested an early start in the morning, otherwise we might be held up for hours behind a slow convoy of trucks.

We were off at seven o'clock the next morning. The service station trucks were all starting up, preparing to transport their loads to Lhasa. It is said that these convoys are not allowed to exceed thirty kilometres per hour. It would better to stay for another night than to be held up behind a long line of trucks.

We were heading towards the Sichuan Tibet highway. On route 318, we went over the Gaoer Temple pass at 4,400 metres, with views over to the king of Sichuan's mountains, Minya Konka. We were soon down to the town of Yajiang. Continuing west, we climbed again to 4,000 metres over the Jianziwan and Kazila mountains. The coach was passing bend after bend, climbing and dropping, and I lost count of all the passes.

DAOCHENG YADING

High Plateau Misery

We stopped for a rest at midday at the foot of a pass with a view over the plain of Litang. There were many concrete buildings in the town and a vast and rather desolate plain beyond, with not much livestock on it. The guide said that every spring and autumn there is a horse racing festival here, attended by Tibetans in their thousands who put up tents and celebrate for days, singing and dancing and enjoying the races. Unfortunately we had just missed it as the festival was held at the beginning of August. Litang is at a height of 4,200 metres, and is known as the 'Town of the Plateau'. It is said to be the highest town in the world. We had lunch here and carried on to Daocheng.

However, as we came down to Litang, I began to feel symptoms of altitude sickness with a constant headache causing me to knit my brow in silence. In fact, many in our group had already been suffering the effects of high altitude. Anti-sickness tablets were passed around for anyone needing them. I was anxious not to rely on medicines, but worried all the time whether I would be able to adjust.

We had been travelling all day in the coach and it was ten o'clock before we reached Daocheng and tumbled into our hostel. It was pleasant enough, but the electricity in Daocheng had failed that evening so there was no hot water which caused us some distress. We gathered round the kitchen window watching the two cooks preparing supper by candlelight, hastily putting some dishes together. We ate by candlelight, cold and damp. I ate as best I could though I had little appetite, and then hurried off to bed.

Clouds had come down outside, and the room was unheated and cold. I was afraid of catching a cold and becoming ill, and I jumped into bed in my clothes, curled up and tossed and turned from side to side trying to get to sleep, but in vain. In the morning, I had a sharp headache and felt sick. All I could take for breakfast was a bowl of rice soup. This was certainly altitude sickness. I did my best to put up with it and then hurried to a chemist's for a box of 'Altitude Peace' tablets. I took two with a can of medicinal juice, wrapped myself up tight in another woollen jersey, and sat on the coach with my eyes shut. Perhaps it was a question of morale, but I gradually felt better and in better spirits.

After breakfast, we visited the picturesque Red Grass Fields, an expanse of paddy fields filled with a red water grass. Behind them was a row of white poplars with Tibetan houses among the trees. Every tourist must see this sight. It is the popular image of Shangri-La that writers promote.

In the afternoon, we set off for our destination, the Last Shangri-La, the Yading Nature Reserve. We arrived at around five o'clock at Yading village, a peaceful village of forty or fifty scattered Tibetan farmhouses, surrounded by fields of yellow barley ready for harvest.

Before supper, although the sun had already dropped below the mountains to the west, it was still light. I went into the fields where the Tibetan farmers were harvesting the barley. They were very friendly and smiled at me. One man saw me watching him, and handed me his sickle. I took it confidently, and stooped over the barley, head down. But after only two or three cuts, I was already aching, and shamefacedly returned the sickle. They said something in Tibetan, and all laughed. I realized that they were amused by my uselessness, but with the best of good will.

Night came, the farmers went home, and the village was quiet. It was only in the guesthouses that people were milling about, and cars were arriving constantly. People were looking for somewhere to stay for the night, the kitchens were busy getting meals ready. It was noisy. This once tranquil village had suddenly become a popular tourist destination, thanks to the 'Last Shangri-La'.

A Sleepless Night

We stayed that night in an old Tibetan house, a farmhouse that had been adapted for guests. Accommodation was rough and ready, each room only having one long bed with space for eight to ten people, and often men and women were in the same room. Provided that there was a space available, someone would occupy it at any time. In the morning there was often a stranger beside you.

After nine o'clock, the owner switched off the only light bulb in each room. We had to make do with torches, lighters and even the LCD light of mobile phones. There was no washing facility and everyone just had to go to bed early without undressing.

In the middle of the night, there were noises of people stomping up the stairs. They banged on the next door. "Any space in there?" someone shouted thoughtlessly. At first no one responded. He kept shouting. "No!!" came a voice. He tried another door. At last someone said, "Yes, two!" A door opened. "You two go in, I'll look for somewhere else," the man said and ran downstairs again.

There was not much that I could have done, there was no space beside me, and I put my head under the blanket to go back to sleep. But it was not that simple. The old wooden door of the house kept banging in the wind, floorboards creaked constantly as people walked to and fro, and mice ran about overhead knocking down dust. Making a fuss would only make things worse. I told myself it was best to relax and to keep my eyes shut and wait for the morning to come.

Five o'clock in the morning and the scene at the reception was astonishing. I have not been to a disaster zone, but it must be much the same. I think that everyone was up at the same time, having breakfast at the same time, and hurrying off to see the sacred mountains at the same time.

At the confined reception, about two hundred tourists were wandering around, the dining room was packed, everyone carrying a backpack, bumping into each other, waiting for breakfast with bowl and chopsticks in hand, sitting down if they could find a seat, hurrying through a bowl of liquid rice, an egg and some roasted peanuts. Meanwhile, the coaches were turning in the narrow lane, ready to set off as soon as their groups were on board for Yading. It was still dark outside, and as soon as I was ready, I put on my backpack and waited outside for my coach.

"Excuse me, would you please look the other way?"

"Certainly," I said, but I couldn't move anywhere, as it was too crowded. So I stood still and acted as a screen for the two girls behind me.

Yading Nature Reserve

We quickly reached the entrance gate to Yading Nature Reserve, and visitors could continue either on foot or horseback. Unfortunately, there were too many tourists and too few mules. Some people were pushing to the front of the queue for tickets, to the outrage of the others who could not get tickets themselves.

There were angry scenes. I was fortunate because friends in the group helped me and I bought the last ticket. It cost 180 yuan, including the service of the groom.

The groom checked my last ticket and told me to mount the last mule, and off we went to the 'last Shangri-La'. Her name was Lamu, and she had been doing this work for fifteen years. She knew her work well, and taking the strong rope, she bent forward and led the way. We were at 3,800 metres and it was quite a struggle going uphill. The mule kept stopping for a drink. I suggested getting down and walking, but after a short distance I was gasping for breath, and Lamu thought we were going too slowly and told me to get back on. There was a small path up through the trees. The mules and horses had made the going very muddy, but Lamu walked on unconcerned.

I rode steadily up through the forest, listening to the birdsong and the streams, with a cold refreshing mountain breeze on my face. Many trees, in their yellow and green shades, tall and very old, were beautifully enhanced by long streamers of pale-yellow lichens hanging from the branches. We were close to the foot of the sacred Mt Shenrezig, and when it came into sight, Lamu gave a slight nod and drew my attention to it with her palm. She explained that it would be disrespectful to point with a finger.

Yading village

We passed Tsengu Temple. There were many tourists on the meadows. Lamu suggested that we should keep going and have a rest here later on the way back. Half an hour further on, we came to Luorong pasture, at the foot of Mt Jambeyang, and this was the end of the horse trail.

I had been lucky. When we set out from the entrance gate, there had been heavy rain, but by the time we reached our destination there was bright sunshine and the whole of Jambeyang was clear before me. It was indeed a perfect cone of snow. Joseph Rock once admired it as the finest mountain that he had ever seen. At this moment, Mt Chanadordje appeared beautifully to the north-east, as Rock described, like a bat stretching out its wings. The fifth Dalai Lama is said to have granted the mountains their honours as the Guardian Buddha, the Bodhisattva of Wisdom and the Goddess of Mercy.

Mt Shenrezig, rising to 6,032 metres, is the highest of all. I saw many Tibetan pilgrims prostrate themselves repeatedly before the mountains, and some went on further to circumambulate them. It was a chance not to be missed. I continued to take photographs until the battery sign was flashing in my camera.

Mt Jambeyang

This reminded me of the last September when I was at the Everest base camp at an altitude of 5,300 metres, and how the sight of the incomparable mountain towering above had given me a feeling of slight disappointment. Its harsh isolation together with the grey surroundings made it a dull and desolate place. Perhaps I was not looking at it from the best angle!

I sat on a little summit and took out my lunch pack. To have these mountains for company in good weather was a joy indeed! Seeing nobody about, I quickly performed a prostration, like a pilgrim before the mountains. But the grooms standing a bit away saw this and laughed. Lamu shook her hand in disapproval and mimicked my action, and I realized that I had made a mistake.

Mani Stone Piles

Treasure Hunting

When we returned to the meadow in front of Tsengu Temple, many of the group were relaxing there. I went over to the river bank and saw a middle-aged Westerner sitting on the grass, counting some money. I nodded and sat down a little distance away. After a while, he very politely nodded to me and said, "Excuse me, do you have any extra renminbi?"

As his Putonghua was not as good as my own, I said, "Do speak English if you wish."

He relaxed. "I'm sorry, I wondered if you could exchange some yuan for me as I only have dollars."

"How much would you like?" I asked.

"A hundred dollars?" he asked.

"I'm sure I can do that, but I don't know the rate."

"It's not important to be exact. Eight yuan to the dollar should be about right."

That was acceptable, and we did the exchange.

"I'm from the States; where are you from?" he asked.

"Scotland."

"Are you here to see Shangri-La?"

"Yes, you could say so," I smiled. "Almost everyone here has come to see Shangri-La. You too, I suppose!"

He smiled. "You will have heard of Joseph Rock, I imagine?"

"Yes, indeed! Many people now associate Joseph Rock with Shangri-La."

"It's true. There are many similarities between Rock's writings and Shangri-La."

"I believe that Rock was the first person from the West to come here. This place was infested with brigands in those days. I admire his courage," I said.

"It would certainly not have been easy without help from the king of Muli," he said.

"Muli! Is that in the south-west of Sichuan Province?"

"Yes, that's it," he said. "Rock paid several visits to the king of Muli and brought him many gifts."

"To bribe him!"

"It did work." He smiled. "What pleased the king most was a copy of the National Geographic Magazine."

"Why was that?"

"There was an article about Rock's previous visit to Muli with a photograph of the king," he said. "Rock then expressed his wish to visit Konkaling, and the king was delighted to write to Drashetsongpen, leader of the brigands, telling his men to leave them alone."

"Did he meet the brigands?" I asked.

"Yes, he did," he said. "To his surprise, the leader assured him of his safety. Rock also learned that he had once been a lama in a monastery at Zhongdian."

"He must have been very pleased with the trip."

"Indeed! Rock was deeply attracted to the natural wonder of this place. Some months later, he wanted to come back. Unfortunately, Drashetsongpen warned that if he ever again set foot in Konkaling he would be killed," he said.

"Why?"

"When Rock left on the previous occasion, there had been a violent hailstorm that had destroyed the whole barley crop, and the brigands thought that the mountain god was angry, and would not allow a Westerner to venture there again." He went on, "I am glad that I can come here today." He smiled and he began to secure his backpack. I knew that he wanted to be on his way.

"I wonder how he handled the goods that he robbed," I pressed.

"His brother was a merchant and sold on the loot. It was said that the king himself enjoyed some of the proceeds, as he let the brigands pass through his region."

"Ali Baba," I said curtly.

"What?"

"Ali Baba and the Forty Thieves, the old story."

"Oh, yes!"

"He must have been very wealthy." I murmured.

"Who?" he asked again.

"Drashetsongpen."

He did not reply, but was busy with his packing. I noticed something that I was familiar with. "I've got one, too." I pointed at the metal detector in his pack. "I'll bring mine next time I come for treasure hunt." I laughed.

He seemed surprised. "How did you know that he left treasure here?"

"I didn't say whose treasure!" After this quick exchange, it appeared he had said something by mistake. Then I went on, "I'm only joking. But possibly, the chief could have hidden his wealth somewhere."

When he heard me, a look of suspicion crossed his face and he smiled reluctantly. "If I say 'yes', would you believe me?"

I was a bit surprised to hear this and I became curious. We were both silent, as he continued to arrange his backpack. Then he stopped and said, "Could I ask you something?"

"As you wish!"

"What does a circle or a triangle mean to you here?"

"The lakes are a circle and the sacred peaks are pyramidal," I said casually.

"Good thinking!" He paused, "There is a rumour that Drashetsongpen buried a large amount of gold and silver coins somewhere."

"Did he?" I stared at him.

"This is something of an open secret in America. It was found in Rock's unpublished notes. It might have been a hoax. Have you heard about it?"

"Not at all," I said. "What did it say?"

"I haven't seen it. It was said to be so simple. Rock had drawn a triangle and a circle. In the centre was marked the location of the hidden treasure – thirty boxes of gold and silver coins."

"Have you any idea where it is?"

"If I knew, I would be very busy right now!" He laughed and then fell silent, his face wary. "Now you know why Joseph Rock wanted to return to Konkaling."

"Who told you this?"

"Oh it's all a rumour," he said. "I'm sorry, I want to be going."

"Where is your destination?" I felt a bit embarrassed to be asking many questions.

"I'll be walking round the sacred mountains, following my dream." He then picked up his pack, and began walking in the direction of Jambeyang. Then suddenly he turned and threw me something from his pocket, "It's a souvenir for you, and thank you for your help!"

I caught it mid-air and found that it was a rusty Chinese silver dollar, in poor condition; but I was thrilled.

"Thank you so much!" I shouted, "May I ask your name?"

"We met only by chance, there's no need for names."

"Have you found Shangri-La yet?" I threw out my last question.

"Yading has the look of it, but it's not quite James Hilton's Shangri-La. For this, you may need to know more of Tibetan history."

I saw him striking a rock with his stick as he walked on. As I watched him go, I wondered what the triangle and circle meant. Was it a sign? He was not playing a joke on me, was he?

TATSIEN-LU

We returned to Daocheng for a night, and the next day made straight for Kangding. We passed Ludingqiao and followed the Dadu River up for about twenty kilometres, with Kangding soon coming into sight. Kangding is the capital of the Ganzi Tibetan Autonomous Region and is a place where Tibetans and Chinese have lived together for many years. The old name of Kangding was Tatsien-lu.

There are various explanations of the old name 'Tatsien-lu'. A popular version is that during the time of the Three Kingdoms (220-280), Liu Bei, the ruler of the State of Shu, occupied Sichuan. His minister, Zhu Geliang, wanted to extend the borders of Shu, and he planned to invite the Tibetan king to a banquet and to request the land that an arrow could traverse. The king did not suspect a trick and readily assented. They agreed that Qionglai was where the arrow would be fired, and that Shu would then extend to the place where the arrow fell. In fact, Zhu Geliang had already instructed his commander Guo Da to ride west through the night with an arrow that had the name 'Shu' cut on it. Guoda covered an enormous distance and was exhausted. He accidentally dropped the arrow into a fast flowing river, and all attempts to fish it out failed. He immediately had a forge make a new arrow. Then he stuck it on a mountain top to the north of the town. After this, the land west of the River Lu belonged to Shu, and the town got the name of Tatsien-lu, meaning 'Arrowhead Forge'. It is said that Zhu Geliang, on an expedition south to settle disturbances on the edge of Yunnan, used the same trick to acquire the areas of Mangkuan and Dehong to the west of the Mekong.

Tibetans have been living there for centuries. Their name for the town is 'Darchedo' which means the confluence where the Dar Chu and the Che Chu rivers meet. In 1908, the Viceroy for the border of Szechuan and Yunnan, Chao Erfeng, petitioned the

Emperor for the change of name from Tatsien-lu to Kangding, meaning 'pacification of Kham'.

Kangding lies at a height of 2,626 metres. A rapid river flows through the town, and there are four stone bridges across it. The famous Horserace Hill rises sharply to 3,000 metres to the south-east. I went up in a cable car, enjoying a panoramic view over the whole town. There were many new buildings. The river was clearly seen flowing through the town. It was a ten minute ride. There is a temple on the top, both Chinese and Tibetan in style, surrounded by tall pine trees hung with many huge cones which were still fresh and green. On the summit was an area the size of a football pitch where the traditional 'Circumambulation Festival' is held in April every year, to celebrate the Buddha's birthday. Some Tibetans were selling horse rides. It only cost five yuan to ride twice around the track, but there were not very many visitors

Many people who have never been to Kangding have heard of the name and the love song. Some years ago, ten folk songs from round the world were chosen and broadcast into space from a satellite. The Kangding Love Song was one of them, '*swift horses racing over the mountain side, a cloud skimming by ...*'

Kangding was the last stop on our tour. We were soon going to be saying goodbye. The group crowded into a small noodle shop for the best meal yet, bowl after bowl of Sichuan beef noodles in peppery sauce, till the vendor's arms were tired. The bill hardly came to thirty yuan in total. When we returned to Chengdu, we felt stiff and tired, and went quietly on our separate ways.

The 'Last Shangri-la' tour was over. Everyone was satisfied, as they had seen a real Shangri-La. It was only myself who felt perplexed. Shangri-La seemed visible but hidden; near but far away; true, yet false. I wondered if this was perhaps the time to call my search off.

I still felt uncertain as to Shangri-La's location. But I kept thinking of the parting words of the American at Tsengu Temple, and my quest for Shangri-La would now take a new turn. I had secretly decided that my next venture would be a treasure hunt.

Tatsien-lu

Kangding

CHAPTER 3

PURSUING …

One day, Lin asked me: "Do you know of the book, 'Irgendwo in Tibet'?

"No, I don't! Who wrote it?"

"James Hilton," she said.

I was a bit surprised. "As far as I know, James Hilton didn't write much about Tibet. What's it about?"

"It's actually the German version of 'The Lost Horizon', and the title means 'Somewhere in Tibet'." She added, "It's obvious, then, that Shangri-La's somewhere in Tibet."

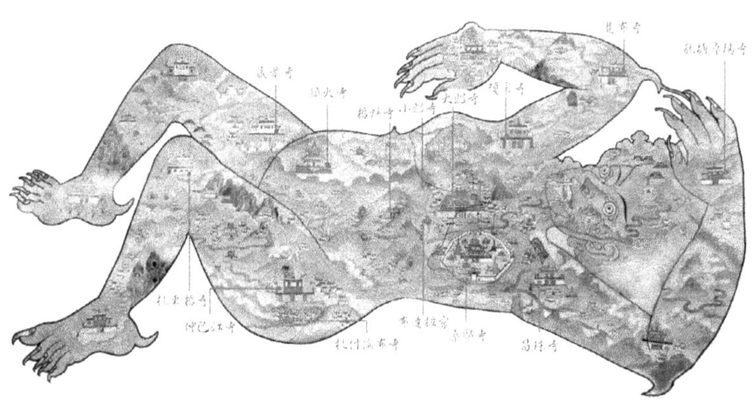

A historic Tibetan tanka showing a demoness lying on her back

ABOUT TIBET

Before I went to Tibet, the Potala Palace and red robed lamas were all that I knew about it. Since Tibet's opening to the outside, more and more visitors have been going there, and information has become much more accessible. Tibet is called the 'Roof of the World' and the 'Third Pole.' It has immense mountains, boundless plains, dashing rivers, tranquil lakes and blue skies. Across it for over a thousand miles run the mighty Himalayas with the highest mountain of all, Chomolungma, at 8,848.14 metres. There is the sacred mountain Kailash, revered by all Tibetans, and the mysterious Yalu Tsangpo river, whose course long perplexed many western travellers.

Frank Kingdon-Ward called Tibet a 'small wonder'. It has captured the imagination of mankind. Its peculiar aloofness, its remote unruffled calm, and the mystery shrouding its great rivers and mountains make an irresistible appeal to the explorer.

People say that you should see Tibet once in your lifetime. But, you can hardly say that you have been to Tibet if you haven't been to Lhasa. Apart from the Potala Palace, there are the historic Jokhang and Ramoche temples, and a host of others. It is the centre of profound Tibetan Buddhism with its impressively devout followers. The first time I knew of Tibet was when I was at school. I used to admire a beautiful picture which I cut out from a calendar, showing the Potala Palace, soaring up from its red mountain top, with meadows and rivers on all sides below. Unfortunately the picture was lost long ago, but its image was buried deep in my heart.

In 2004, I went as a tourist to Lhasa for the first time. I had not read up at all beforehand. I managed to visit most of the popular attractions. It was rushed, like *looking at flowers on horseback*, and I felt a bit dazed by the end.

The following year, I flew to Lhasa again from Chengdu. As the flight passed over the high plateau of eastern Tibet, there was much excitement. Everyone was scrambling for cameras and filming at the windows. Last year, on the same route, I was unprepared, and after thirty seconds looking out felt dazzled and faint, almost blinded. I had to close my eyes for a while to recover. This time, I put on my sunglasses, and could comfortably enjoy the views of the highest ranges of all. I saw from the map that flying from Chengdu to Lhasa, if you were lucky, you could see Omei Shan and Minya Konka Shan in Sichuan Province. We would pass over the three parallel gorges, Mt Namcha Barwa and the great U-bend of the Tsangpo. At this moment, I saw ridge after ridge of snow and ice rising like wolves' teeth to the horizon. There were rivers twisting along the valleys. For nearly an hour, we were still over glaciers and snowfields. I was wondering how long one could survive in such an environment.

In October 1922, the 54 year-old explorer Alexandra David-Neel and her adopted son Yongden set off from the north-west of Yunnan disguised as beggars. They secretly crossed these icy wastes down below us, avoiding the attention of officials, eluding murderous bandits. At one time, they were so hungry that they had to boil up shoe leather for food. It took them 16 months over a tortuous route that was more than twice the normal distance to reach the forbidden city, Lhasa.

In 1924, Kingdon-Ward explored the hidden region of the Tsangpo Gorges. The expedition discovered a great waterfall which they named the 'Rainbow Falls'. They reached the famous U-bend in the Gorges, and marvelled at what appeared to be the greatest drop in altitude of any river in the world. He believed the Brahmaputra in India to be the same river as the Tsangpo in Tibet, and this was later confirmed.

Kingdon-Ward also gave some details of the Tibetan sacred land – Pemako, among the Tsangpo Gorges. He wrote, "Pemako is the Promised Land of the Tibetan prophecy. A land flowing with milk and honey, where the crops grew of their own accord.

Most races have their promised land, and such legendary places must necessarily be somewhat inaccessible, hidden behind misty barriers where ordinary men do not go; otherwise people would quickly explore the land and explode the legend." His book *The Riddle of the Tsangpo Gorges* attracted much attention.

Pemako is often said to be the Shambhala of Tibetan myth. An American newspaper in 1999 had the bold heading, 'Explorers in world's deepest gorge find Shangri-La'. It described how two Americans in Pemako had found an eighty foot-high waterfall behind which, they were told, there was a hidden cave that led to the sacred Shambhala.

In fact, many other western explorers had left their footprints in this part of Tibet. From the beginning of the seventeenth century, missionaries, explorers, botanists and scholars, whatever their motivation, went to great lengths to penetrate to the Roof of the World, and especially to reach the forbidden city of Lhasa.

Before the mid-twentieth century, 'Tibet' to western people generally meant where the Tibetan people lived. This included the whole of Qinghai, the south of Gansu, the west of Sichuan and the north-west of Yunnan Provinces -- in other words the whole of the Qinghai-Tibet plateau. Over four and a half million Tibetans lived in this area, more than 95% of the total, the rest being Han, Mongols, Monbas, Lopas, Naxi and Moslems.

Before the roads into Tibet from Qinghai and Sichuan opened in 1956, the routes were formidable. People had to travel on foot or riding horses and yaks, crossing rivers in coracles and on inflated hides, rope bridges and pulleys. Everything had to be carried by people or by animals, and this was slow and dangerous. Today there are roads into Tibet from all directions. The construction of the Qinghai-Tibet railway is now complete. There are daily flights from Lhasa Airport to many destinations. Groups of explorers and climbers arrive from all quarters. The veil of Tibet is slowly being drawn aside.

LHASA

On 24 September, I arrived at the airport of Lhasa at about 7.30 in the morning. I always enjoy being a backpacker as there is no need to wait by the conveyor belt for luggage. I was probably the first to leave the terminal. It was already busy in the airport and outside, and there were many foreigners. A bus was waiting outside the main exit. I asked in Putonghua a Tibetan standing beside the bus, "Excuse me, is this the bus for Lhasa?" He didn't answer and just gestured impatiently to me to get on.

Once the seats were all taken, the driver piled up the luggage in the gangway till there was no room to move. It took about one hour and twenty minutes to the Lhasa central bus station. Absurdly, the driver, not saying a word, simply opened his door, got out and walked off, leaving us all jammed inside. Impatient passengers had to clamber over the top of the luggage pile to get out of the stuffy bus. The others had to help pass the bags forward one by one before they could enjoy a breath of fresh air. There was nothing that we could do about our surly driver.

Lhasa lies in central Tibet. It is the capital of the Tibetan Autonomous Region, and its political and economic centre. Lhasa is the cradle of Tibetan Buddhism, and every Tibetan hopes to see it once in his lifetime. The elevation is 3,650 metres, the climate is dry and bright, not particularly cold in winter and temperate in summer. It is known as 'Sunshine City', as it has 3,000 hours of sunshine each year. Recently, Lhasa was acclaimed as one of the most favoured destinations for European tourists, and many foreigners can be seen here.

Today, Lhasa is gradually modernizing. The streets are busy: there are many cars, shops and restaurants, internet bars and places of entertainments. There is much construction as new hotels and other buildings go up to meet the demands of the tourist industry. Most of the streets are surfaced with asphalt or concrete and are clean and trim.

In the Past

Thomas Manning, the English traveller, visited Lhasa in 1811. He found it bleak and dispiriting: "There is nothing striking, nothing pleasing, in its appearance. The habitations are begrimed with smut and dirt. The avenues are full of dogs, growling and gnawing bits of hide that lie about in profusion and emit a charnel-house smell; others limping and looking livid; others ulcerated; others starved and dying, and pecked at by ravens; some dead and preyed upon. In short, everything seems mean and gloomy, and excites the idea of something unreal."

Nearly a hundred years later, Lhasa did not seem to have changed very much. Edmund Candler, the British reporter had found the city squalid and filthy beyond description, undrained and unpaved. Not a single house looked clean or cared for. The streets after rain were nothing but pools of stagnant water frequented by pigs and dogs searching for refuse.

At that time, Lhasa's streets were full of beggars whom the local people called ragyabas. Apart from begging, their daily task was removing dead bodies to the sky burial sites where they chopped them up and fed them to the vultures and stray dogs. Another of their responsibilities was to catch lawbreakers for the authorities. The ragyabas rampaged through the town, and nobody dared offend them. They lived in gruesome houses covered in cow and sheep horns, with yak hides over the roof.

Visitors to Lhasa all had revolting accounts. Sarat Chandra Das, the Indian explorer, wrote: "On the streets I met numerous bands of ragyabas, or scavengers, wandering from place to place, clamouring for alms from every newcomer or pilgrim they saw. If no attention is paid to them, they thrust their dirty hats in the stranger's face."[1] Even worse, they would curse: "When you are a

---

[1] Sarat Chandra Das: Journey to Lhasa 1902

corpse, we will tie a rope round your neck, and drag you like a dog outside the gates and tear you to pieces."[1]

When Spencer Chapman was in Lhasa in the mid 1930s, he could still see the ragyabas carrying corpses on their backs to the cemetery where they were laid out on flat stones and cut into small pieces. They were then thrown to the vultures and ravens which crowded round waiting for their share of the meal. [2]

In the eighteenth century and before, apart from the difficulties of the journey, Tibet was not inaccessible. It is evident from the Capuchins' reports that Tibet was not then a closed country. Not only could the fathers come and go as freely as the weather and transport allowed, but there is mention of other foreign visitors, including Russian traders, a French merchant, a Dutchman, as well as Armenians. The Capuchins recorded Lhasa as a busy market-city of some 80,000 inhabitants.[3] But I am surprised that Austine Waddell gave the population[4] in 1904 as just over 10,000. It seems strange to me that the population should have declined so over the years, and I think the Capuchin figure may be too high. In recent years, there has been great change to Lhasa. The present population is more than half a million, and thousands of tourists from all over the world arrive every day.

On my second visit to Lhasa, I intended to find out more about the ragyabas. I went to Lingkor North Road, the circular path for pilgrims in the north and followed it round to the southern side of the city. Here were many butcher shops, with whole carcases of pigs, cows and sheep displayed outside waiting to be cut up and sold. It was a busy place. A century ago, this part of the city was a butchers' centre, and a place where the ragyabas hung out. Many of their cow horn houses were here, especially by a sky

[1]   Graham Sandberg: Tibet and the Tibetans 1905
[2]   Spencer Chapman: Lhasa the Holy City 1940
[3]   Hugh Richardson: A Cultural History of Tibet 1968
[4]   Austine Waddell: Lhasa and its Mysteries 1905

burial site in the south-east corner. It was said that every day at least one corpse would be sent to this site to maintain its prestige, otherwise bad luck would befall Lhasa. The bodies were cut into pieces and fed to scavenging pigs, dogs and vultures. These pigs, they said, were especially delicious to eat.[1] Today, the ragyabas and the stray dogs have gone, and where the horn huts stood there are now schools and office buildings.

THE POTALA PALACE

Seen from a distance, the Potala reminded me of Edinburgh Castle. Both have massive walls and old buildings towering high on a hilltop, but the Potala seemed more imposing and mysterious with its religious character. A writer described it well by comparing it to the portrait of Mona Lisa. Wherever you stand, it seems to be watching you. It seems to be sending a message to you, a summons that enthrals you and does not let you go, a sight that you will never forget.

In the year 637, the Tibetan king, Songtsen Gampo built the original palace on top of the red hill. Through many centuries of disaster and destruction, the palace fell into ruin. Then, in the middle of the seventeenth century, the fifth Dalai Lama rebuilt the palace, and it was gradually extended to its present impressive appearance.

'Potala', its Sanskrit name 'Puto', means the residence of the Bodhisattva Guan Yin. The palace is very clearly in two parts, the white and the red. The Red Palace is where the stupas of the deceased Dalai Lamas are placed, the White Palace is where the Dalai Lamas resided. Since the fourteenth Dalai Lama left Lhasa in 1959, the White Palace has been empty, and is now visited by tourists in their thousands.

---

[1]   Graham Sandberg: Tibet and the Tibetans 1905

The Potala Palace

1667 by John Grueber

1904 by Thomas Holdich

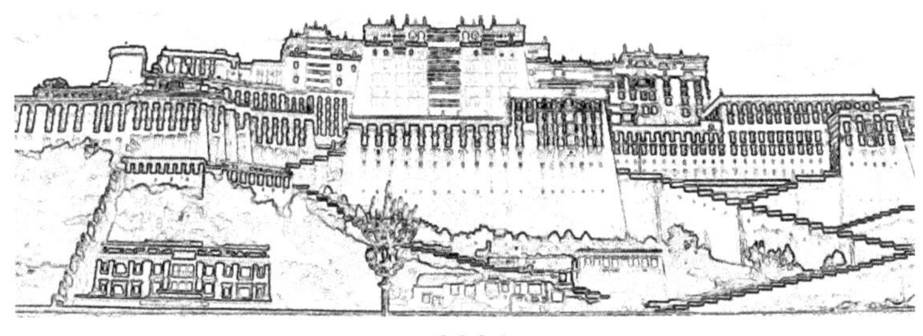

2004

There are few pictures surviving of the Potala Palace in early times. Perhaps the earliest is the drawing by the Jesuit John Grueber in the book *China Illustrata* by Athanasius Kircher published in 1667. In 1645, the fifth Dalai Lama began the rebuilding. The White Palace was finished in 1653, with its central part rising thirteen storeys, and the Red Palace was completed in 1693. Father Grueber came to Lhasa in 1661, long before the Red Palace had been built. His drawing shows the White Palace on the mountain top, but it is hard to make out anything of thirteen storeys; the very tall part seen today is the Red Palace. It is generally said that Father Grueber drew this picture from memory, and it does look somewhat fanciful.

On my first visit to the Potala Palace, I was affected by altitude sickness for the first time, and felt dizzy and miserable, and groggily followed the guide through the doors and corridors. The Palace was all very dark and indistinct. There were wall paintings and *tankas* (hanging scrolls) in great quantities, relating to Buddhism and to Tibet's history. They illustrated the beginnings of relations between Tibet and China, and the receiving of the Chinese princesses as brides was vividly portrayed.

When the fifth Dalai Lama was building the Potala Palace, the Chinese Emperor Kangxi sent hundreds of craftsmen to assist with the construction works. His title, the fifth Dalai Lama, was conferred on him in 1653 by the Emperor Shunzhi and confirmed him as the spiritual leader of Tibet. In the Palace there are ceremonial boards displayed high overhead bearing the calligraphy of the Emperors Qianlong and Tungzhi and presented by them. There is a portrait of the Emperor Qianlong and a tablet with 'Long live the Emperor!' on it in the Han, Tibetan, Manchu and Mongolian languages.

Today, the Potala Palace, this most remarkable icon for Lhasa, has become one of the hottest attractions on earth. Every day, thousands of visitors pour in to see the beautiful city which used to be so remote and seemed out of reach. On the highway in front of the Palace, Tibetans drove expensive four-wheel drive vehicles carrying young people and foreign tourists, the boots filled with backpacks, coming and going in all directions, off on another day of exploration.

On the pavements were many Tibetans, especially old people, prostrating themselves in rapt concentration before the Palace, muttering prayers. Others were moving along the side of the Lingkor Road, the outer circular road for pilgrims, kneeling and prostrating repeatedly, circumambulating the Palace in a clockwise direction. They ended their circuit at the Jokhang Temple where they worshipped before the statue of the Buddha, Sakyamuni. In this way they accumulated merit.

The Jokhang Temple

THE JOKHANG TEMPLE

In the year 641, the Chinese princess Wen Cheng was married to the Tibetan king. She brought with her a precious dowry of a life-size statue of the Buddha Sakyamuni when he was twelve years old. When they reached the north of Lhasa, the cart with the statue of the Buddha stopped itself and could not be made to move forward. The princess, who was skilled in divination, discovered that the spot was in communication with the underworld, and that there was a crystal palace inhabited by the Nagas dragon deep in the earth underneath this place. She then recommended to the king to have a temple built here for the Buddha, to suppress the evil dragon and bring good luck to the country. The temple was called 'Ramoche' meaning 'Big Chinese Mansion'. Its Chinese name is 'Xiao Zhao Si.'

At about the same time, the Nepalese Princess Bhrkuti also brought a statue of the Buddha with her when she came to marry Songtsen Gampo. She knew how Princess Wen Cheng had built the Ramoche Temple, and asked her for help to build a temple. Princess Wen Cheng discovered that the topography of Tibet was like a demoness's body; Lhasa was situated at her heart, and the water of Lake O-Ma-Thang was her blood. She recommended that the lake be filled in with earth which must be carried by sheep, which were regarded as propitious. A temple was built here in 647. Its original name was Ra-sa, meaning 'sheep earth'. It was later called 'Jokhang' because of the statue of the Buddha, Jowo, that it housed, and its Chinese name is 'Da Zhao Si'. Westerners normally call it 'The Cathedral' [1]

It is said that Princess Wen Cheng planted a willow tree in front of the Jokhang Temple. More than a thousand years later, the tree remained. In a photograph taken by Perceval Landon in 1904, a

---

[1]   Austine Waddell: Description of Lhasa Cathedral 1895

tall weeping willow can be seen. Until 1950, the willow tree was still flourishing, and it is shown in Heinrich Harrer's book. A stone tablet under the tree was framed with brickwork topped with tiles, like a little shrine, in their photographs. Today, there is just a small and vigorous white poplar tree. The bricks and tiles have disappeared, and just the tablet itself remains.

The tablet was set up in 1794 during the reign of the Chinese Emperor Qianlong. It is called the 'Smallpox Stone'. Smallpox was rampant in Tibet, and the Qing government official Helin petitioned the emperor to be allowed to put up a tablet encouraging people to be vaccinated against it. The tablet appears to be in poor condition and badly defaced; it would be very hard to read. To the right is another stone which was set up in the year 823 by the husband of the Princess Jin Cheng, Chidezuzan, and the Tang Emperor Muzong, the 'Peace Treaty Stone': the Tibetans and the Chinese called each other 'cousins' and would not attack each other. The inscription is cut in Tibetan and Chinese, and is evidence for the history of treaties between the two States. The two stones are now protected behind a high wall, and it is not easy to see them closely. It would be hard to prove their authenticity.

Peace Treaty Stone

Smallpox Stone

In front of the Jokhang Temple, there were many pilgrims, coming from all places, most of them Tibetan men and women of all ages, ceaselessly prostrating themselves. Their hands clasped high above their heads, they chanted the mantra, *Om Mani Padme Hum.* They were continually repeating their prostrations, sitting on the ground for a rest when they were tired. Over the years, the stone paving has been polished by these pilgrims till it shines.

For centuries, the Jokhang Temple has been one of the holiest places of Tibetan Buddhism. Tibetans' lifelong desire is to come to worship here and to lie outstretched on the ground in veneration before the statue of Sakyamuni. They present a white *khatag* (scarf) and some butter oil and *tsamba* (roasted barley), and finally they touch with their foreheads the lotus throne of the Buddha. Then their desire has been accomplished and very great merit gained.

A Young Pilgrim

I was sitting in a corner of the perimeter wall intently watching the actions of the worshippers, and taking the opportunity for some photographs. A Tibetan boy sat down beside me and wanted to see my pictures. I handed him my digital camera, and showed him how to press the button and see them. He was very pleased, and held up the camera wanting to take a picture of me.

"What is your name?"

"Zhaxiciren. I'm sixteen." His Putonghua was a little stilted.

"Where do you come from?"

"Naqu, three hundred kilometres from here." He seemed to know what I was going to ask, and I expect he had been asked these questions before.

"How did you come here?"

"I came prostrating myself all the way. It was just me that came on my own." He kept telling me more than I had asked him.

I looked at him. "How long did that take you?"

"It took three months and sixteen days," he answered precisely.

"Why did you do it?"

"To worship Buddha, and to pray for good health."

In Lhasa, Zhaxiciren was staying in the Ramoche Temple, for half a yuan a day. He was often at the Jokhang Temple and sometimes I saw him prostrating along Barkor Street and receiving alms. His parents were farmers and he had brothers and sisters at home. He told me that after a while he would continue prostrations into Nepal, where there were many Buddhist temples, and he was hoping to study Buddhism and to return home to the temple in Naqu and to be a lama there.

I looked at the lump on his forehead, and thought about the long road to Nepal and even more the high Himalayan passes that he would have to cross, and wondered if he would live to return to Naqu. I did not understand whether he was superstitious or overzealous, but I could not but deeply respect his uncompromising fearlessness, his religious certainty and his devotion.

Barkor and Langkor

There were many pilgrims on Barkor Street, the middle circular road for pilgrims, holding prayer wheels and chanting scriptures, some prostrating themselves all the way as they circumambulated the Jokhang Temple. All along the street were shops and stalls, and many tourists. There was shouting of wares, haggling over prices, arguing and spectating. Many vendors were selling ornaments and antiques, mostly imitations, and almost every stall sold the same goods. After a while, one had seen enough of them.

I bought a ticket and followed the crowds into the temple. Before the main sanctuary there was a courtyard open to the sky, not big but very crowded. Many groups of tourists were listening to their guides' stories. It was like a session of the United Nations, with snatches of English, French, German and Japanese, not to mention Chinese.

The courtyard gave access to the various chambers of divinities. Worshippers were going from one to the next carrying plastic bottles filled with butter oil, and some were in the courtyard bowing to the sanctuary. It was strange to see that the pilgrims were from time to time swarming together from one place to the other, so fast that you wondered if something had happened. Suddenly a new swarm left for the Langkor, the inner circular route for pilgrims, and I joined in to see what was going on. I found that the pilgrims were all off to the prayer-wheels. In the press, one couldn't slacken the pace until we had turned all one hundred and eight wheels. It was tiring work, and I went back into the courtyard feeling weary and dazed.

I sat against one of the great pillars looking at them supporting the upper storey and it reminded me of Das. He described these pillars as the most remarkable feature of the Jokhang Temple. The large teak pillars, he said, were decorated with branch and flower pattern carvings, and at their base there was said to be gold and silver treasure buried; other pillars carved with dragon heads had charms buried beneath, to ward off illness and to destroy the powers of spirits hostile to Buddhism; others carved with lion's heads had charms buried to ensure good harvests. I looked carefully at the carvings on each of these wooden pillars, but saw none that matched Das's description. Had the pillars been replaced and was I sitting above hidden gold and silver treasures? I wondered.

A MYSTERIOUS GIRL

I observed the movements of each pilgrim, and presently my eye fell on a Tibetan girl, sitting quietly by the entrance to the sanctuary. She looked young. She seemed a little unusual compared to the other pilgrims, dressed in Tibetan costume with a scarf that concealed the whole of her head and face except for her eyes. She looked tired, sitting head down and hugging her knees, often looking attentively towards the entrance. She noticed my gaze, and appeared awkward, glancing often across in my direction. Soon she put together the bag beside her and joined the crowd entering the sanctuary. I looked up and saw her quickly disappearing among the others.

Though the pilgrims and tourists were here in great numbers, they were orderly and not bumping into each other. After a while, I filed into the sanctuary too. I went along a dark narrow passageway, turned to the left and passed round the main chamber in a clockwise direction. The sanctuary was filled with statues, and in the dim surroundings, they seemed all the more menacing. The statue of the Buddha was placed in the centre to the back. The chamber was packed with pilgrims. They were in line, waiting to complete the final climax to their arduous journey.

The light here was very dim; everything was indistinct. Visitors are hardly able to make much out. Some ten lamas were sitting on thick rugs, bending forward, reading and reciting scripture with their distinctive deep low voices. I was amazed that they could see to read in the gloom. I moved slowly forward in the crowd and could hardly stop. There were many pillars glossy black in colour and they felt like metal when I tapped them. The wood is said to be all the original timber, worn smooth as copper by hands passing over the surface, as for many centuries these pillars have supported the temple. The noise of scripture recitation and of bells ringing never stopped, every corner was filled with people, the air was stale, with a pervasive smell of butter oil, and I felt suffocated and nauseous, and hurried out.

In Trouble

After I had walked round inside the temple, my eyes were becoming accustomed to the obscurity, and it was becoming easier to make things out round about me. When I came back into the narrow corridor, it was less crowded than before, and I could slow down and look about more closely. On either side were two towering figures with glaring eyes. The ceiling was worn and had not been painted. I saw a bell hanging from the rafter, about 25 centimetres across. It looked like a church bell. I examined it as carefully as I could, but it was not easy to see in the dim light.

I had before read about an old church bell that was said to be still hanging in the Jokhang Temple, and I wondered whether this could be the one. If it was, then it was of great interest. The bell was hanging on its own, looking rather out of place.

Standing in the corridor by myself, I glanced to left and right, hesitating about taking a photograph. Whom could I ask? I thought for a little while. I slowly took out my camera, off went the flash, and the trouble began! A fuming lama strode across. Though I did not understand what he said, his meaning was clear enough.

I explained to him in Putonghua that it was a harmless photograph, and hoped he could bend the rules just this once, but that I could delete the picture if necessary. But the lama would hear nothing of this, and he angrily put out his hand to take my camera. Just when I didn't know what I could do, someone behind said, "Do you need help?"

I looked round, and saw that it was the girl I had noticed earlier. I told her what had happened, and asked if she could explain to the lama.

She listened, and then spoke to him. After a short conversation, the lama went quietly away. Then she said to me: "He thought you were taking a picture of the altars, and there was a misunderstanding because of language. Everything's fine."

This was a relief, and I was very grateful to the girl. I smiled and thanked her warmly, but she made little response.

"Are you from Lhasa?" I asked.

"No!" she said, and took no further notice of me. She was looking up and down at the bell.

I could not see the expression on her face, but, from the way in which she was observing round about her, she appeared very alert. I did not want to embarrass her so I thanked her again, said goodbye and walked up the steps to the upper floor.

Lhasa's Setting

At the front on the upper floor, I could see the Potala Palace standing sublime on the Red Hill. Right in front, there was a large public square filled with stalls and crowds of pilgrims, prostrating themselves continuously before the Temple. There were many tourists, holding their cameras ready for a good shot of this unique scene. Pilgrims were used to the cameras and took no notice of them. People standing by the tall wall did not seem to be aware of the ancient tablets behind them. From where I stood, they were clearly seen. With the golden wheel on the roof of the Jokhang and the magnificent Potala Palace in the distance, they seemed to echo to each other the glorious history of Lhasa.

Lhasa is situated in the centre of Tibet, and the Jokhang Temple in the centre of Lhasa. It is referred to as the 'Holy of Holies'. Standing on the balcony, I could see the mountains all around the city.

Lhasa is perceived to be lucky in its setting, like an eight petal lotus flower, a wheel with eight radiating spokes, and hemmed about by eight treasures. These are the wheel, the lucky knot, the lotus flower, the vase, the golden fish, the umbrella, the white conch shell and the banner.

The Eight Lucky Signs

I looked hard and strained my imagination, but I could not see any of these. I just turned my face to the sky with my eyes shut and took a deep, propitious breath. As I lingered on the balcony taking photographs, I sensed that I was being followed. I assumed it was the lama, and he must be observing me. It would be best to keep to the rules, and to pay no attention to him. It was not long before I discovered that it was the girl who had just rescued me. I pretended not to have seen her and left to buy some mineral water at a stall. I sat down on a step and rested.

I heard a voice behind me, "May I sit here?"

I looked round, though I already knew who it was, and quickly said, "Of course, please sit down!"

She sat down, a little way off, and was silent. She was looking down, wiping fresh blood on her finger. Though she was looking at her finger, I saw that she was wondering how to open a conversation.

"What's happened to your finger?" I took the initiative.

"Nothing! I scratched it."

"Don't do that! If it gets dirty, it may go septic," and I reached for a piece of plaster out of my bag.

I opened the plaster. "I'll put it on for you."

"I'll manage."

"But you've only one free hand. Let me do it."

She slowly stretched out her hand. "Thank you," she said quietly.

"Thank you for helping me just now. I don't know what I could have done without your help."

"You need friends when you're away from home. It was nothing."

"One minute!" I ran over to the stall and bought a bottle of mineral water to give her with a straw. She gladly took it. Her movements and eyes and speech were now much more relaxed.

"Were you studying the geography just now?" she asked.

"Why do you say that?"

"You were gazing at all the mountains for a long time."

"Ah, right! I read something interesting in a book." I raised my voice a little and tried to engage her in conversation.

"What was it?"

"Look and see what that mountain looks like." I pointed to the south-west.

She looked up for a while and said, "It doesn't look like anything to me."

"Doesn't it look like a vase?"

She hesitated. "No, it doesn't."

"What about that one?"

"No, it doesn't look like anything either." She was puzzled.

Actually, I couldn't make anything out myself. I gave a laugh and she probably thought that I was teasing her. Most of the time she kept her face down and she only raised her head a little when she was talking to me.

Checking on me

She looked at my digital camera and said, "May I see your photos?"

"Of course!" I switched on the power and handed her my camera.

She looked at my pictures one by one. "You've been to Daocheng and Yading?"

"Yes." I looked from the side. It was a photo of me on the horse at Yading in front of Mt Jambeyang. I was thinking, Yading was over two thousand kilometres away from Lhasa, and she knew the place at once and seemed familiar with it; where was this girl from? She kept on looking at the photographs, much more lively now, and sometimes she paused to examine a photograph in detail. Soon she was studying one, and I heard her mutter, "The bell's nothing special." I knew what photo this must be.

"There was nearly trouble just now," she said. "Do you realize that you could easily end up in the police station?"

I drew in my breath. "I know!"

"Why did you take a chance? Was it worth it?" She seemed to press me for the reason.

"Yes, it was simply out of curiosity," I said. "I heard long ago that an ancient church bell was hanging in the Jokhang Temple, and I was looking for it. It seems curious, don't you think, that this famous thirteen centuries-old Tibetan Buddhist Temple should have something from another religion hanging in it. That was why I took the photograph."

"But you know that photography is not allowed."

"Had the bell been hanging in the sanctuary, I would never have photographed it." I was excusing myself to smooth things over. Intuition told me that she knew where the bell was from.

"This is only a traditional Tibetan bell, not anything unusual."

"Really?" I was surprised.

When I was taking the picture, the passageway was dark with no lighting, and I couldn't see the bell clearly. She handed over the camera and I began to feel disappointment. The picture plainly showed the bell's shape and decoration, not like the picture of the church bell at all that I had seen in books. I thought for a little and tried not to show how I was feeling. I wanted to find out more from this girl, so I made no further comment, "Are you sure?"

"Yes, quite!"

"Have you seen that church bell?" I asked.

"No, but I've…" and she stopped. What was she about to say?

"Might they have moved the church bell?"

"I've looked everywhere and have not found a trace."

"Have you asked the lamas in the temple?"

"They always say they don't know. If you ask them too many questions, they become suspicious," she said.

We fell into silence, and glanced at each other. Her headscarf was still wrapped tightly about her face, and when she had a sip of the water, she carefully drew it aside from her mouth. I looked away to save her any embarrassment.

"Do you often come to Lhasa?" I asked.

"It's the third time."

"And you've never seen that bell?"

She looked at me sharply, then lowered her head pretending to be sucking the straw, and said nothing.

"Are you a Buddhist?" I deliberately changed the subject.

"Yes, I am."

"I've heard that Tibetan Buddhists come great distances to Lhasa to worship the Buddha in the Jokhang Temple."

"Yes, it's the greatest wish of every Tibetan."

"You seem a little different from the other pilgrims."

"You seem to notice me."

"You are rather unusual."

She lowered her head and looked elsewhere.

Some time went by. "Your hat's nice. You do not look like a local person." She seemed to be wanting to change the conversation.

"It's made in Scotland." To reassure her, I explained who I was. "I'm from Scotland."

"Scotland!" she sounded a little surprised, "so you are Scottish." She suddenly switched to English. Though her spoken English sounded a little wooden, I was surprised.

"I am not a Scot, really I'm a Scottish Chinese," I said.

"All right!" She seemed to be thinking about something.

"Do you know where Scotland is?"

"Of course I know. My fa …" She stopped again.

"Who taught you to speak English?"

She looked down and did not answer my question. "Why are you in Lhasa?" she asked.

"I'm a tourist!"

"Oh, really!" She didn't seem to believe me.

I hesitated. "I'm here to pursue my dream."

"And have you found it?"

"Not yet."

"What is it?" She sounded curious.

"Shang - ri - la." I said this slowly, and watched for her reaction.

When she heard this, she looked at me attentively. "Is this your occupation?"

"What occupation?"

"A book writer perhaps, searching for the story of Shangri-La."

"I'm not a writer, though I might be in my spare time if I knew the truth about it. In fact, I am working in an elderly centre, helping and looking after old people." This seemed to reassure her about me.

"How long will you be staying in Lhasa?" she asked.

"About five days."

"And then?"

"I'm not sure yet. I have to be in Lijiang by the 29th," I said.

"Do you like hiking?"

I nodded, and there was a pause. It was cold now, with fine rain beginning to fall and a slight wind. I had a mild headache. Perhaps it was the smoke from the butter lamps in the temple that was still affecting me. I kept frowning, and she noticed.

"You have altitude sickness symptoms," she said. "Take it gently, don't rush about; don't worry, Lhasa is only at 3,600 metres, not really high and you should adjust soon."

I kept my eyes closed and I was thinking about how high 3,600 metres was. The highest mountain in Britain is Ben Nevis in Scotland, at 1,344 metres. Lhasa was almost three times that! The year before when I was in Lhasa for the first time, I had felt miserable with altitude sickness, but had tried to cope without medication and recovered within a day. Then I had gone much higher and felt fine. This time should be no problem.

Since 4 o'clock that morning, I had been rushing to Chengdu airport for the flight, then scrambling for the bus, and arriving at the Jokhang Temple without stopping for a rest. I was still carrying my backpack, feeling very tired and sleepy. I leaned against a pillar with my eyes shut, hoping that I would soon feel better. For a moment, I seemed to hear her talking to someone in Tibetan.

Pursuing my dream

"Wake up! Follow me."

"Where to?" I was half asleep.

"Somewhere that you won't feel altitude sickness."

"There's no need. I'll rest and be fine."

"Didn't you say you were pursuing your dream? Well then, come with me!'"

"Are you taking me to Shangri-La?'"

"No, but to somewhere as good." With that, she picked up the bag beside her, and turned confidently to go. She seemed quite certain that I would go with her. Her words were like a tonic to me. I felt renewed spirits, picked my pack up, and followed quickly after her out of the Temple and then to the right into Barkor Street. The courtyard in front of the Temple was as crowded as ever. She walked lightly, and never looked round to see if I was following. I think that she was listening to my footsteps, and sometimes she slowed down to let me catch up a bit. My backpack seemed to be getting heavier and heavier, and I rushed on panting like a dog, now turning left, then right, then left again, going I didn't know where. At last we arrived in a small street.

"Wait for a little." She looked round, and went over to a small car. It didn't look like a taxi. The driver seemed to be waiting for her. She said something to the driver in Tibetan and waved to me to get in. Where were we going, and for how long? Would I be safe? I held back a little, and then made up my mind, and got into the back.

She slipped into the front seat and asked me, "Are you worried?"

I paused for a moment. "No, I'm fine! Perhaps I was running too fast, and my head is aching a bit." I took a deep breath and tried to relax. She opened a compartment at the front and took out a flask. She poured out a hot drink for me. It was butter tea. I had tried this several times before and recognized it right away.

"This is not the usual butter tea. It's a secret recipe handed down in my family for altitude sickness. Do you want to try it?" she said, and slowly poured me out a full cup. "It will help to calm you down."

"Thank you!" I took the cup and drank it. It did taste different, salty with something of a tart fruity flavour. It was refreshing.

"Take a rest, and when we're there I'll wake you."

I first checked my watch. It was a little after seven o'clock. Out of politeness, I closed my eyes, but I tried to keep wide awake, and was thinking over what had happened that day. The car set off, it was getting dark, and I peeped to try to see our direction. My eyelids would not stay open. At first, the two of them were talking in Tibetan and sometimes laughing, but I understood nothing that was said. Fairly soon, they were silent, and I felt the car jolting over an unsurfaced road, the engine roaring constantly, climbing and descending, speeding up and slowing down, continuing into the night. I seemed to have taken a sleeping potion, a deep sleep came on and overwhelmed me.

CHAPTER 4

MYSTERIOUS JOURNEY

"Are you awake? We're nearly there!"

I woke up and looked out. It was murky grey, except straight ahead where dawn was appearing: we were driving east. I looked at my watch. It was just after seven o'clock. I felt puzzled that I could have been asleep for twelve hours without any awareness of what was happening or of the car stopping during the night. My companion in the front had now removed her scarf and I could only see her hair from behind. Though I was keen to see her face, I restrained my curiosity and did not wish to appear impatient, to avoid causing embarrassment to her.

Soon we turned off up a rough mountain track. On both sides were scattered patches of scrub. It was a desolate scene. The road was slippery, with the endless noise of stones thrown up by the tyres. It wound for about five kilometres and then stopped. "That's as far as the road goes. Let's get out!"

She got out. I took my pack beside me and got out too. I stretched myself. The air was fresh, damp and very cold. She spoke to the driver and he turned and drove off at speed.

"Well, how do you feel? No headache anymore, I trust!" She turned her head and looked at me.

I saw her face for the first time. After a moment, I replied, "Excellent, the headache's gone."

A pair of familiar eyes, black and bright, a fine round face, long elegant hair woven into many small plaits, and two slender coloured necklaces; she was about 1.65 metres tall, wearing black

Tibetan costume and a long thick robe. Her complexion was paler than that of many Tibetans, and on her cheeks two red patches were faintly visible. These usually appeared on the faces of inhabitants of the high plateau due to the strong sunlight.

I was looking at her involuntarily. She seemed a little ill at ease, and said, "Well, I don't look like a bad person, do I?"

I promptly smiled as a reply.

"My name is Padma. Welcome to my home and be our guest!"

"Sam Chau. I'm so pleased to be invited." I nodded and put out my hand to shake hers.

"We still have a long way to go. You can manage, can't you?" She seemed to have doubt on my ability.

"I'll try my best," I replied. I felt a little sour on hearing this, and could imagine that it would not be an easy journey ahead of us. Wasting no time, I immediately shouldered my pack and said, "Off we go!" I followed behind her on a small, winding path.

"Why don't you ask where we're going?" Padma asked, without looking round.

"Well, I'm here, and what comes next is up to you; you honour me with your attention," I said.

"Well then, we'll first have something to eat at the village in front, then continue," Padma said, as she pressed on.

"No problem at all!" I replied light-heartedly.

A Little Church

By now, the sun was rising from behind the mountains, and all at once it was full daylight. We had been walking for about thirty minutes when a small village appeared on our right on the mountain side, with its houses scattered here and there among banana trees. We followed the path into the village. There were about thirty houses and most were built of mud brick in three floors. There were also two-floor houses of wood and bamboo. This was a mixed village of Tibetans, Monbas and Lopas and the villagers were already up and working.

By the entrance, there was a notice: *Do not enter without permission.*

"Padma, do you see the notice?" I was a bit worried.

"Don't worry, just follow me!" Padma strode into the village and she seemed to know the village well. The villagers all waved and greeted her when they saw her, and gave me friendly smiles.

"How many people live here?"

"Just over a hundred."

Padma took me to a Tibetan house. The host was standing at the door waving to invite us inside. It was a spacious house. I was surprised to find many chairs neatly set in rows and I saw on the wall a cross. It was certainly a meeting place, I guessed. "Is this a church?" I asked.

"Yes, it's also Baibuqi's home."

"Is he a priest?"

"Well, yes; he has not been baptised, but his father was," Padma replied.

"Who baptised his father?"

"An evangelist called Brinklow."

I thought for a little. "I certainly know the name, but don't remember clearly."

"After his father died, Baibuqi carried on his work as an evangelist."

"Are there many Christians here?"

"Around twenty." Padma answered every question I asked. She seemed to know everything about the village.

"None of them baptised?" I couldn't stop my curiosity.

"Does it matter?"

I shrugged my shoulders. Now Baibuqi indicated to us that breakfast was ready. Porridge, boiled eggs and pickled vegetables had been laid out on a low table. We sat on the floor beside the hearth and ate our breakfast. It was a simple but delicious meal.

Padma told me to eat a bit more, as we still had quite a difficult journey ahead. I felt that Padma was watching the time, as she picked up her bag as soon as she had put down her bowl and chopsticks. I knew she was hurrying me, and so I ate quickly too.

"Can we spend some time here?" I suggested.

"Yes, we can, if you don't mind arriving in Lijiang after the 29th."

"Then let's be on our way!" Padma seemed to have made plans for me already.

As we were leaving the house I heard, "Dang, dang, dang." Baibuqi's wife was tolling the bell which hung high under the eves.

"What's that about?"

"Today's Sunday, don't you remember?"

"Of course, there's a service!" People were now walking over. We then said goodbye and were on our way.

Restricted Zone

Not too far away from the village, there was another notice board: *Restricted zone, all tourists stop!* I paused for a moment and looked around the area. "What does it mean?" I asked.

"There are poisonous snakes and wild animals, landslides and swamp. It's very dangerous. Are you afraid?" She spoke easily without any worry on her face.

"If you're not, why should I be?"

"Well then, follow me!"

Though I had said that, I felt somewhat uneasy and remained on high alert. At first, the going was straightforward, and we were talking and laughing.

"Are you Tibetan?" I asked.

"You've guessed half right, my father is Han Chinese," Padma answered straight.

"Why then do you have a Tibetan name?"

"My father says we should respect the local traditions, so I was given a Tibetan name."

"What does it mean?"

"Lotus flower."

"What a pretty name! How old are you?" I asked.

"Tuesday will be my twentieth birthday."

"Well, then happy birthday to you when it comes!" I picked a spray of flowers and put it on her backpack. She was pleased and smiled.

"What date is Tuesday, Padma?"

"September the 27th."

I thought a little, "What a coincidence! It's Holly's birthday as well."

"Who?"

"Oh! my daughter," I said. "She's older than you, in fact."

"Is that so? You don't look old at all," she stared at me with a little doubt. "Then I should call you Uncle Sam!"

"That's okay!"

Suddenly, I realized that I was stepping into an awkward age, I could not pretend that I was young, and I was not prepared to be old either. I was still fit, but to be called 'uncle' was a reminder that I was getting older, and that there was now a distance between me and young people. Time is merciless and cruel. It was a prompt to me to make good use of time, doing things that make life significant. No use regretting!

"Do you not feel lonely travelling on your own?" she asked me.

"Yes, sometimes," I said. "A wise man said, '*Silence separates more than distance.*' If you are travelling with someone that you are not able to communicate with, you will feel lonelier than if you were travelling alone."

Padma looked at me seriously. "What about now?"

I looked at her and didn't answer. Then we both laughed. "How much further do we have to go?"

She pointed to a mountain top far in front. "Behind that

mountain, another twenty kilometres or so."

"It's not far, another five hours walk perhaps!" I spoke light-heartedly.

Padma gave me a little smile. "Come on, let's go!" She didn't answer my question.

Pilgrim Couple

We were walking on a faint winding track that was overgrown with shrubs and creepers. There were many springs in the lush forest, but no sign of humans around.

"It looks as though no one has been along this path for a long time,"

"You're right!" Padma said. "People in our valley very seldom use this path."

"Is that so?" I said. She was perhaps suggesting that there was another route.

"This is a shortcut," she tried to explain.

This raised doubts in my mind. When I travel alone, I am often on the alert and safety comes first. The present encounter had been sudden, and I had been making contingency plans and repeatedly considering the situation. I was going with a young girl that I had just met to visit a distant place. If she was scheming something, why would she need to bring me so far? This thought reassured me, and I walked more easily.

The untouched beauty around me was enchanting, and I stopped often along the quiet path among the woods and flowers to take photographs. Padma however was anxious and objected, "If you carry on like this, we won't reach home tomorrow either. Watch where you're going or you'll be in trouble!" When I heard her tone, I at once put the camera away and kept up my pace.

The gentle gradient of the mountain path had made a pleasant journey so far. Padma told me that the worst of the rainy season was over, and the weather was getting finer every day. Autumn flowers were blooming. At times, we were walking over meadows decorated with millions of dots of white and yellow flowers.

The mountain side was now thickly forested, and it looked scary and full of dangers, perhaps of wild animals attacking or an encounter with brigands. I constantly looked around to assess any risks. Padma was not talking, but from the way she walked she seemed quite at ease. The two of us on the mountain path were like a couple of pilgrims, one in front and one behind, trekking onwards.

Danger Zone

My backpack seemed to be getting heavier, walking was becoming more laboured and my pace was slowing down. It was windy and the air was very damp, and now and then drops of water were hitting my face. At this moment, Padma now had her scarf back on. I followed behind her in silence with my head down, panting, and I watched as her regular steps threw up little sprays of mud. I was struggling to keep up.

Although the view on all sides was obscured by thick mist, it was a beautiful scene which I could not resist and I took out my camera for a few shots. When I lagged a bit too far behind, she would turn round to check. "Uncle Sam, you must follow me, don't stray. There is treacherous ground here. You wouldn't be able to get yourself out if you fell in." Padma seemed to know the way very well, bearing to the left or to the right expertly.

We came to a suspension bridge which looked rather primitive. Padma examined it for a while and then said, "Uncle Sam, are you alright with this?"

"Er," I didn't give an answer. I was looking at the bridge with concern.

The bridge was about twenty metres across, constructed with steel cables and planks. The cables, fixed to the rock, were quite worn. Two cables were for holding on to, and wooden planks a metre long were laid across the two cables below. The bridge was about ten metres above the river, swaying gently in the wind. I went over to inspect the cables where they were fixed, and when I looked round, I was startled to see that Padma was already in the middle of the bridge, and in no time she was on the other side.

"Okay, your turn," Padma shouted.

Sometimes you just have to do things you don't want to do. This seemed to be the only way forward and returning was quite impossible. There was no avoiding it. I gritted my teeth and stepped out onto the lurching bridge. When I saw the water surging below, my legs felt weak. Step by step I moved gingerly forward, and eventually I was across. Standing by the cliff, my legs were quivering.

"Sit and have a rest! We need to be well prepared."

"What for?" I looked at her for an answer.

"In front, there is a stretch of forest. The bushes are full of bloodthirsty leeches. The slightest gap in your clothes and they burrow in and suck your blood. However careful you are, they'll always find a way." Her words sounded frightening.

In the luxuriant forest, the old trees soared up to the sky. Innumerable creepers clung to their trunks and tied tree to tree. Thick and fine suspended roots hung from the trunks to the ground, and others drifted in the air like an old man's beard. Deep in the forest, only faint dappled sunlight filtered through the thick foliage; the forest ground, surprisingly open and relatively easy to move about, was lit here and there by the golden beams pouring down from above. Amidst the unceasing bird calls, strange sounds were often heard from the depths of the thickets. I had to remain calm, follow Padma and walk briskly forward.

There were leeches everywhere clinging to leaves and twigs, bending their long bodies and waiting to lunge. I picked a leafy branch and made sure that it was uninfested, and used it to swipe my clothes and brush my face. When Padma saw me doing this, she giggled and said, "Don't get so worried!" Padma seemed very experienced. She walked along the centre of the path carefully avoiding contact with the bushes. I followed her rhythmical footsteps, and nimbly kept clear of the undergrowth. Apart from leeches attacking, I was all the time having to wave mosquitoes away from my face. One careless touching of nettles by the path, and red sores appeared on my hands, stinging like a painful burn. There was some discomfort, but at least I wasn't bothered by the leeches, and we encountered no poisonous snakes or wild animals. When we came out of the forest, we looked at each other to see that all was well and then continued

Orchard in the Wild

It was about midday. The wind had died down. Though the cloud had disappeared, the sun was weak and the weather looked unpromising.

We walked through a narrow valley. The view had opened out. A brook flowed down the glen with its ribbon of water winding lazily between the long green grass on both sides. On the hill slope were scattered pine trees, their fresh green aroma filling the air.

We followed a path gently downhill. Suddenly, it looked as though we had entered an orchard. Fruit trees were everywhere. It appeared that no one had ever collected them. I saw apples, oranges, peaches and walnuts growing in profusion. Oranges and peaches were not quite ready yet. The apples and walnuts didn't taste good at all.

Along the path were many kinds of wild berries. Among the bushes I found a solitary pomegranate tree. Though short, it was growing exceptionally well. Its branches were strung with big red fruit. Many had already ripened and split open, and the ground below was covered in seeds. It made my mouth water. I picked one to try. It was sweet and juicy. It seemed a pity that no one would be able to enjoy this beautiful fruit in such a remote place.

A poet wrote:

In the deep mountains the pomegranate has ripened,
opening its mouth and smiling at the sun;
Deep in the mountains few come to collect them,
rubies and pearls rolling away.

Padma much enjoyed the blackberries. We picked and ate as we walked, and this helped to boost our morale. I saw a kind of blueberry which looked familiar to me. When I was a boy in the countryside, they grew all over the hills, and I used to eat lots. I picked one and put it in my mouth.

"You can't eat those!" Padma shouted.

"What, are they poisonous?" I at once spat it out.

"Not exactly, but if you eat them, I may have to carry you."

"It's a blueberry, isn't it?"

"No, it's not. We call it a 'numb berry'. We use it as an anaesthetic and a sleep inducer."

"Who taught you that?"

"My father."

So Padma knew about medicinal plants as well. This was the second, perhaps the third mention I had heard from her about her family. Who else was there in her family? What was her home like? What kind of reception would I find? All sorts of queries kept floating in my mind. It was not so easy to feel relaxed.

A Rope Slide

"How much further is it?"

"Over the rope slide in front and we're there."

"At last! Hurrah!" I was overjoyed.

"That's just to where we have a rest. Our final destination's further on."

"Oh, no!" I suddenly felt a bit disappointed.

"You're sorry you came, are you?" Padma sounded impatient, perhaps she was exhausted.

"No, not at all, just a little tired. Actually, the rope slide is fun. I used to play on them when I was little, and I can try it again."

At the river bank, I was relieved to see that it was not as bad as I had expected. The river was calm and only about ten metres wide. A rope was suspended about five metres above the water. I imagined that if I fell in, I could still swim ashore easily. I was amazed to find that the rope was made of twisted strands of bamboo. It seemed that the lubricant on it had dried out long ago. I could still smell the faint pungent scent of butter oil. There was only a single rope, dropping gently to the other bank. Looking across to the other side, the first query that came to my mind was, how could I get back across when I returned?

From nowhere, Padma had found two strong wood sliders which fitted well over the rope. A raw hide yak strap was fastened to the slider as a seat. Looking at the long rope bending over the river, I said boldly, "Let me go first!" Padma smiled and helped me sit on the strap, telling me to hold tight to the hanging rope, then she gave me a push, and off I shot over the middle of the river, with a smell of singeing wood from the slider running over the rope. In no time I was on the other side. Padma quickly followed.

After crossing the river, a faint track led us over a stretch of marshy grassland. Things were not cheerful for us at all, not only did our feet keep sinking into the mud, but clouds now swept swiftly across the sun and it started drizzling. Trying hard to pull our feet out of the mud while trudging through, we were totally exhausted. I could hear Padma panting heavily in front of me. We finally got over to the solid ground beyond. Our shoes were now probably double the usual weight with all the mud sticking on them. We had to wipe it off before we pressed on.

A REMOTE HOMESTEAD

The rain now was more than drizzling. The wind grew more and more violent and the rain was blown on my face like stinging needles. Padma had to keep her head down as she surged on. After a short distance, I was surprised to see a good path ahead of us going up to the ridge. I also saw crops of peas and beans on both sides. Though Padma did not say a word, I could imagine that this was an inhabited area. I at once felt much relieved.

Over the ridge, we saw a dense thicket of green bamboo and beside it was a solitary wooden house. A puff of grey smoke was rising from the roof. I could hear the muffled sound of a dog barking. I followed close behind Padma, walking with a much lighter step.

As we approached the house, a Tibetan mastiff barked and growled at us viciously. It was chained to a thick wooden pillar by the door, straining frantically, trying to break loose and attack us. Padma looked a little scared and hesitated to make a forward step.

At this moment, a Tibetan man came out of the house and shouted at the dog. It at once quietened down and lay on the ground. The man then indicated to us to go inside. Padma evidently knew him.

We climbed up a short wooden ladder which was simply made from a large notched tree-trunk. When we went into the house, we saw a woman and a child there. Padma introduced us. Our host was Danji and his wife Sangmei. She was sitting by the hearth brewing tea and the child was playing beside her. When she saw us, she smiled and nodded, and motioned to us with her hand to sit by the fire.

It was three o'clock in the afternoon, the sun still hiding behind the clouds. It was a reasonably bright day, but very dark inside the house. Other than the open fire, there was only a glimmer of daylight coming through a small window. The yak-dung fire smoked evilly. A big cloud was hovering under the thatched roof, waiting to find its way out. This might be a good way of getting rid of the insects.

"It's still early, we'll first rest here a while!" Padma said.

"Okay!" I replied.

We quickly took off our soaking wet shoes and socks to dry them by the fire. The woman courteously gave us butter tea that had just been brewed. It was very hot, and I held the brimming wooden cup in both hands, and slowly sipped the tea. I felt the warm liquid flowing inside me slowly reviving my energy. I am not very fond of butter tea, but there was no other choice. When Padma had drunk her tea, she sat beside the hearth with her eyes closed. She seemed quite tired.

In the dark room, the flickering firelight played on Padma's face and figure. Her appearance and her costume were more Tibetan than Han Chinese. Though only twenty, her manner was very mature and assured. Once again, a host of questions welled up in my mind. Who was she? Where did she come from? Why did she want to take a stranger to her home, and why were we taking such a remote and difficult route? What was her motive? What was she thinking just now? She did not seem to have any doubts about me.

Danji was leaning against the door repairing a farm tool, his wife was busy with her chores, and the child was sleeping by the fire. All was calm.

Suddenly, it became dark and a wind rose. The distant sound of thunder came, and squalls of heavy rain pattered on the roof. Danji said to Padma in Tibetan, "The weather's not very good; I want to go to see how the river is." He put on a straw cape and went out.

Padma stood up and gestured to Sangmei, and then she said to me, "We will go out while we still can to get some vegetables for supper. Could you stay and keep an eye on the child?"

When I saw the little child fast asleep, I felt that I could not refuse. "That's fine!" I answered.

They both put on straw capes and went out, closing the door after them and leaving me with the child.

Inside the House

I looked all around me. The furnishings were very simple. There was a rather large bed, made of wooden planks, piled with blankets of yak felt. It looked like the only place where the family could be snug. There was a low table and some little stools. In the corner, there was a pile of logs and dry yak-dung. The fire was in the middle of the room, and this was where they cooked. There was an iron cooking basin, a wooden churn for making butter tea, a stone hand-mill for grinding corn, several bamboo basket, wooden bowls and bamboo mugs. By the door were placed some old wooden farm tools and hunting gear such as a cross-bow and a long knife. Many golden corncobs, red chilli peppers and strips of dried meat were hung by the door; the fields grew many vegetables. They did not seem to be short of food.

This was a two-floor house. Downstairs were the animal quarters and upstairs was the family's home. There were only three small windows round the house. Doors and windows were of rough workmanship, and dapples of light came in through crevices in the log walls. They had no chimney, just a small hole in the roof. Much of the room had been smoked to a dull black.

On the beam above hung something very strange. It looked like a phallic carving with red paint dimly visible at an end. This must be something related to the Monba religion, a prayer for a thriving family. Sangmei must be a Monba.

My eyes moved slowly across the wall and came on a tattered black and white photograph. This was of two Tibetans with a middle-aged western woman, with the Potala Palace in the background. There was a faded and seemingly incomplete signature in the right hand bottom corner, 'A… and … 192…' Who were they?

There was a small shelf on the wall with some empty bottles, cans and other objects. Among these was a small pile of stones in various colours: red, yellow, blue, and green. I stared at them, and could not help picking up a red one for a closer look. The stones had not been polished, but they were translucent like gemstones. Though I am not an expert, these looked valuable. There were about twenty, the size of small marbles. There were some smaller grains of gold, too. I imagined that this amounted to considerable wealth, and wondered whether the owner realized this. Anyone seeing them would be fascinated. I played with the red stone for quite a while, and then put it back in its place.

Just then, Padma and Sangmei came in the door. They took no notice of what I was doing. Sangmei was carrying a large basket with the vegetables which they had picked in the field, cabbages, potatoes, and tomatoes, and she went straight into the kitchen to prepare supper whilst Padma took her pack and dried her wet clothes at the fire. The rain was becoming heavier. Danji returned, in his soaking straw cape, and spoke in Tibetan to Padma.

"The rain is too heavy, and the river is very rough. We would not be able to cross it. We should spend the night here," she said.

What else could I do now? I must not cling too hard to my hopes. I could only nod my head in acceptance.

For supper, unexpectedly, we had boiled chicken with potatoes, green vegetables and rice. It was long since I had had such a fresh and delicious meal, and I had a good appetite. So had Padma. Through the translating of Padma, we talked and laughed while we were enjoying our meal. Sangmei clearly had a speech difficulty. She asked many questions about my family through signs to Padma. Sometimes I was not sure where the questions were coming from, but they were contented with my replies.

The little boy was just four and kept close to his father most of the time. He liked the chocolate and the crisps that I gave him, and kept asking me to show him the camera. He was overjoyed to see his own digital images.

"Who are the people in the photograph?" I asked of a sudden.

Danji looked at the photograph, then took it down from the wall and pointed the people out. "This is my father and my uncle. This is a Ladakhi woman. She has blond hair."

"Could I take a look?" I took the photo and examined it for a while. "How did they meet each other?"

"My father told me that they met the Ladakhi woman and a young lama when they went to Lhasa to sell barley. The lama invited them to visit the Potala Palace and offered gladly to be their guide. After the visit, my father gave him a few copper coins as alms. The woman asked to take a photo with them and took down their address. Six months later the photograph was received through the post."

"Have you read about this woman?" Padma asked.

"I am not sure."

Padma looked at me, and didn't ask further.

'Miguel'

By half past seven, it was already dark outside. Sangmei cleared the table and gave the floor a sweep. Then she spread thick felts by the fire for us to lie down on. The rain was falling steadily outside.

Intermittent flashes lit up the room, and every so often our conversation was broken by the thunder which seemed to be getting closer and louder. Suddenly, right above the house, there was a sharp flash of lightning followed by a huge clap of thunder which shook the house. We were all quiet.

Suddenly from deep in the valley came a long and high-pitched animal cry. Everyone froze and listened. The little boy clung to his father's leg. The cry was repeated a few times, and then ceased.

"It's Miguel." Danji looked nervous.

"What Guel? Do you mean a ghost?" 'Guel' sounds like 'ghost' in Chinese.

"It's not a ghost, it's 'Miguel'. Miguel is a wild creature that is half human and half ape."

I asked Danji if this was just a rumour. "No, no," he said, "It's real. About ten years ago, I came across a creature covered all over in brown hair. It was well over two metres tall and it walked like a human. I followed it quietly through the woods, but it realized and turned back to scream at me: 'Kwei Kwei'. I didn't dare go any further, and he quickly disappeared in the forest." Danji spoke with excitement, "They usually come out hunting in the forest at night or in the rain. A couple of times, the garden fence was torn down and some of our livestock were killed and went missing. I suspected that it was Miguel."

In fact, there have long been accounts of a wild man in the dense forests in the Himalayas. It is also known as the 'yeti'. There have been many expeditions to the Himalayas to look for it. They have taken hi-tech equipment deep into the forests, and have kept watch for nights on end, but they have never found firm evidence.

Attempting to put our fears at ease, I proposed in fun that we should organize yeti discovery tours. I would publicize them abroad, Padma would be responsible for bringing in the tourists, and Danji would be the tour guide. There would be plenty of business, more than we could cope with. The three of us drank to this proposal. I took a bit of charcoal out of the fire and drew 'B & B' on a wooden board.

"What does that mean?" Danji asked.

"It means a bed and a breakfast. It's very popular business in Scotland, providing inexpensive accommodation for visitors. If you put up a sign at your door, foreigners will come to stay. That is the first stage in our joint venture."

We were laughing, drinking yellow wine and eating roast potatoes, and slowly we fell silent.

A Night in the Wilds

When night came, the room was very dark with only light from the fire and a dim butter lamp. I could not see and gave up trying to write my diary. The cold wind penetrated through the crevices in the wooden plank walls. It was bitterly cold and damp. The wind was roaring outside. A snapped branch of a banana tree beside the house was slapping the wall like torn sails and heavy raindrops were pattering on all sides of the house.

Often the low, spine-tingling sounds of wild animal cries could be heard. It was as though I was suddenly back in the ancient times; a peculiar sense of remoteness overwhelmed me, in the darkness of the night, staying in a lodging in the wilderness, danger lurking on every side. Looking back on the day's journey, I seemed to have been learning a new lesson in my life, and I was glad that at my age I had been physically able to cope so far.

The wood in the fire sparked and crackled, and the firelight played on the wall like ghost shadows. With eyes half closed I lay in my sleeping bag, listening intently to Sangmei lightly turning a prayer wheel. Though Sangmei could not talk, she could still utter from her throat a slight noise of chanting. How dignified and devout she was. Padma was sleeping with her back to me, and I could make out the sound of her deep breathing. She must have been very tired and had probably fallen asleep. Danji's snoring was now rolling across. The wood fire was burning low. I carefully put on a piece of yak-dung, and the fire burned up more brightly. I gazed into the fire, thoughtfully, listening to the trickle of rain from the thatch. The room was very still for a long while. The fire had burned down quickly and would soon be out, the chill was growing. From downstairs a faint smell came up between the floorboards from the animals. But I felt exhausted, and burrowed down into my sleeping bag, and drifted off to sleep.

I awoke to the sound of dogs barking and cocks crowing. The fire was blazing up, the wood crackling away again and giving off a rich warm smell. Padma was folding her bedding. Danji and his wife must be working outside. I had slept well and felt ready for the day. I rolled up my sleeping bag and went out to enjoy the morning freshness. The rain had stopped, and the wind had died down. The sky was still dark with streaks of dawn light sometimes coming through the thick layer of cloud. Mist was rising from the gorge like a wad of cotton wool and it blotted out the view completely. The river was out of sight far below, and only its rumbling could be heard.

Mastiff Wong Wong

The mastiff that had barked at me yesterday now wagged its tail. I threw it a piece of biscuit, and it caught it in the air. When I put out my hand to stroke the huge head, it put out its tongue to return the greeting. I hadn't expected that we would be good friends so soon.

When Danji saw me playing with the dog, he came over and began to praise him: "Wong Wong has saved our lives. Once when I took him hunting in the forest, we met a large bear. We were too close to avoid it, and I just had to stand still. Wong Wong was like a tiger, barking ferociously at the bear till it turned and left us. Another time, Sangmei was working in the field when two wild dogs broke in. Wong Wong chased them off, he bit one badly, and since then there has never been any sign of wild dogs again." Danji expressed himself with words and gestures.

When I heard this, I took out a piece of dried meat that I still had in my pocket and presented it to Wong Wong as a prize.

Yaks are known as the ships of the high plateau, and these mastiffs are the guards. Born in this harsh environment, they are the loyal companions of the Tibetans, protecting them and their property. They are brave and aggressive, and are said to be a match for leopards and wolves. They are often portrayed as the sacred guard dogs of the Living Buddha.

Breakfast today was rice porridge and pancakes. The little boy was playing while he ate. He was bashing stones together, and the louder the noise, the happier he appeared. I noticed that they were the stones that I had admired. Danji and his wife were sitting watching with delighted smiles, but the noise was a pain to my heart.

When he saw me staring, Danji said, "These are stones from the river under the cliff."

"Are they? They're beautiful," I said with admiration. It was an expensive game though.

In this very isolated place, there was no other habitation in sight. Everything that Danji's family had was what nature provided. Warmth, food and safety were their greatest blessing, and everything around them was valuable and would bring them satisfaction.

"We need to be going again. Are you ready?" Padma asked.

"Yes, Madam!" I replied lightly, and she smiled.

UPHILL DOWNHILL

Saying goodbye to Sangmei, we took our packs and left the house. The rain was off and the clouds were light. The air felt fresher than ever. From where we stood by the cliff, there didn't seem to be any way forward. "We have to go over there." Padma pointed to the mountain on the other side of the gorge.

Down to the River

Danji led us across the field behind the house and we passed through a hidden palisade. We followed a path down intermittent flights of stone steps, turning through thick bushes. We seemed to be going deeper and deeper, into the core of the earth; and it was getting warmer gradually. It took about an hour for us to descend to the bottom of the gorge, down some five hundred metres.

Before us was a fast river, about twenty metres wide. The waves dashed against the cliff face with a frightful force, spray thrown in every direction in a deafening roar. I wondered how we were going to get across. Danji reassured me, and led the way upstream. After we had clambered over a big boulder, we made our way up through a knee-deep meadow for about half a kilometre, when suddenly the scene changed as if by magic. Unfamiliar plants clinging to the banks were flowering in profusion. The river was broad here and flowing smoothly. Danji now said something to Padma, said goodbye to us, and went back the way we had come.

The Boatman

There was a boat here tied to a wooden pole on the bank, but no one in sight.

"Uncle Sam, wait here, and I'll look for the boatman. Whatever you do, don't wander off." Padma went off into the bushes.

I strolled along on the bank. At a bend, I saw a middle-aged man sitting fishing. He had a long bamboo rod that reached almost to the middle of the river, with a piece of coarse string at the end of it. It seemed a rather crude way to fish. After a while, he raised the rod, and I saw that it wasn't a hook at the end of the string but a small long net. Seeing the net was empty, he lowered it into the river again.

He looked round and saw me. "Who are you?" and, before I had time to reply, "What are you doing here?"

I was wondering what to say, when he continued, "Ah! You're a treasure hunter."

"What treasure?"

"Don't you fool me! Everyone who comes here is treasure hunting." At this moment, the string seemed to be tugging. He pulled it up at once, and there it was, a yellow stone in the net. He held it up to the light and muttered, "Not bad!" tossed it into a corner, and let down the net again. It looked like one of the stones that I had seen in Danji's home.

I looked into the corner. There I saw a small pile of different coloured stones, all the size of marbles. Now I knew what he meant by 'treasure'.

"Are these all from the river?" I asked.

He did not answer. He was intent on manoeuvring the rod. However, I had to wait for Padma, so I sat down nearby and watched. After a while, the man said to me, "Could you take the rod for me and I'll have a rest." It seemed a bit abrupt.

I had nothing else to do, so I gladly agreed, "Delighted!"

"I'm Dorje, who are you?"

"I'm Sam. Pleased to meet you!"

He handed me the rod. He told me to keep the rod up, otherwise the net would be swept away. Then he sat against a tree and had a rest. Soon he was on his feet again. "I'm feeling hungry," he said, "I'll go and find some fruit."

"There's no need!" I said, "I've water and biscuits in my pack.

Just help yourself!"

"Thank you very much, then." Dorje at once opened my pack and inspected the contents for a while. "I'd prefer fruit. Wait here, and I'll get you some fresh mangoes to try." He didn't wait for a reply, and went into the trees.

This man's behaviour seemed odd. I wondered how long he would be away. Padma had been away half an hour, and I hoped that nothing was wrong. I held on tight to the rod, feeling a little disquiet. When I thought of Danji's family, their behaviour was curious too, and so was Padma's. Were they all connected? I was a bit confused. I must just be patient!

I was looking at that wonderful pile of stones, yellow, red and green. Suddenly the rope was tugging, and I knew that I had caught something. I retrieved the net. At once I saw it, the size of my thumb, a clear sapphire. Though not cut, it had been washed and scraped in the river till it shone. I held it up to the light. The even blue was fascinating. It was a real gem. I admired it so much, holding it and feeling its coldness against my face. All at once, I felt indecisive. I held on to it for a while, and eventually I put it with the others in the pile, and let out the net again.

Immediately, Dorje reappeared carrying an armful of wild mangoes. He urged me to try them. He took over the rod and tied it to the pole. Then I heard Padma shouting, "Uncle Dorje, Uncle Dorje! Where are you?"

"We're here!" Dorje cried out loudly. When I got up to look, Padma had already joined us.

"Uncle Dorje, where were you? I've been looking everywhere for you!" She sounded a little annoyed.

"My dear Padma, I've been here all the time, waiting for you both." Dorje spoke softly, "Come on, don't be angry, try some mango."

Their conversation was confusing. How had Dorje known we were coming? He took out a ripe mango and handed it to Padma, then threw me one. He started eating hungrily. Though small, they were very juicy. Padma and I ate two each while Dorje had probably consumed four.

"You've met Uncle Sam, then. Can we cross the river?"

"Yes, of course!" Dorje stood up as he spoke.

"Shall I help you stow the net?" I asked.

"No, thank you. I will come back here to wait. You never know, I might hook a big fish."

Dorje was enigmatic. There seemed to be a further meaning behind what he and Padma said to each other. I tried not to think about it too much, nor ask what they were not ready to tell me.

Crossing the River

The wooden boat was some five metres long and slender. I sat behind Padma in the middle. Dorje quickly turned the boat into a small channel. Here the water was quiet, and we moved gently forward. On either side were tall reeds, taller than a person, at times almost blocking the way and making it hard to see where we were going. But Dorje stood confidently at the stern wielding the pole, turning the boat now to the left and now to the right.

After about thirty minutes, the boat touched the shore. "Here we are."

"Uncle Dorje, thank you." Padma took her pack and leapt for the bank.

Dorje held out his hand to say goodbye. "It's been a pleasure to meet you, Sam."

At this sudden cordiality, I at once put out my hand to shake his. There was something hard in his hand. "This is for you," he said.

When I felt the coldness of the object, I realized what it was.

"Oh no, you shouldn't! It's too precious," I said at once.

"Of course I must. The river's full of them. It's a souvenir for you."

I was thrilled, and thanked him over and over.

"What a beautiful sapphire! Favouritism, Uncle Dorje!" said Padma.

"My dear Padma, you already have a red one. We mustn't be greedy, must we!"

"I was just kidding, Uncle Dorje! Take care of yourself. Goodbye!"

We saw Dorje steering the boat away and slowly disappearing among the tall reeds.

"Where does he live?"

"We've been to his home," Padma said. "He is Danji's brother. They live together."

"Does he not have a family yet?"

"Yes, he does. Sangmei is his wife."

"What? Didn't you say that Sangmei was Danji's wife?"

"Yes, she is!" Padma confirmed.

I might not have heard right. It was perplexing, and best not to think about it too much. We had to press on.

Through the Clouds

All around us were high cliffs. I had doubts as to whether we could continue.

"Over the top and we will reach my home," Padma told me.

"How are we going to get over the top?" I doubted.

"Don't worry. Follow me."

In the cliff face behind the bushes, there was a hidden cleft, wide enough for us to squeeze through. After a few dozen paces, we saw a flight of stone steps, straight up like a ladder into the sky. These had been cut out of the rock, and there were iron posts and a chain to hold on to. I followed as close as possible behind Padma. Some stretches were extremely steep, and required hands as well as feet to scramble up. The steps varied in width and height with the changing profile of the cliff, and the going required great effort. On both sides were immense drops, and one felt dizzy looking down.

"Keep climbing and don't look down; watch out for wet and slippery patches," said Padma.

"How many steps altogether?" I hadn't told her that I was afraid of heights.

"Two thousand maybe, or more."

When I heard this, I was sorry then that I had come. If I had had the choice, I would have abandoned my dream, and stuck with my safe routine at home. There was no use for blame really at this moment; it was the problem in front of me that demanded attention. I peered down, and my knees went weak with vertigo. I gripped the hand chain and panted heavily.

"How many steps so far?"

"About five hundred," Padma replied.

"Oh no, another fifteen hun ..."

"Don't count! Here, give me your hand."

Padma was pulling me up. I don't know how many times we stopped to rest. I gradually became aware of the cold damp air and the cloud drifting past.

"Nearly there!" Padma was panting too.

By now, I was too tired to speak. Suddenly, I felt that time was chasing after me and I was getting old. How much further would I be able to go?

Another thirty odd steps, and the clouds suddenly cleared, and I began to feel the warmth of the sun. It was as though hope was with us again. We were at the top of the staircase. At this moment, I felt that every cell and fibre in my body seemed worn out. I was near to collapsing, and slumped to the ground, eyes shut and panting.

"Uncle Sam! Uncle Sam!" Padma anxiously shook my shoulders. She thought that I had passed out.

"I'm fine, I'm fine. I just need a little rest," I told her. At this she relaxed and sat down nearby to rest too, still keeping an eye on me. After a while, I sat up, and we both laughed.

Padma said, "There is an old saying among the villagers: *'Up the mountain we go through the clouds, down the ravine we cross the river. Though we could call to each other from opposite sides, it would take all day for us to meet.'* Now you understand what these verses mean."

I nodded with a smile.

A poet wrote:

> *Half way up the cliff,*
> *we see the sun over the sea of cloud.*
> *Through the air*
> *comes the crow of the heavenly cockerel.*

We were not yet at the summit; but we looked over the restless sea of magnificent and impenetrable cloud, like a silvery platform lit up by the sun, endlessly varied and stretching to infinity. To be able to see this was a real reward for the hardships that we had passed through.

After a little rest, my energy slowly returned. In front of us was a gentle path. "Right! The path's easy from now on," Padma said cheerfully.

Beyond a corner, the scene was all of a sudden filled with sunshine. We were standing on a gentle slope with a broad plain before us surrounded on all sides by high mountains. A village encircled by dark green forest was in the centre.

"Through the wood in front, and we will reach my home." Padma's face lit up as she gazed at the village ahead of us. Her smile expressed her joy in returning home. To me it looked no different from other villages. Could this be the place that I was looking for? It was only curiosity that had driven me here. Yet I did not hold out too much hope.

"Well, let's go!" My tiredness made me a little despondent.

Padma looked at me, and she encouraged me saying, *"If you've not had the chilling cold of the winter snow, you will not smell the fragrance of the plum blossom."*

Though Padma was young, her words were really impressive; I couldn't but make a renewed effort.

Butterfly Gathering

We continued along the path, dropping perhaps two hundred metres. Suddenly, it was as though we had entered a tropical garden. The grass and trees were luxuriant, and hot vapour was rising from the streams floating like mists among the trees. The heat was oppressive.

"My, it's hot!"

"There's a big hot spring over there. The temperature is high. It's our natural bathing place." Padma indicated to the right.

Because of the perennial vapour from the hot spring, the vegetation was lush and flowers flourished everywhere. The birdsong and the sound of insects were delightful, rising like waves from here and there, high to low, louder to softer. Bright sunshine pierced through the trees in thick and fine rays of light, striking the undergrowth like arrow shafts.

Suddenly a beautiful butterfly alighted on Padma's head, contrasting with the colours of her plaits.

I said to her, "Padma, you have a new travelling companion!"

"Have I?" she looked round.

I pointed to the top of her head. She carefully brushed the butterfly away with her hand. Then she looked at me and said, "You have several yourself."

I stopped. "Where?"

"On your hat, on your pack, and your shoulders. Lots of them!"

It was a new experience to have all the butterflies clinging to me. I did not disturb them and continued to walk gently on.

In no time, a cloud of butterflies fluttered up to greet us. Some were large, others small, in different colours and markings. They were all around us, on the path, on the grasses and flowers, on the leaves and branches. Their numbers were growing and they were obstructing our way. We needed to brush them aside constantly and walk with great care. Padma signed to me to keep calm.

Ahead of us, we found beneath a great tree myriad butterflies gathering on a piece of damp ground. All the time, more and more were joining them, and the area they covered kept expanding. A breeze through the grass and up they all rose into the air, then suddenly down they all dropped back again. Tens of thousands of pairs of brilliant wings pulsated before my eyes. It was a radiant, mysterious phenomenon. I felt that I had entered a fairyland. Padma raised her head and spread out her arms to let still more butterflies settle on her, her eyes quietly admiring this beautiful sight.

"The Butterfly Gathering is a natural phenomenon in our valley. It happens once a year. No one knows when or where it will be. It's very seldom that we see this. You are very lucky; perhaps it was meant to happen for you." Padma smiled as she spoke.

I looked at the butterflies filling the sky, and for a long time did not want to leave.

The Watch Tower

When we came out of the wood, a brick tower came into sight on our left. It rose into the blue sky like a ship's mast at some thirty metres high. It was surprising to see such a tall building in this remote place.

"It looks old," I said.

"About sixty years."

Someone called out, "Padma, you're home!" The voice came from the top of the tower.

"Yes! Baiduo, I'm home! Is everyone well?" Padma shouted back.

"Everyone's well. Welcome to your friend!" and the man waved to us.

"Hello!" I waved back.

"It's Baiduo on guard today," Padma said.

He looked as though he was armed. "Are there brigands here?"

"There used to be."

As we went on, the scene was changing. There were more and more signs of activity. The place was seemingly visited by people frequently. Traces of footsteps and piles of yak-dung could be seen. Bees were buzzing around among the flowers.

Padma began to sing: *"A place of beauty where all long to go, grass and trees forever green, a place without sadness, this is Shambhala, a place where immortals dwell. ..."* The song was lovely, and the words were beautiful, too. Her light heartedness showed on her face.

"Are you taking me to Shambhala," I couldn't help interrupting her song.

"We are human beings, not immortals, we cannot go to Shambhala," Padma said. "Shambhala is a mythical place in Tibetan Buddhism, a world of bliss. Only fully enlightened beings can attain to it."

"Is Shambhala Shangri-La?"

"It's not the same. Shangri-La is a more ordinary place, where people enjoy a tranquil life of freedom, but they need to work, and they pass through the normal cycle of life."

"Do you know, then, where Shangri-La is?"

"Uncle Sam, wasn't this why you came with me?"

It seemed that Padma, wise beyond her years, did not wish to disclose more than necessary. It was better for me not to ask further questions, but to tell myself to be patient and to wait for the answer to come.

Our Destination

There was a small village half hidden in the bamboo groves, a dozen fine wooden houses scattered here and there. Around each of these little houses was an orchard. There was a strong aroma of ripe lychees. Great numbers of banana trees were covered in hands of light green fruit. My favourite jack-fruits were already as large as a fist. There were other varieties that I did not recognize, covered in buds that were ready to open. It seemed strange that so many kinds of fruit could be grown here, some of them seemingly out of the normal season.

"It's mild here all year round, with plenty of sunshine. Plants grow very well," Padma said.

"How high are we here?" I asked.

"One thousand metres lower than Lhasa."

"Is rice grown here?"

"Yes, of course, and barley too."

Before the village was a wide paddy field, with rippling golden grain. A line of young women was off to work in the field. They wore short close-fitting jackets and cylindrical dresses with silver ornaments. Their faces were shielded by their tilting grass hats. Each had a small bamboo basket hanging from her waist and on her shoulder carried a long thin pole, bouncing along with straw panniers hanging at both ends.

They walked elegantly along the ridge. The whole picture was pleasant. I felt mystified by the place and I stood transfixed.

"Uncle Sam! Come on, they're waiting for us!"

I came to with a start. "What? Who's waiting?" I asked.

"Our villagers," Padma said.

"And how do they know we're coming?"

"Baiduo has let them know!"

"Oh! Has he got back to the village before us?" I said.

"No, we have our own way. Come on! Let's go."

When I looked back to the tall tower, I saw a puff of smoke rising from the top and Baiduo was still standing there on guard.

Walking for another five minutes, our destination was before us. I suddenly grew nervous. What sort of place was it? Was this the place of my dreams? What reception would I find? I wondered as I went, keeping close behind Padma to the entrance to the village. About twenty people wearing different folk costumes of brilliant colours lined up to greet us with radiant smiles. They started to sing and to dance. Two pretty girls brought us three cups of tea. It was strange, as there were only the two of us.

"Please drink your tea," Padma said.

"Yes, thank you! But you drink too!" I said to her.

"No, it's all for you, you are our guest."

"Alright, thank you!" I said, helping myself to a cup.

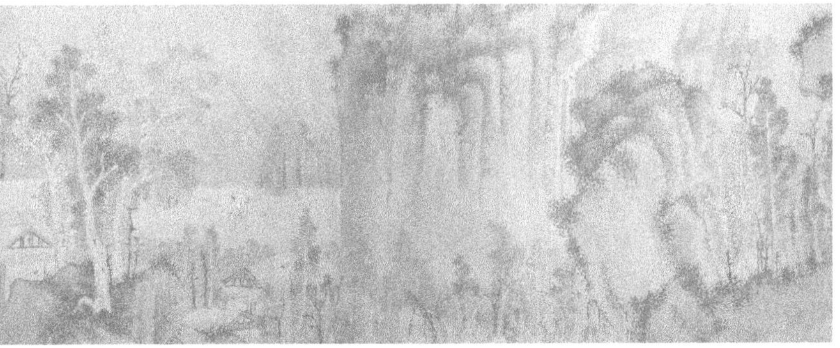

"No, Uncle Sam, start from the left."

I followed Padma's instructions, and drank each in one mouthful. The first cup was bitter; the second sweet; and the last was a mixture of both. I had not come across this tea drinking ritual before; it was very unusual.

"This is the traditional way in which the Bai people in our valley welcome guests," Padma went on, "Don't you like the sweet taste coming after the bitter is over?"

I understood her meaning, and just answered with a smile. Such an imposing welcome made me feel rather pampered, and I kept bowing to everyone and thanking them.

The Tibetan words of greeting 'Zhaxi-dele!' made me feel at home. Some came up and shook my hand and said hello, some stuck their tongues out at me, clasping their hands before them. Padma said that this was how Tibetans expressed their welcome to guests.

Some said in low voices, "That's the guest from far away that Padma's brought home with her."

The children in particular seemed very happy, capering and prancing behind us.

A woman dressed in Mongolian costume came over and said to Padma, "When you have the time, bring your friend round and be our guest, please."

Padma told me her request, and I nodded assent.

"Yes please! Thank you for your invitation, Hameina!" Padma answered in her language. The woman walked away pleased. Padma looked satisfied. She was smiling. I thought that these people were most friendly and civil. It was the first time that I had been in an unfamiliar place and felt completely secure.

CHAPTER 5

A PLACE BEYOND

PADMA'S HOME

Up on a little hill, one could enjoy a spectacular view over the valley. There was lovely wooden house built on top of a gentle slope. A little stream was flowing beside it. In front of the house, many herbal plants had been hung out to dry in the big courtyard. The family seemed to be herbalists. Behind the house was a thick green wood.

"This is my home!" said Padma. She led me in and quickly poured me a cup of hot green tea. "I'll go and get my parents. Please sit down for a while." Padma stepped quickly out into the back garden.

The room was full of dried herbs, scattered around. There were two glass cabinets standing by the wall. One was filled with ginseng and caterpillar fungus and some other medicinal materials; the other held western medicines like painkillers and antibiotics. I was surprised to see these and supposed that someone here would know how to use them. All at once, someone behind me said in English, "Welcome to the valley."

I turned and saw a middle-aged couple dressed in Tibetan clothes. Padma was behind.

The man held out his hand, "How do you do? I am Tserin."

I shook his hand while Padma stepped forward and made the introduction. "This is my *Apa* and my *Ama*."

"I hear that you are from Scotland."

"Yes, I am."

"How long have you been in Scotland?" He beckoned me to sit down on a wooden chair.

"Thirty-three years."

"Well!" he said. "In fact, I went to Scotland before you."

"Oh! Is that so?"

"Yes, I remember it was in 1965."

"Where was it in Scotland?" I asked.

"I stayed in Glasgow and Edinburgh for a short while. Then I travelled to Inverness."

"How did you find it there?"

"Glasgow looked monotonous with its dark buildings, and it was always so smoky. They said that this was the coal fires. Edinburgh seemed fresher. The castle was magnificent, a little like the Potala Palace. It was so rich in Scotland's history. Scotland's scenery was lovely," he said. "By the way! Have they found Nessie yet?"

"It's hard to say. I've been there a few times and I've never seen the monster," I said.

We all laughed. Now I understood why Padma told she knew of Scotland when we met in the Jokhang Temple. Padma was listening and smiled. She clearly understood what we were saying. Her mother seemed a little quiet, but I was assured a warm welcome by her friendly smiling face. Tserin looked at her and realized that she had been left out. He changed to speaking in Putonghua.

"Padma's given you a hard time, I imagine!"

"Yes, she has. It was a real challenge for me." I smiled and looked at Padma. "Did you teach Padma English?"

He looked at her. "A poor student!"

"Just lack of practice!" Padma said as an excuse.

"Padma told me that you were Han, but you are wearing Tibetan clothes," I ventured.

"Yes!" he said. "But it's only my clothes and they don't have much significance. I suppose that you sometimes wear a kilt?"

"It's true," I said.

His wife said graciously, "Mr Chau, welcome to our home. I will go to prepare supper. Please make yourself at home here." With this she nodded and went to the kitchen.

"I'll help you, *Ama*." Padma followed. She seemed a child with her parents.

Someone outside the door called out, "Dr Tserin, are you at home?"

"Here I am, please come in, Zhuoga." He asked her to sit down and then inquired how she was feeling today.

"Much better! But I've still a slight headache," she said.

Tserin felt her pulse. I was surprised when I saw him using both his hands, holding up each of her wrists. He listened quietly, and asked her to open her mouth for him to check. "Zhuoga, your cold is almost better. Drink the herb potion one more time tonight and that will be enough. If in the morning you still have a headache, take one painkiller!" Tserin took two painkiller tablets out of the cabinet and gave them to her. "Remember, if you don't have a headache don't take these!"

Tserin's patience and his professionalism as he examined the patient filled me with admiration. The woman took the medicine and went out satisfied. I wondered why Tserin had not asked for any fee or recompense.

Potato Story

Padma came out of the kitchen. "Uncle Sam, try some snacks Ama has made specially for you." She placed a dish of potato chips in front of me and a bottle of homemade tomato ketchup.

"This is the staple food of the westerners," I smiled and said. "I remember when I first went to Britain, my mother told me that British people ate only potato chips. Being considerate, my mother had prepared a little bag of rice, a bowl and a pair of chopsticks in my baggage."

"Your mother is very thoughtful."

"Yes, she was!"

"Come on, try our local produce." Tserin poured out some tomato ketchup into a little dish, picked up the chips with his fingers and invited me to join him.

"They taste fresh and delicious," I said. "I usually think that potatoes can only be seen in western countries. I never thought I'd be eating them here. Are they grown here?"

"You call them 'potatoes', and we call them 'earth beans'. They never used to be here, but now you will see them everywhere. Have you heard how they came? It's connected with your home country."

I felt uncertain. "My home country?"

"I mean Scotland. *'Live long in another country, and it becomes your country too.'* I hope you don't mind my talking like that."

"No, not at all. Actually, you are quite right!" His words deeply affected me: without my realizing it, I had become another country's man. "But what is this to do with potatoes?"

"Potatoes entered Tibet in the eighteenth century. Have you heard the name George Bogle?"

I thought for a while. "He was a famous Scot and he was in fact a Glaswegian. Is there a connection?"

"Yes, I would say so. In 1774, Warren Hastings, the Governor of Bengal, appointed George Bogle as a special envoy to the Panchen Lama to initiate trade between the Raj and Tibet. He instructed Bogle to plant potatoes at the places where he stayed along the way, for future convenience, perhaps. Later, potatoes were widely planted in Tibet. They spread quickly east, as far as Sichuan and Yunnan, and became an important part of the people's diet."

"So that is why I've been able to eat potatoes wherever I've been," I said. "It was not a bad achievement at all for Bogle. I was told that, in the early days, Glaswegians called potatoes 'tattie Bogle'. I seldom hear this nowadays." I ate a few more. "Bogle was the first British emissary to Tibet. Did he go to Lhasa?"

"No. He only went as far as Shigatse, and became a close friend of the Panchen Lama. He did ask if he could go on to Lhasa, but the permission was refused, and he returned within a year to India."

"We all know that the Dalai Lama is the spiritual leader of Tibet. What is the standing of the Panchen Lama?"

"He is the most revered religious leader next to the Dalai Lama," he said. "The Dalai Lama lives in the Potala Palace in Lhasa, and the Panchen Lama in the Tashilhunpo Monastery in Shigatse. Since the early Qing Dynasty, they have ruled the two districts of Tibet as living Buddhas."

"Was Bogle's mission successful?" I asked.

"To be honest, the mission didn't achieve much at that time, but it did open the door to Tibet and pioneer the way for later Westerners," he said. "Bogle kept a detailed record, and there is a picture of the audience that he had with the Panchen Lama. In this painting, Bogle is wearing a native costume and a white scarf is presented to the Panchen Lama. It was an impressive occasion."

"Have you seen the painting?" I asked.

"Yes, I have. It was painted in 1775 by a well-known contemporary artist Tilly Kettle, and it is now in the Royal Collection." He went on, "When I was in London, I went to Windsor Castle, and saw it there. It was very true to life. Have you been to Windsor Castle?"

"Several times," I said, "but very unfortunately I did not notice that painting. I do hope I can go again, and I will look out for it, if it's still on display."

"Sam, you have lived many years in Glasgow: have you heard about Bogle's family?"

"Yes," I said. "I've heard that Bogle came from a well-known family, and that he was brought up in Glasgow; his grandfather was a successful businessman, his father a well-respected rector of Glasgow University. I heard that the Mitchell Library in Glasgow is preparing an exhibition about him. I have seen in the library some of his original letters written to his brother."

"When I was in Glasgow, I especially went to see Daldowie House where Bogle was born, but unfortunately it had passed out of the family; ten years ago it was converted into a crematorium." Tserin looked disappointed. "I asked people living nearby about his descendants, but sadly they hadn't heard of him."

"It's really sad," I echoed. "I think people have short memories, and that he's just another forgotten hero."

Tserin's information about George Bogle impressed me very much.

The Chinese in Scotland

"Yes! Tell me how the Chinese are faring in Scotland!" Tserin had moved to a new topic.

"In what respect?"

"That year when I was in Scotland, there were only about five hundred Chinese and they were dispersed all over. I was told that they were called the 'silent community'. This sounded rather sad. Has the situation changed?"

"This was all because of the language problem," I said. "Owing to their ignorance of English, when they came across any problems, they had to resolve them without asking for help from outside. That's why local people referred to them as 'hidden'. Following the increase in numbers in the new generation of Chinese, the situation has gradually improved."

"What is the present population?"

"Twenty thousand, I guess."

"That many! Are they still in catering?" Tserin asked.

"This is still where the Chinese excel," I said, "but there has been a different trend among Scottish born Chinese."

"Does the younger generation speak only English? What about their mother language?"

"English has become their first language. They find the mother language hard to acquire," I explained.

"Do they have the opportunity to learn Chinese?"

"Yes," I said. "The first Chinese school was established in 1972 in Glasgow. Today, Chinese class is offered all over the country. Chinese has now become a new trend in language study."

"Teaching Chinese and promoting cultural exchange is very worthwhile indeed. This kind of enterprise is so commendable," Tserin said. "How about the old people, do they have support in their old age?"

"The welfare system in Britain is very good; the old people's interests are secured."

"Is there a problem of race prejudice?"

"For the Chinese community, this is not really a big issue. Many instances are due to misunderstanding," I said.

Tserin seemed reassured. "There's something though that puzzles me. Many people in Britain use the term 'Asian' so loosely. Sometimes it's not clear who they are referring to. We all know that Asia includes more than 40 countries. It's common knowledge!"

"Yes, you are quite right. I am confused too."

Meanwhile, Padma and her mother were still busy, and aromas were wafting through from the kitchen. I was starving, and my stomach was complaining. Soon, a big supper was ready. There was lamb curry, fried shredded potato with egg, green vegetables, chicken soup and boiled rice. I hadn't expected that I could have such a good meal in this remote place. After many tiring days, I at last felt refreshed.

Conversation with Tserin was immensely satisfying. After days of difficult travelling, my tiredness evaporated. "Your room is all ready. Please have a good rest, and in the morning Padma will show you round. I hope that you will enjoy staying here," Tserin said kindly.

A Night Scene

The two-floor house was built of bamboo and timber. It was sturdy, but spacious and light. The furnishings were simple. My room was small, but very tidy. Apart from a bed, there was little else, and this simplicity added to its freshness. When I had washed, I felt a little less tired. It was only ten o'clock. I lay down with my eyes closed, and the events of the last few days passed one by one before me.

Intermittently, a mournful wail of a bamboo flute came from the distance. I was tempted to get up, and pushed open the window. The night was still. The occasional sparkle of fireflies and the all-pervading noise of insects made me feel relaxed. A gleaming moon hung high in the sky, like a solitary lamp lighting up the whole valley. I could see people coming and going between the houses.

Not far from me, I saw three old men sitting quietly in front of a gourd trellis. Some dry grass was burning beside them with a strong smell, presumably to keep off mosquitoes. One of them was repairing a basket; one was fanning himself; and the other one was lighting a smoking pipe. One after another, they shared the pipe between them. I could hear water bubbling from the pipe, and their faces were then lost in a cloud of smoke. All of a sudden, one of the old men said, "Today, Padma brought home a guest from distant parts. People said he was from Mr. Con's place. We've not had a visitor for a long time."

I reckoned that the guest must be myself; but who was this Mr. Con? Again, the sad strains of the flute and singing were heard, accompanied with the faint sound of weeping. The old man spoke up again. "Lhaba died this morning. There will be a sky burial in two days time, the arrangements have been made."

A few more words were spoken, and then they were back to silence, smoking their water pipe, at peace with the world. I watched them quietly, only sometimes wiping their faces and brushing away mosquitoes. What were they thinking about? Were they recollecting the days when they were young, or reminiscing about their home long ago?

At midnight, the whole valley was in silence. I told myself that I must rest, as I was hoping for more adventure the next day. I blew out the lamp, lay down and burrowed under the cover. I was exhausted. I closed my eyes, listening to my own deep breath, in… out… in… out… .

At about four o'clock, the cocks began to crow. There was still pale moonlight over the valley. I shut my eyes to go back to sleep. Gradually the crowing of cocks and the barking of dogs pervaded the whole valley. I looked at my watch; it was just after seven.

A poet wrote:

The moon shines brightly above,
Under the pine trees
*   the window frames look still.*
The sun rises among the clouds,
With the crowing of the cocks
*   and the barking of the dogs.*

A Busy Morning

"Good morning, Sam. Have you slept well?" Tserin asked when he saw me coming down the stairs.

"Very well, thank you," I said, "good morning, everybody!"

Tserin's family were sorting a large quantity of caterpillar fungus and ginseng, with the help of five other villagers. Padma was working with some dried fruit, and I went forward to have a good look.

"Do you know this fruit?" she asked me.

"Numb fruit," I recognised it straightaway.

"Correct! This fruit has all kinds of properties. It's very good for insomnia."

"And it's good added to mountain sickness draught, isn't it?"

Padma just smiled and didn't answer my question. At this moment, a few patients came in to see the doctor. Tserin courteously invited them to sit down, examined them and prescribed medicine. Then taking the medicine with them, they made their way out.

"We don't use money here." Padma understood my query. "All our services are free, and everyone helps each other." I saw a villager come in with a basket of eggs, put it down and leave; another person brought in some meat and vegetables.

"Mr Chau, breakfast's ready, Come, Padma." Mrs. Tserin was always in her polite manner. "After breakfast, Padma will show you around. I hope that you will have a very happy day!"

"Thank you, madam."

FESTIVAL ON THE MEADOW

It was a sparkling, clear day, fresh and cool. Padma took me for a walk through the village. I found the place was very pleasant. Some of the houses were built of earth and stone, others of bamboo and wood. They were beautifully constructed but not in the least pretentious.

Each house was separated from its neighbour by a large garden. Various kinds of vegetables were growing in profusion with lots of red and green chillies and aubergines. The quantity they grew was probably just a little more than a family's consumption. Pigs, cocks and hens were raised in an enclosure in the yard. At the back of the houses were plantings of millet, rice and barley in good quantity. Farmers were busy at their work.

There were also many kinds of fruit trees. A man climbed high up a tree and shouted to us, "Padma, want to try some pears? Catch!" Padma immediately caught two in her hands before she could reply. "Thank you! Uncle Gytso." We ate the pears as we walked on, fresh, juicy and delicious.

We walked past some little shops, a tailor, shoemaker, carpenter, and a gold and silversmith, too. Most houses had a wide open door, and one could see the villagers at home relaxing or quietly at work. There was no sense of rush. When they saw us passing, they waved and came outside to greet us. Sometimes we went into houses for a quick chat and were kindly received.

The children all delighted to walk along with us, and when I aimed my camera at them, they were not shy but posed for me, and then thronged round to see their digital images, laughing and asking a lot of questions. Old people came across to join in the fun. They showed more interest in my clothing materials and they smiled to themselves when they saw so many pockets on my trousers. They all invited us into their homes, but time was short, and Padma declined their invitations.

"Are the children not at school?" I asked.

"Today's a holiday. Everyone's off to the festival on the meadow. We'll be going there."

The great meadow by the lake stretched right to the foot of the mountains like a green carpet, providing rich grazing and a natural sports ground. This was a peaceful place on other days, but now it was quickly filling with activity. Tents were being put up; horses rubbed down and saddled; people were bustling around in their colourful costumes. Everyone was streaming out, the very old assisted, babies carried, with cooking pots and stoves, tea, butter, meat and other supplies, setting up on advantageous spots and preparing their picnics to celebrate the festival.

Shaolin Impressions

As we approached the tents, we heard the noise 'Hei,…Hoo,… Hei,…Hoo!' From where the noise was coming, a monk was leading a group of youngsters practising martial arts, moving smartly together and roaring defiance.

"Is he from the Shaolin Temple?" I asked.

"Yes, he is." Padma said, "This valley used to be troubled by the bandits. Some thirty years ago, Master Shi happened to pass by, and he sorted the problem out. Master Shi was deeply affected by the life here, and he stayed on to teach martial arts, both for physical training and for the defence of our homes. Most of us, me included, have been his pupils." She went on, "Have you seen Shaolin martial arts before?"

"Yes, I have," I said. "Some years ago, Shaolin monks came to Scotland to perform martial arts."

"Shaolin monks are reaching out now, aren't they? I've heard that they have organized a football team."

"Shaolin football team!" I was amazed. "If this is true, I'm sure they will become a strong opponent of Manchester United," I said.

"Manchester United?"

"Yes, a world famous football team."

"Are there many westerners learning martial arts?" she asked.

"Yes, there are," I said. "The Shaolin monks are no longer just the guardians of their temple. They have stepped out to the world. They take part in commercials and films, winning fame and fortune. Nowadays, 'Shaolin' is a brand name that is widely exploited to draw in students and make huge profits, and its quality can be poor."

"Is it that bad?" Padma seemed surprised.

"The Shaolin Temple now has its own website, and soon it may be offering distance learning," I said. "Some people are greatly enthusiastic, going all the way to the Shaolin Temple for training. When they graduate, they go home and open schools. Their performance is astonishing. Their commitment and high aspirations mean that in time a western tradition of Shaolin martial arts may develop and be imported back into China."

The Caravan

'Ding, dang, ding!' from the distant horizon rang out animal bells. 'Ding, dang, ding!' Everyone on the meadows raised their heads, looking in the same direction towards the far distance. They all seemed to know what was coming. As the sound grew, a long caravan came into sight. There was a column of about fifty mules over the green plain, under heavy loads, swaying from side to side, advancing towards us. All at once, villagers were all excited, men and women, boys and girls were on their feet, surging forward to line the way in welcome. Padma and I joined in.

The leading mule was decorated beautifully, an embroidered mask with a piece of shining metal for head protection, tied with colourful tassels. Hanging from its neck was a large bell, swaying and jingling. The mules following wore decorations too, but less spectacular. The man in charge was smartly dressed in Tibetan costume with a cow-hide hat. Sitting high on a horse and with a long rifle on his back, he appeared a man of authority. When he saw us, he called out, "Padma, you are ahead of us."

"Yes, Uncle Gesang, we used the short cut," Padma replied and smiled while he looked at me.

"Zhaxi-dele, welcome to the valley!" Gesang greeted me.

"Zhaxi-dele," I replied.

"This is our own caravan. The men have been buying provisions, and have hurried back for the festival," Padma said.

"Do they do this regularly?"

"Every three months; but if need be, they go off at any time."

The caravan halted at a bare piece of ground beside the lake, presumably where they usually unload. More and more villagers were milling round. The caravan men dexterously slackened the ropes and spread the bundles on the ground. Then they opened each package one by one and neatly laid out the contents. There were a variety of Chinese and foreign goods, foodstuffs, clothes, household utensils, sweets and toys, anything that might be needed. It was like a travelling shop, and brought much excitement to the quiet village.

The villagers must have placed their orders in advance. The leader brought out a list of names which he then called out one by one and people came forward for their share, and quietly made selections from what was left over.

Great numbers of people were now covering the plain, tents here and everywhere, flags fluttering, the smoke from stoves rising on all sides into the air. All the men and women were dressed in colourful costumes, rich in ornaments and bright headgear. It looked extravagant, and their movements seemed to be slowed down by their unwieldy and heavy dress, but they were relaxed and smiling as they made their way through the crowds. Among them, many red-robed lamas were helping to keep order.

I was fascinated by the various costumes. "What people are these?" I asked Padma.

"Those people covered in strings of agates and stones are Tibetan people; the ones wearing high silver crowns are the Miao; the ones in long blue robes are Mongols; the costume with five white spots on the back belongs to the Naxi; that's the Yao," Padma went on, "our Han costumes don't look so special."

"That's what I thought, too."

"Do you remember those people with the tilting round hats?"

"Yes, I do. We saw them yesterday in the forest. They are the Dai people."

A strapping young Khamba Tibetan stood on a raised piece of ground. He looked magnificent in his full traditional costume, yellow brocade clothes, a blue satin gown, leopard-skin jacket, and fox-skin hat. All over him were pearls and coral and agates of various colours; he wore a chain of precious stones and ornaments of silver and gold. His right hand held a sword inlaid with red amber and blue sapphires and attached to his waist, and in his left hand he raised a rifle to the sky and fired: 'Bang!' and the festival commenced.

The competitors filed into the arena, sturdy men and graceful women, each to his and her place. There was wrestling, horse racing, archery, and shooting. One unusual event was the yak race. About twenty yaks pounded off towards the finish, scurrying as though chased by snapping wolves, with a deafening, earth-shaking, thunder of hooves.

As well as athletic contests, there were resplendent folk dancing competitions. Team after team gave their best to their unique traditional dances. To the music, they danced lightly and unconstrained, smiling without affectation, an emotional performance that blended into the atmosphere of the whole plain. It was an effect that could not be matched by any performance on a stage.

Padma led me through the throng visiting the tents. We drank countless cups of butter tea and barley wine, tasting traditional dried meats and *tsamba*. Everywhere we went, we were received with kindness.

The cheers of the crowds came in wave upon wave, gongs rang and drums rolled, music from the dancing, shouts and laughter, welling up here and dying away there. The happiness under the bright sunshine and white clouds was rising to fever pitch, and the whole valley was filled with joy.

At a Mongolian Yurt

Beside the river were some Mongolian tents. Light smoke was rising from the tops, and a woman standing in front of the door was waving friendlily to us. I recognized that it was Hameina. She beckoned to us to come in, and we gladly went over.

Her husband, Baersi, placed a white scarf on me and on Padma's shoulder and bade us enter. Inside, carpets were spread out on the floor. Apart from Baersi and Hameina, there was an old lady sitting on a thick cushion. We sat round in a circle, and our hostess offered us bowls of hot milky tea. On a small red table, all kinds of cheese, cakes and biscuits, together with butter and sugar were placed.

They did not speak Putonghua, and I was dependent on Padma's translation for limited communication with them. They said that they had come from Hulun Buir in Inner Mongolia some thirty years before, and had been here ever since.

"Have you seen the great grass plains of Inner Mongolia?" the old lady asked.

"No, I'm sorry, I haven't. If I can make it, I will certainly go."

"I was told that there was a disastrous blizzard four years ago affecting three thousand families, and that livestock perished in enormous quantities. I don't know what had happened last winter."

I felt sorry, as I was not able to reassure her, and could only say, "I have heard that the Government took many precautions last year to protect people and animals. I don't expect there should have been a problem. Do you still have family in Inner Mongolia?"

"Not any more. But it's still our hometown!" Her eyes glistened, and love and concern for her homelands were very apparent.

When we had drunk tea and eaten the cakes, Hameina poured out wine. Padma at my side guided me how a guest should behave.

When a cup of wine was poured for me, Padma told me first to flick a few drops with my index finger, up and down, left and right, then drink a little and pass the cup to the host. He then raised the cup to his forehead, and passed it on to his left. Padma returned the cup at the end to me, and told me to drain it. As I did so, there was a long, low hum of good wishes. Everyone's attention was focused on me. Their kindness moved me close to tears.

"Uncle Sam, you are our honoured guest!" Padma said thoughtfully.

"Thank you." It was all that I could say.

"Mer..er..er!" We heard a sheep cry from outside. Just then, in ran a teenager in great excitement, "Granny, I was first, I won!"

"You won? Batu, fantastic! What's the prize?" The old lady glanced at me a little shyly.

"I won a sheep! It's tied at the door," Batu said jubilantly.

Baersi stood up and hugged the boy. I stood up at once, shaking his hand to congratulate him. Batu then sat down with us for some milk tea and cakes.

"Saren isn't home yet. I wonder how she's done in the dance."

"Ama, don't worry, she'll not disappoint you!" Baersi said.

The old lady's hopes for her granddaughter brimmed over. The family's kind faces were often smiling. The old lady was treated with honour, her cup and her plate frequently replenished.

This reminded me of a traveller's account, telling that Mongols were neither dutiful nor respectful to parents or old people; it was not uncommon for them to turn their aged parents out of the tent and leave them to die or a son would often kill his father when he had become a burden to him. When I saw the happiness in Baersi's home, I found it hard to credit the writer's strictures.

"Is there support here for the old?" I asked.

"We have a family support system," Padma said. "Sons and daughters are responsible for providing for their parents. The children contribute to meet their parents' needs. It is the traditional Chinese way of respecting the old."

"What if the children's ability is inadequate?"

"We will provide help moderately."

"Moderately?"

"Yes, moderate help, not indulgence." Padma looked serious. "I was forgetting, Uncle Sam, that you work in an old people's centre; you must know a great deal about services for the old."

"Welfare service for the elderly is comprehensive in Britain. The children have no need for anxiety on that account."

"You are very fortunate."

THE LAMA AND THE BRIDGE

Away from the Mongol yurt, and as we were walking downstream along the river, suddenly a flash of gold caught my sight. Just off the bank was an enormous prayer wheel in brilliant gold, inset with rubies and emeralds, constantly turning. It was some ten metres high, much the biggest that I had ever seen. The wheel was held in place by a strong wooden frame and it was driven by running water, turning slowly. A line of pilgrims standing on the platform held onto the wheel as it rotated.

On the wheel were the sacred words *Om Mani Padme Hum.* As the sunlight struck the wheel, the golden light was constantly refracted across the valley in every direction; as though the sacred words were being transmitted to every household of the valley.

"There is a great amount of scripture stored inside the wheel. When people turn it through one revolution, that is the equivalent of reading it one time and merit is compiled," Padma said.

"Is this real gold?" I asked, looking at the size of the wheel.

"Gold is abundant in our valley."

"It's heavy though."

"It weighs more than two tons."

"Two tons! Goodness me!" I exclaimed. "Is it made here?"

"Yes, of course!"

"It's certainly worth a lot of money." I tried to come up with an estimate.

"In our valley, it is meaningless to think of things in money terms." Padma sounded pretty serious.

"Oh, I beg your pardon. It's a failing of us city people. You are right."

We sat down on the grass for a rest. Before us, the river flowed quietly into the lake. It was a good-sized lake, though not big in relation to the whole valley.

Some thirty Tibetans were making their way along the shore, their thick clothing touching the ground, headscarves fluttering in the wind, and their shadows were reflected in the quiet water. It was indeed an inspiring picture of pilgrimage.

"How long does it take to go round the lake?"

"A little more than an hour," she said. "Usually they go round three times, and then to the lamasery."

"A lamasery here?"

"Certainly. I'll take you there."

Just then, I noticed that there was a lama twenty metres away, sitting quietly beside the river, his scarlet robe a vivid contrast against the green grass. He was motionless, holding a line out over the water.

"Is he fishing?"

"No, lamas don't eat fish."

"He's netting precious stones, then." I thought of Dorje by the river.

Padma smiled. "Wait and you'll find out!"

At this moment, the lama started slowly to draw in the line. At the end was a wooden board floating on the water. He did not bring it right in, but let out the line again and the board floated off. He kept doing this, and sometimes would take a handful of barley or millet from a bag beside him and cast it into the river. He was watching the board steadily and chanting.

Padma explained that there was an image of the Buddha and scriptures cut on the underside of the wooden board, and that the lama was imprinting these on the surface of the water for it to carry forth. This too was an act of merit.

"I think it's amazing that the lamas know the use of water power to assist their religious practice. And yet someone made a comment that it was a matter of misdirected energy. What do you think?" I asked.

She paused for a while. "When did the Westerners invent hydroelectricity? Was it in the 1880s?"

"I suppose so."

"You know, long before that the Tibetans were using water power to turn prayer wheels, and this was remarkable. Though the use is not the same, it may be that the Tibetans have derived the greater satisfaction." She went on, "In fact, the Tibetans built their first hydro-power station in 1928." Padma's knowledge was striking, and though what she said was a bit far-fetched, she did have a point.

All at once, there was spray splashed up midstream.

"Monster!" I said in fun.

"Don't tease! This is not Loch Ness!"

I couldn't help laughing when I heard this.

Something was beginning to emerge. First it was like a stone, and soon after a head came out, and a body followed. By now I saw that it was a lama, still wearing a red robe and slowly making his way towards the bank.

"Padma, how long have we been sitting here?"

"About thirty minutes."

"But we haven't seen anyone going into the water. That means he must have been under the surface for at least thirty minutes. It's hard to imagine." I kept staring at the lama.

The lama took off his soaking robe. He skilfully swung it round above his head and it then dropped perfectly back on to his body. He sat down on the grass. He closed his eyes and seemed to be doing religious exercises, completely motionless like a Buddhist statue beside the river. After about twenty minutes, I saw that the red robe was giving off steam; after another twenty minutes, the lama stood up and again flourished his robe, holding it out fluttering in the breeze, and it was almost dry.

"I have heard that lamas have magic powers. Is that so?" I asked.

"Uncle Sam, this isn't magic, the lama's been practising *thumo*. With the art of *thumo*, they can raise their body temperatures at will. It's useful for resisting the cold in their frequent journeys in the high mountains."

Padma continued, "My father told me that there was a woman explorer who practised *thumo*, and she wrote about it in her book."

"Yes! That was Alexandra David-Neel, the 'lama lady'. She was the first western woman to reach Lhasa, in 1924." I thought for a moment. "I remember now! We've seen her."

"What? We saw her? It's impossible!"

"Yes! in Danji's house."

"How would that be?"

"I mean that photograph, the one of Danji's father and the woman. That was her."

She seemed to remember. "Didn't his father say she was a Ladakhi woman?"

"She actually disguised herself as a Tibetan by staining her hair with Chinese ink."

Padma seemed to understand, "Was that so? I must tell Danji."

"Don't worry, I'll tell him when I go back."

"Okay, perhaps you could," she murmured with her head down.

Clear Mirror Bridge

The two lamas were still there in the sunshine, printing on the water and sitting in meditation reciting.

The placid river was about ten metres across. A delicate and picturesque old stone humped bridge crossed it in a single arch. There was constant traffic of villagers coming and going over it, leading oxen, driving sheep, carrying baskets with babies in them, children and the old. The river was not very deep, and the bottom could be seen. The reflection turned the semicircular arch into a full circle, like a big round mirror, and this was aesthetically very satisfying.

"This bridge is called 'Clear Mirror Bridge'."

"That's very apt," I said, looking at the great round mirror.

"It was built thirty-nine years ago, and it's as strong as ever. There was no bridge before that, and the villagers had to wade across. Then there was an incident.

"One day, three lamas were on their way back to the temple. When they came to the bank, they saw a very beautiful Miao girl standing there faltering. She wanted to cross, but the water would come up to above her knees, and she did not want her lovely dress to be soaked. The lamas looked at each other for a while without a word. The youngest finally stepped forward and politely offered to carry her across. She gladly accepted.

"When they were across, the senior lama was very angry, and told the young lama that he was wrong to have contact with a woman; he had broken the rules, and when they got back to the temple he would report him to the head lama. As they walked back, he kept muttering and telling the man off. The third lama had so far been quiet in order to keep himself clear of trouble.

"The culprit patiently endured his colleague's lecture. Finally, he had had enough. 'My respected brother,' he said, 'I put the woman down already, but you are still bearing her!' The senior lama had no answer to that.

"When the news reached the lamasery, there was a stir. Everyone was debating the rights and wrongs. In the end, the High Lama made a tranquil pronouncement:

'The sixth generation leader of Chinese Buddhism, Zen master Liuzu Huineng once said:

Enlightenment is not the tree of enlightenment;
It is the clear mirror, not the mirror stand;
It is not an object at all;
Whence then is this dust?

'To have a heart for helping people is pure like a clear mirror, without any uncleanness or blemish. On the other hand, keeping yourself clean and out of trouble while holding on to something in the mind and not letting it go, whatever a person's wisdom and cultivation may be, is an evil root.'

"When they heard this, everyone understood. Three years later, the young lama succeeded the high lama of the temple.

"The year after that, he instructed that a stone bridge be built for the convenience of the village people. He commissioned a skilled engineer from Suzhou to design an arched bridge and he named it the 'Clear Mirror Bridge'."

When Padma told me this story, I was impressed that though still so young she could tell it with such vividness and depth. So I asked her how he had been qualified to become the high lama.

"It's because he had a heart to help people," Padma answered, and her simplicity was again apparent.

I found this story enlightening, too. Fame and fortune are evanescent in our lives, and when the right time comes they should be set aside. But there are people who cannot put them out of their minds.

"Let's go to the lamasery now," Padma said, "The High Lama will be so glad to meet you."

"Why is that?"

"There is so much he wants to talk to you about."

I would be delighted to be received by the High Lama, but Padma's words often puzzled me. "I'm not yet thinking of becoming a lama, you know," I said in fun.

Padma laughed, and I laughed too.

Lao-tze, the founder of Taoism, wrote:

Stretch a bow to the very full,
and you will wish you had stopped in time.
Temper a sword-edge to its very sharpest,
and the edge will not last long.
When gold and jade fill your hall,
you will not be able to keep them safe.
To be proud with wealth and honour
is to sow seeds of one's own downfall.
Retire when your work is done, such is Heaven's way.

CHAPTER 6

THE LAMASERY

The lamasery was situated at the east end of the valley, about 300 metres up on the hillside. We followed the groups of pilgrims up the slope. Among them there was a couple who made their way up continually prostrating themselves.

I intended to slow down my pace so that I could observe carefully the sequence of the prostration. They placed their hands together above their heads, then down to their chests; they walked three steps forward, lay flat upon the ground, then rose, and where their outstretched hands had touched they repeated the action again, all the time murmuring scriptures. As I watched their disciplined movements, I remembered Zhaxiciren in front of the Jokhang Temple, and wondered whether he was already off to Nepal, prostrating himself all the way.

At bends on the way up, there were *mani* cairns, to which each of the pilgrims added a stone. *Tsamba* and butter oil were also left by the cairns as an offering to the mountain god. All over the cairns scripture pennants were set at all angles, fluttering in the wind. Smoke pungent with the smell of cypress was rising from nearby stoves.

A little cascade was plunging through a crevice on the mountain face to a pool at its foot. Pines were flourishing everywhere. They were all beautifully shaped as though twisted in various styles like miniature *bonsai* trees, poised on the edge of the cliff, clinging to the rock face, overhanging in mid-air, bending their bodies and reaching out their arms as though they were waiting for an important guest to come.

Under the shade of the pine trees, we followed the path a little further up and very soon a wooden building came into sight. This was an imposing two-storey structure with symmetrical wings on either side. The roof was covered with semicircular tiles in light grey colour, beautifully arranged over an immense area, supported by massive beams, struts and pillars. My first impression was that it was like a Chinese temple, and yet with its restrained decorations and colour, there was a refinement and simplicity that was somehow a touch of Japanese character.

The lamasery was built high against the mountain face and commanded views over the whole valley. Its giant door was wide open and the pilgrims were streaming through. I followed Padma inside. Down a passageway we came to a winding corridor about three metres wide. At every corner was a wooden statue of a divinity, about human size, the faces full of expression, each different but all well proportioned and very lifelike. Everything was made of wood, with a lightly applied varnish that beautifully brought out the grains in golden yellow. As I walked over the shining floor, there was a sensation of harmony. The corridor ran round a sunlit grass quadrangle, most carefully tended, a place of elegance and peace.

"Do I need to take my shoes off?" I asked Padma quietly.

"No! This is not our custom," she replied.

The entrance to the main temple was off the corridor. Inside was where the lamas read their morning prayers and recited scriptures. There was a statue here of the Buddha. A constant stream of worshippers was going in bearing butter and white scarves. This place looked very like the Jokhang Temple, though the structure was simpler, the air fresher and brighter. The interior of the temple was easily seen. Many *tanka* scrolls were beautifully displayed on the walls. It surprised me that I did not see any of those huge fierce images.

My attention was caught by the complex *dougong* structure of supports and beams below the eaves, built up one above the other, the ends projecting out like logs from a woodpile, and bearing the weight of the whole roof. Padma told me that no nails were used in the whole construction. It was certainly an astonishing achievement.

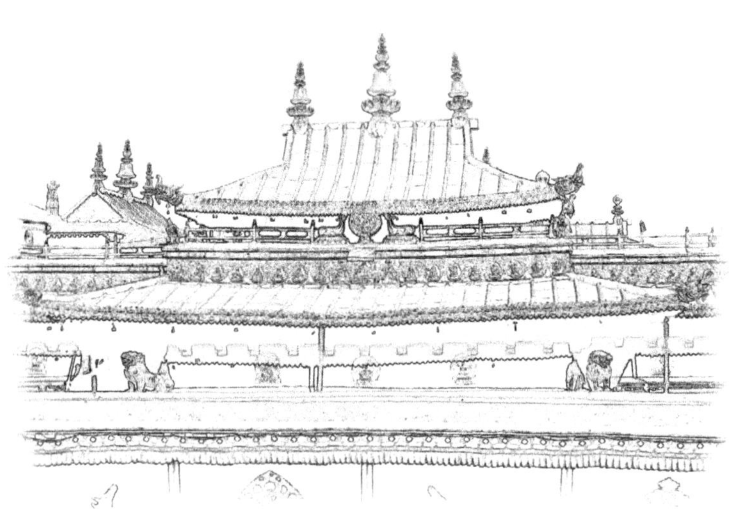

THE HIGH LAMA

As I admired the architecture of the building, a voice behind me suddenly said, "Sir, welcome!"

"Good afternoon, Lama Wangdui. This is Mr Chau," Padma made the introduction.

"Good afternoon. Please come this way, the High Lama is waiting for you."

I bowed slightly. Padma looked excited, and I felt a little nervous. We followed him up a flight of stairs to an open area on the upper floor, and into a room opening off it. "This is the High Lama's drawing room. Please sit down. I will tell the High Lama that you are here." Wangdui gently held the door open and then left.

Works of Art

The room was well lit and ventilated. Though the two windows were half opened, there was still a wafting smell of butter. Through the window, one could look over to far distant peaks and across the villages below in the valley. The room itself was fitted with simple furniture in Tibetan style. There was also a small bookcase full of Chinese art books. On the walls were water colours and items of calligraphy which seemed to have been done recently and not yet mounted. This must be a connoisseur of Chinese art, and evidently someone who was also fond of butter tea.

My eyes were drawn to a pair of small and elegant olive shaped vases, decorated beautifully with birds and flowers on a yellow ground, only about twenty centimetres high, sitting on top of the book shelf. I examined these for a while, and asked Padma, "Do you know about ceramics?"

"No, not at all."

"This could well be a pair of enamel vases from the imperial kilns of the Qianlong period. Do you know their value?'

"Uncle Sam!" Padma reminded me.

"I beg your pardon, there I go again: money has no meaning here, does it?"

This seemed to mollify Padma. And yet, I was making mental calculations. If I remembered right, some years ago at an antiques auction a pair of similar vases had sold for over ten million Hong Kong dollars. I inwardly felt nervous, because the vases were unprotected, and if they chanced to be knocked off, that would be that. Two Chinese scrolls on the wall were valuable too; the ink was faded and they seemed to have been torn in places and looked very old. There were calligraphy materials on the table, and a horizontal scroll of four big characters in standard script. These must have been just completed, as they were still wet.

I was silently admiring the calligraphy, when I heard it suddenly declaimed from behind me, "Tian Di Ren He!"-- Heaven Earth People in Harmony! I had not noticed the venerable lama appear at the door, with Wangdui respectfully following behind. He was about six foot tall, wearing a yellow gown, with a deep red robe over one shoulder. His kind face was shining and red, with a white beard. His bearing was dignified and noble, his presence commanding, his voice was clear and strong, like a booming gong. Wangdui said something quietly to him, and then went out.

Padma introduced him forthwith. "Our reverend High Lama Dazhi."

I immediately bowed with both palms together, and said "Zhaxi-dele!"

"Zhaxi-dele, Mr Chau. Do you like calligraphy?" the High Lama enquired, moving to the table.

"Yes, I do, but I am not good at it at all."

"The practice of calligraphy is most valuable. It gives pleasure and it nurtures the spirit, purifying both the body and the mind; it trains the aesthetic and critical faculties, strengthening character and the will. Would you agree?"

"Well!" The unexpected question was a little disconcerting and I paused to recollect myself. "The Song dynasty master Su Dongpo said that calligraphy was achieved through the coordination of the heart, the eye and the hand. Someone has said that calligraphy is like practising *taiji* on paper, vigorous and yet gentle, with endless variation."

"That is a good description. You must be a fine calligrapher yourself." The High Lama seemed pleased.

"Oh, not at all, Sir!"

"Mr Chau, please sit down here." He motioned to two chairs.

"Thank you." I was nodding respectfully each time I responded.

"Padma, do sit down, please. You have been working hard. I must say you've grown!"

"It has been my duty, Sir!" Padma's face lit up when she heard the High Lama's appreciation.

The High Lama turned to me with a smile. "It is such a pleasure to welcome you, and I do hope that you will enjoy your visit. Please do feel at home here."

"I am honoured to be here, thank you very much." I was sitting about two metres from the High Lama, with Padma beside me. A teapot and cups had been set out on the little table in front of us, with small saucers filled with dried apricots, almonds and walnuts. These were common delicacies in Tibet, but there were also fresh, ripe mangoes. "Are they grown here?" I showed a little surprise.

"Yes, they are. Though we are at an altitude of 2,600 metres here, conditions are ideal."

"It's a fine variety," I said, looking at those big golden mangoes.

"This is thanks to Bogle. He introduced potatoes to us, and he also brought us mango seeds from Punakha, and they have become a speciality of our valley," he explained.

"Where is Punakha?" I asked.

"Bhutan."

The Classic of Tea

We had not been sitting long when Wangdui served tea and quietly went out again.

"Please drink tea. This is the best green tea in our valley. It used to be presented to the Emperor, I was told." The High Lama raised his cup to invite us.

I appreciated the High Lama's kindness. "This is a treat, but I must admit that I am not a connoisseur of teas."

"Mr Chau, have you heard the story of Kou Kai Tchou, in the fourth century, eating sugar cane?" he asked me with a smile. "Whenever he ate a piece of sugar cane, he would nibble it gently and slowly make his way to the best part of it. Drinking tea is like that, it needs to be savoured to arrive at the finest taste."

"That is very true." We raised our cups again, and I said, "I thought the people here would only drink butter tea….I mean the Tibetans!"

"Yes, indeed. The Tibetans normally drink butter tea, and it helps to revive their strength. But we are not restricted to traditions, and the people of the valley are fond of green tea too and find it refreshing. Sometimes I like a change and drink English tea with milk."

"English tea with milk!" I was surprised.

"Yes, indeed. And if you wish, we will make you a cup. We have a variety of teabags, Typhoo, Tetley; and we even have, Scottish ... Blend." He slowed down his speech as he said these last words, and was watching for my reaction. "And don't worry, it's nice and fresh. It's available in all the supermarkets."

To hear the High Lama listing names of teabags was a surprise. "It is very kind, but no, thank you."

"Mr Chau, perhaps you could tell me the correct way to make English tea? I can never make it satisfactorily."

"I should say this is simply a personal preference. I would prefer a good balance of the strength of the tea and the quantity of milk. To make a good cup of tea, it may also require patience as well as good will.”

“Good will! I didn’t realize this was important.”

“It is indeed!” I said.

Getting to the Point

“Padma has told me that there was nearly trouble when you wanted to take a photograph in the Jokhang Temple.”

I had not expected that the High Lama would change the subject so suddenly. “Yes. Do you mean the church bell?”

“It must have been that,” he said.

I thought for a while. “It was all my curiosity.”

“How do you know of the bell?”

“I read about it,” I said. “Several western travellers have mentioned the bell. If it really is a Christian object, it is incongruous. For it to be hanging in the Jokhang Temple, there must be a special reason, and it was this that intrigued me.”

“It is indeed a Christian object. Do you know where it came from?”

“I would like to find out,” I said.

“Have you read about the missionaries who came to Tibet in the early days?”

“Not in detail, but I did read a story that gave a simple account.”

“Which story was this?” he asked.

“*The Lost Horizon*, by James Hilton.

“Ah! It’s a story about Shangri-La.” The High Lama seemed to know it well.

“That’s it.”

“And this is the dream that you are pursuing, perhaps!” he said.

“Yes, it really is.” I kept my voice down a little, feeling a little embarrassed.

“Do you believe it, then?”

"James Hilton states that Shangri-La is on the Tibetan plateau. I have visited many places and seen much, but it all seems inconclusive."

"Most people concentrate on the scenery and the topography of Shangri-La, and they do not study evidence from the past," the High Lama said. "To look for Shangri-La, you must begin with the history of Tibet. Are you familiar with it?"

"Just a very little."

"I haven't spoken about it for a long time, and I am so happy to find someone to talk to. Would you like to refresh my knowledge with me?"

"I shall be delighted to be your audience," I replied.

CHRISTIAN MISSIONARIES IN TIBET

"You may not know that our valley people have had a long association with missionaries from the west."

"Is that so?" I was surprised and I realized that what he was saying was significant.

"As long ago as the early seventeenth century, missionaries from the west were already beginning to come to Tibet. They were sent by the Roman Church for evangelism. But another reason was, as *The Lost Horizon* describes, to look for surviving remnants of Nestorian Christians."

Nestorian Christianity

"I have heard very little about the Nestorian Church," I said. "What is its origin?"

"Nestorianism is a branch of the Christian church, and it begins with Nestorius who was a patriarch of Constantinople in the fifth century. He was accused of heresy for his different interpretation of the Incarnation. In 431 he was expelled and exiled to Egypt and died there.

"After his death, his followers slowly spread to the East. The number was expanding in Syria and Persia, and by the beginning of the sixth century they had reached Xinjiang in China. In the Tang Dynasty, the Nestorian church was known as the Jing religion or the Persian faith, and it flourished greatly. But for some reason, from the beginning of the tenth century, there was no word about them in China for many years."

"So that was why the missionaries went to China, to look for them," I said.

"There were other reasons too." The High Lama continued …..

The Christian King, Prester John

"In about the year 1140, a beautiful story was circulating in the West that somewhere in the East there was a Christian king called Prester John who ruled a great Christian kingdom.

"At that time, the Christians in Europe were embroiled in a long war with the Moslems. The Pope fervently hoped that Prester John could support him in the recovery of the lands that had been lost. At a critical time, the Patriarch of Constantinople received a letter signed by Prester John in which he declared that he would raise an army to march against the Moslems. This letter was a great boost to the morale of the Crusaders, and the news spread quickly throughout Europe. Even the Moslems were all convinced, and feared that the day would come when Prester John would march west to the sacred city of Jerusalem.

"The Pope then wrote a reply to Prester John and sent it by a special emissary. Unfortunately, nothing more was ever heard. It was later suspected that the letter was a Christian forgery, written to encourage martial spirit in resistance to the Moslems. But the story did not go away; in fact it only became more fascinating.

"In the thirteenth century, the Mongol armies in the East appeared in great strength, conquering in all directions. The Church had never forgotten Prester John, and wanted to find out who the Mongols really were. In 1245, the Franciscan Giovanni Capini was sent to the East to investigate. He claimed to have seen the Christian king, and had also found many Nestorian Christians living in Mongolia. Whatever the truth may be, his account did attract many explorers and missionaries towards the East."

The Nestorian Tablet

"In 1625, a great stone tablet, nearly eight feet tall, was unearthed in Changan, known as Xian today, relating to Christianity. The tablet was set up in 781 and is inscribed with a heading of nine Chinese characters which mean 'The Propagation of the Roman Nestorian Religion in China'. The text, in Chinese and in Persian, introduces the doctrines of the Nestorian church and its transmission into China starting from 635.

"The Nestorians had been evangelizing for more than two hundred years, and churches were built in many places in China. In the year 845, Buddhism was suppressed and the Nestorian Church was implicated, churches were destroyed, and believers were forced to abandon their practices. After the collapse of the Tang Dynasty in 907, Nestorianism seems almost to have disappeared in China. However, there is evidence that remnants of Nestorianism persisted in the north-west until the thirteenth century." He went on …..

Missionaries to the East

"When news of the Tablet spread out, western missionaries were all the more attracted to China, both to search for the Nestorians and also to expand the work of evangelism. Gradually, their ambitions were extended towards mysterious, remote Tibet. When they discovered the simple Tibetan people with their own exclusive form of Buddhism, they wanted to try all means to be able to stay in Lhasa and to preach there. They hoped that one day the Tibetan Buddhists would all become Christian, and that would be a magnificent victory for the Church in Asia.

"Tibet is a high plateau, surrounded on all sides by high mountains with a harsh climate and difficult communications. Approach from any direction is like climbing into the sky. The friar Odoric of Pordenone is said to have been the first European to enter Tibet, and is claimed to have arrived in Lhasa in 1325, though this is unconfirmed.

"Some three hundred years later, the second European that we know to have visited Tibet was the Portuguese Jesuit Antonio de Andrade. In 1624, he and Fratello Manuel Marques set out from

Agra in India, crossed the Himalayas, and reached Tsaparang in the kingdom of Guge, but they didn't go to Lhasa."

"Who, then, was really the first to reach Lhasa?" I broke in to let the High Lama know that I was still listening.

"Sam, if you had stayed quiet, I would have wondered if you were still awake," he said smiling. I noticed that he had called me by my first name. "The first Europeans who certainly entered Lhasa were two Jesuit fathers, John Grueber and Albert d'Orville. In 1661, they left Beijing, crossed the Gobi Desert and via Xining came to Lhasa.

"Grueber's *China Illustrata* was published in 1667. It was the first book to introduce Chinese culture, natural history, geography and mysterious Tibet to the West. It was widely distributed and aroused great interest." He raised his teacup and gestured to me to drink. "After that, it was the Capuchin Fathers who were the first to initiate work in Lhasa."

"The Capuchins! They are mentioned in Shangri-La. Who were they?"

"You seem especially interested in anything to do with Hilton's story."

I could only smile in reply. Padma and I took a sip of our tea gently. Most times when we paused in our conversation, Wangdui would come in to refill our teacups, then he left the room quietly without the least interruption.

The Capuchins

The High Lama continued, "The Capuchins were founded in the early sixteenth century by Friar Matteo da Bascio, who wished to reform the Franciscans and to return to the primitive way of life, the solitude and penance practised by Saint Francis. They are also called the Friars Minor, as they humbly referred to themselves as 'little brothers'. The Italian word *'cappuccio'* means a hood, as they wore tall, pointed hoods, and this is where their name comes from."

"Nowadays, people know about cappuccino coffee, but not about the Capuchin monks," I said.

"Really? What's the taste like?"

"I find it a bit watery, and prefer a stronger coffee," I said. "There are capuchin monkeys too, did you know?"

"Is that so? Why are they called this name?

"It's because the coffee colour and foam are like the Capuchin hood, and the monkeys have a tuft on their heads like a hood, too."

"I've never realized it was such a popular name," the High Lama said, smiling.

"When did the first Capuchin missionaries come to Lhasa?"

"It was in June 1707. Two Capuchins came across the Himalayas from Nepal."

"Hilton's book mentions four Capuchins setting out in search of the Nestorians in 1719 from Peking. I wonder if they were the same persons or somehow related." I had a little doubt.

"Quite frankly, we have no records whatsoever about those four Capuchins." He saw the look of doubt on my face, as he went on, "This information is confirmed by a letter written in 1713 by the Capuchin father Domenico da Fano."

"Who were the two men?" I then asked.

"They were the fathers Francois Marie de Tours and Giuseppe da Ascoli."

"The environment must have been harsh for them."

"It was certainly not easy." The High Lama gazed out of the window. He recollected himself, and slowly looked round again into the room. "When they arrived in Lhasa, they pretended to be on their way to somewhere else. They at once offered free medical care to the people so that no one would suspect their motives."

"Were they well treated by the people?"

"They were well respected and highly commended by the king, Latsang Khan, who couldn't understand how these 'white lamas' could make such a difficult journey to his people, dispensing medicines and asking for no money, doing good only for the honour of God. News of their work soon reached as far as Beijing, and it was reported in the official Peking Gazette."

"Had they any language problem?" I asked.

"Surely they had. But they studied Tibetan assiduously and at the same time prepared for their evangelistic work. After a year or more of hardships, the money that they had brought with them was finished. Francois Marie returned to India because of poor health, and Giuseppe stayed on alone in Lhasa.

"In May 1709, Father Domenico da Fano and the lay brother Michelangelo di Borgogna, arrived in Lhasa, and the three set to work. But very soon, they were again in financial straits. Two of the men decided to leave, and only Domenico remained, continuing to treat the sick without remuneration. In May 1711, Father Giovanni da Fano arrived to support him."

"Their object in Lhasa was to evangelize, but they had to give up because of money, and yet they still refused to accept any payment. Weren't they being a bit inflexible?" I asked.

"This was a part of their religious discipline. The Capuchins stuck to the principle of Saint Francis, promoting temperance and poverty in their preaching." The High Lama went on, "Their medical work undoubtedly won the trust and support of the people, but they wanted to avoid any suspicion of having ulterior motives and so they declined to take any payment or recompense. Again, the two fathers were quickly at the end of their funds, and finally on Christmas Day 1711 they left Lhasa."

"It seems a shame that after more than four years of toil they had to quit," I said.

"In fact, Domenico had not given up hope. After he returned to Rome, he wrote a long report describing the many problems that the mission had faced. He petitioned the Pope to restore the work in Tibet and he finally won support.

"In October 1716, Domenico returned to Lhasa, and with him were two other priests, Francesco Orazio della Penna and Giovanni Francesco. Soon after, they were joined by Father Angelico and Father Bonaventure. But in less than a year's time, because of ill health, three fathers had left, leaving Domenico and Orazio in Lhasa.

"The Capuchins realized that to spread the Gospel more effectively they must study the Tibetan language and scriptures. With the patronage of Latsang Khan, Francesco Orazio, together with a Jesuit Father Ippolito Desideri who was then also in Lhasa, were allowed to study in the Sera Monastery."

Father Ippolito Desideri

"Just before the Capuchins returned to Lhasa, Ippolito Desideri had already arrived. He was equally welcomed by Latsang Khan and likewise granted permission to preach. He was also allowed to study in the Ramoche Temple, and to make use of its library. He soon had written a book refuting Tibetan Buddhism."

"How did Father Desideri get on with the Capuchins? Was there friction between the two orders?"

"A good question." The High Lama continued, "They actually lived together. There were the odd disagreements, but everyone was able to stay on good terms. On the surface, all was well, but in fact there were tensions over territory, and both parties submitted closely argued petitions to the Pope, claiming their right to missionary work in Lhasa. The final ruling went against Desideri, and in April 1721 he withdrew from Lhasa."

While listening to the history of the missionaries, I was amazed by the High Lama's memory. "I hope you don't mind if I ask, Sir, what are the sources of all these details?"

"They are from the letters of the missionaries. Most of them are recorded in Luciano Petech's I *Missionari Italiani nel Tibet e nel Nepal* and Adrien Launay's *Histoire de la Mission du Thibet*. Other details come from Sandberg and Vannini."

I was so impressed by High Lama Dazhi's knowledge. I believe it was true that he had not spoken about the history of Tibet for a long time. He looked a little anxious while talking about the Capuchins' story and he seemed eager to press on.

Capuchin friar

FRANCESCO ORAZIO DELLA PENNA

"In December 1717, the Mongol army took Lhasa. Latsang Khan was killed, and the soldiers ransacked the city. Desideri escaped away from Lhasa. The Capuchins' house was turned upside down, and the fathers were hung up naked and beaten.

"Because of the chaos, remittances from Rome were not getting through, and their missionary work became almost impossible. Domenico's health was gradually breaking down. In 1719, he was succeeded by Francesco Orazio as head of the mission and he later left. In May 1721, Father Gioacchinoda San Anatolia arrived with new hope to the flagging mission. He had brought with him a thousand gold scudi which would assure living and contingency expenses for the Capuchins for the next several years.

"In 1720, the Qing army drove the Mongols out of Lhasa and restored order to Tibet. Kanchenas was appointed to replace Latsang Khan. Again, the priests were treated with courtesy by all ranks of officials. This greatly improved their morale and the scope of their work was increased.

"Gioacchinoda was mainly involved in medical work. He went out looking for herbs, prepared medicines, saw patients, and carried out surgery. The sick streamed in to the clinic, fifty or more every day. There were nobles, lamas, officials and ordinary folk. Many came great distances to see him. And yet the priests adhered to their original principle, accepting no payment and treating everyone regardless of status. They became very well known and much respected.

"Francesco Orazio was active in evangelism. He would visit men of high rank, befriend them, and take every opportunity to preach his religion. He translated books of Christian teaching into Tibetan. One of these was '*La Dottrina Cristiana*' by Saint Robert Bellarmine, and this was widely read. Christianity became for a time the subject of much debate and study among the lamas.

On one occasion at the Sera Monastery, a lama read out from this book to a gathering of about four hundred people, and there was considerable excitement.

"The Capuchins won the support of Kanchenas and of the seventh Dalai Lama. Francesco Orazio often visited the Potala Palace to expound Christian teaching."

"The Dalai Lama was the leader of Buddhism in Tibet. Did he not resist this newly arrived Christian religion?" I asked.

"The Dalai Lama chose to be tolerant, and he patiently tried to appreciate the good in it. The two men often set out and discussed the doctrines of Buddhism and Christianity. The Dalai Lama once wrote a letter to Francesco Orazio saying that he did not accept that 'God created the heaven and the earth.' He argued that if this were so, God lacked compassion: He had brought suffering and sickness upon many people, and the dead were equally His creation; but He had given others prosperity and enjoyment. This was partiality. Buddhism on the other hand considered that suffering came from wrongdoing, and that one's circumstances in this life could be understood in terms of the transmigration of all living things from previous existences.

"Francesco Orazio realized the importance of preaching through the written Tibetan language, and he worked hard at translating Christian teaching into Tibetan. The Dalai Lama gradually changed in his regard for Christianity. In February 1724, he issued a decree permitting the missionaries to work freely, and allowing religious choice to the Tibetan people. The decree also allowed them to buy land to build accommodation for themselves and a church. Nobody could obstruct work on these buildings and they were to be exempt from paying taxes and duties."

Building a Church

"Ever since they first arrived in Lhasa in 1707, the Capuchins had always rented accommodation, and they were determined to build a church and convent. In March 1725, they eventually bought a piece of ground which consisted of a square of twelve *colonen* on each side, to the east of the Jokhang Temple, for eighteen pieces of silver.

"How big is a *colon*?" I asked.

"A *colon* is equivalent to 18 Roman feet."

"And how much is a Roman foot?"

"296 millimetres, just a little shorter than an English foot."

I made a rough calculation. "That must be at least 4,000 square metres. Was there a site that big on the east of the city?"

"It's very hard to know. There were not as many houses then as there are now."

"It sounds a bargain for eighteen pieces of silver."

"The actual value then was said to be one hundred pieces of silver. The Capuchins were certainly given special favour. When some of the senior lamas saw the generosity of the Dalai Lama and of the King towards the missionaries, they resented it, and they were convinced that they presented a threat to the standing of Buddhism in Tibet. They began to oppose the Christian religion, they prohibited contact between lamas and fathers, and slowly a force became apparent that was against Christianity.

"In August 1725, there was torrential rain in Lhasa. The Kyi Chu River burst its banks and the whole city was flooded. The lamas then incited the people, saying that the flooding was caused by divine anger at the building of the church. They led a crowd to the site, and wanted to destroy the newly laid foundations of the church.

"The fathers had to produce the edict issued by the Dalai Lama and were able to keep them temporarily under control. The instigators did not stop, and several times brought back angry crowds wanting to drive the missionaries out. Finally Kanchenas told the crowd that he had consulted the oracle at the Samye Temple, and it had declared that the flooding was divine punishment upon the people for their own wrongdoings. He warned of other punishments and ordered that the 'white lamas' were not to be further disturbed.

"The convent and the church were finally completed in September 1726. There was a solemn service of consecration on 4 October, the exact five hundredth anniversary of the death of Saint Francis. Many people came to give their good wishes. The Grand Lama of Lhasa, Sempa Chembo, came to offer his congratulations and he even exclaimed: *Your God is truly a great God.*"

"What was the church like?"

"It was only a small building, about five metres tall and eleven metres in length. There were altars in the church, a small sacristy, and a small room for singing and prayer."

"What about the convent?"

"It was about the same height in two floors. Downstairs was a refectory, a dispensary and a kitchen; upstairs were eight rooms and a small drawing room. The rooms were very small, and one could touch the ceiling."

"Was this the first church in Tibet?" I asked.

"I would say the first church in Lhasa." He continued, "When the church had been built, all continued as usual. Francesco Orazio and Gioacchinoda shared responsibility for evangelism and medical work, and the church became a place frequented by the people.

"However, war broke out in 1727. Kanchenas was killed, and the convent and church were looted. Fortunately the successor Polhanas recognised the privileges which had been given to the Capuchins, and he treated them with greater respect, proclaiming an order that they and their church should be protected in perpetuity.

"In 1731, Francesco Orazio completed his Tibetan-Italian dictionary, containing 35,000 Tibetan words translated into Italian. In the next year, he translated Nicholas Turlot's *Le Tresor de la Doctrine Chretienne* into Tibetan. The missionary work appeared to be going well, with much support expressed by nobles and high officials, but in fact there were many hidden problems.

"The church now only had two missionaries left. For many years they had had no news or funding from Rome, and no new missionaries had come to support them. They once again were in financial straits. The climate on the high Tibetan plateau was severe. There was always fighting and unrest. They faced hunger much of the time and were in poor health. The old momentum had gone and they wanted to leave.

"The Living Buddha rGyal-Sras Rinpoche, hearing that Orazio was intending to leave Lhasa, approached him with a request that he might take a group of young monks to Rome to study Christian doctrine. Since the future of the Capuchin mission in Tibet was so uncertain, Orazio declined.

"After many years of missionary work, Orazio was frail and often sick, and finally he was persuaded to leave. Before he departed, Polhanas gave him a written undertaking that he would look after the church property until they returned. Orazio left Lhasa on 25 August 1732. The following year, Gioacchinoda made preparations for his own departure, stored away the church and convent belongings, left the keys with Polhanas and sadly left."

"Where exactly was the church?" I asked.

"A good question!" The High Lama then raised his voice. "For more than a century, many people have tried to find it, but no one has succeeded. I suppose that you are busy looking, too!"

"There's so little information on this point."

Persevering

"After the Capuchins withdrew, Christian evangelism in Lhasa completely stopped. Even so, the missionaries retained hope. In 1738 the dogged Francesco Orazio made a successful proposal to the Pope for the revival of the missionary work, and a year later, the Capuchins set out once more.

"After travelling for sixteen months, Orazio and six companions arrived at the convent in Lhasa, in January 1741. The buildings were unharmed. They were received once more by the seventh Dalai Lama and Polhanas who were delighted with the European gifts from Pope Clement XII. They at once issued a decree, restoring freedom to preach. Their old friend Sempa-chembo used to drop in for a cup of tea.

"On their return to Lhasa, the Capuchins received the full support of the officials and their hard work met with much success. More and more people were coming to the church each day and some were baptised. But the more rapidly their work developed, the closer they were to latent danger. Some of the leading lamas were well aware that if the Capuchin missionary work proceeded unchecked, the privileged status of Tibetan Buddhism in the country would be threatened. So at all times they looked for a pretext to attack Christianity.

"There came a chance. In April 1742, a newly baptized Christian called Putserin was sent to the Potala Palace to attend a ceremony. While presenting gifts he did not allow the Dalai Lama to touch his head in blessing, and in front of all, he cried out that he now believed in the true God of the white lamas and could not accept any other form of blessing. Though the Dalai Lama made no comment, some of the lamas bitterly criticized Putserin's disrespect and said that it was insulting to Tibetan Buddhism. There were others too who refused to recite the important Mani prayer. The lamas had finally lost patience, and they campaigned to have Christian preaching banned and the missionaries expelled.

"The situation quickly grew worse and the lamas turned against Polhanas. All at once, four hundred angry lamas from many temples gathered outside the king's palace, and denounced his partiality towards the Capuchins. The king realized that the situation was serious and, frightened, he capitulated. He told the crowd that he would have no further dealings with the missionaries, that he would issue a decree forbidding them to preach to the Tibetan people, and that converts would be arrested.

"Quickly, five Tibetan Christians were arrested. Wooden collars were placed round their necks and they were taken to be exposed in the public square. Father Orazio went several times for help, but Polhanas refused to see him. The judge condemned the five men to twenty lashes each for insulting Tibetan Buddhism. After this, the Capuchins were ridiculed, Tibetan believers could only come furtively to the church, and fewer and fewer people came for medical help.

"Eventually, Orazio did have an audience with the Dalai Lama and the king, but it was hard now to alter the proscription on conversion. He knew that times had changed, and in August 1742 three missionaries left while he remained with the rest of the fathers. With a great final effort, he printed two further books against Tibetan Buddhism which he presented to the two leaders. This certainly exasperated the hatred of the lamas against him, increased the pressures on Polhanas, and served to isolate Orazio yet further.

"Orazio was now old and frail. He finally realized that the missionary work in Lhasa had completely failed. In April 1745, they departed in great sadness, and the mission closed. Three months later, Orazio died in Nepal. Capuchin missionaries never set foot again in Lhasa, and no one seems to know what became of the tiny number of Tibetan converts who were left.

"Not long after his death, it was reported from Tibet that the church and the convent had been demolished. Two years later,

Polhanas himself died. No more was said about the Capuchins and their church." High Lama Dazhi sighed softly, then he asked, "Sam, you have now heard the story of the Capuchin missionaries, and I wonder what you think about it?"

"If I may reply from a neutral standpoint, it is a sad story. Nowadays, one can fly from Rome to Lhasa in a matter of hours, but in those days, the Capuchins took three long years or more, and it is hard to imagine how difficult a journey it was. Their indomitable spirit is very impressive. They laboured for so many years, but finally it all ended in failure. What a pity!"

"Could you imagine that there is a connection between the Capuchin missionaries and James Hilton's story, or Shangri-La perhaps?"

I knew that the High Lama was guiding me to the subject. While listening to the Capuchin story, I had been trying to establish the link between the two. "I think Orazio and Perrault, the High Lama in Shangri-La, have something in common. Perhaps James Hilton wrote about Orazio under the name of Perrault." I said, watching for his reaction. His eyes shone, as though he could read my thoughts. He looked at me smiling and then his gaze moved to Padma. She listened with eyes wide open, intently.

Disclosing the Secret

"Padma, you are twenty already. Has your father told you about Orazio?" The High Lama seemed to know Padma well.

"No, he hasn't."

"Very well then, let's explore it together, and you can learn more about our valley." Once again, he was connecting the valley with the missionaries.

"Tell me, what have Orazio and Perrault got in common?" He turned to ask me.

"They were both Capuchins, learning the Tibetan language,

translating works into Tibetan and writing books refuting Buddhism. They both built churches and made several converts." I went on, "But the date, 1719, of Perrault's arrival in Shangri-La confuses me a little. The year Orazio arrived in Lhasa was 1716."

"James Hilton was perhaps affected by some writers who had mistaken the date of Orazio's arrival in Lhasa," the High Lama explained.

"What about Perrault's age? His birth year could be worked out as 1681, but it is said that Orazio was born in 1680," I asked.

"Not much difference, is there? Perhaps it's only a calculation mistake," he said. "Nevertheless, Orazio's birth is given as 1681 in the Catholic Encyclopedia 1907. Though there are slight discrepancies in the years, Hilton's facts are essentially correct." The High Lama was looking at me. "I can see that now you are beginning to understand the story."

"Yes, I believe that James Hilton made use of the Capuchin story as the background of Shangri-La," I replied. "How did he come by magical powers such as clairvoyance and levitation?"

"From a scientist's standpoint, this is all but impossible," the High Lama said, "but Tibetan lamas who have undergone prolonged training have faculties beyond the normal, and adepts can reach 'Shambhala'. The people of Shambhala are all said to live to a great age. They can fly and they can predict the future." The High Lama went on, "James Hilton could well use this as material for his book. A novel does not need to be completely true to history otherwise the reader may find it insipid. Having said that, the oldest person in our valley was one hundred and thirty-three. There are many centenarians."

"Then Perrault's great age was fiction?" I said.

"The great age is a little excessive, but it was not altogether fiction, just a bit of poetic licence on the novelist's part."

171

Pieces of Evidence

The High Lama drew a deep breath. "Let me tell you something that many people have overlooked. In 1741, when Orazio and the fathers returned to Lhasa, they brought with them many precious gifts and also some necessities for the church. Two of these were of great importance."

"What were these?" I was excited.

"The first was a Tibetan printing press. Over the years, Orazio had been translating Christian writings but he had not been able to disseminate them effectively. He knew that with a printing press, Tibetan tracts could be quickly produced. A printing press was given to him by Cardinal Belluga. Under his supervision, two sets of Tibetan metal type were made. One set was kept in Rome and the other was taken to Lhasa together with the printing press."

"What was the second?"

"It was a bell," he said, watching me, "the bell that you are looking for."

"The church bell!" I exclaimed.

"That's right, a small but heavy hanging bell."

"That's amazing! How ever did they bring that and a printing press to Lhasa?" I asked.

"It was certainly a terribly hard job, one could imagine. In those days, all things could only be carried on people's backs. They separated their goods into small loads for porters to carry. There was so much that it was more than six months after the missionaries reached Lhasa that all the luggage arrived. Orazio hung the bell in the church that he had built fifteen years before. Even more significantly, the hymn of praise to God rang out, the *Te Deum Laudamus*."

"*Te Deum Laudamus*!" I exclaimed, "Those were the Latin words inscribed on the bell."

"That's it!"

"What does it mean?"

"It is a hymn of praise to God. The words are *Te Deum laudamus: Te Dominum*. They mean, 'We praise Thee, O God, we acknowledge Thee to be the Lord.'" He went on, "Remember, Sam, what it says in *The Lost Horizon*?

> *'...On all such pilgrims Perrault bestowed his blessing - forgetful, it might be, that they were lost and straying sheep. For 'Te Deum Laudamus' and 'Om Mane Padme Hum' were now heard equally in the temples of the valley.'"*

"Yes, I do remember. I suppose this could be the key to the mystery of Shangri-La, don't you think so?" I asked the High Lama quietly. He nodded gently.

"What is the meaning of 'Om Mane Padme Hum'?"

"They are words of praise to the Lord Buddha," he said. "Its general meaning is 'Praise to the jewel in the lotus!' The lotus symbolizes the glory and the holy purity of the Buddha. The six syllables form the basis of the chants of praise for Tibetan Buddhists."

"So this was how the hymns of praise of two religions could be heard in Shangri-La!"

"That bell was hung for more than two hundred years in the Jokhang Temple. Few people have asked about it. What drew your interest to it?" he asked.

"It was the Latin words of praise which could also be heard in Shangri-La. I don't think that this can be coincidence."

The Significance of the Bell

"How did the bell end up in the Jokhang Temple?" I asked.

"As soon as Orazio left Lhasa, a group of angry lamas descended on the church, claiming that the missionaries had deliberately buried many *Kangyur* scriptures beneath the door so that people would trample over them when they entered the building, a calculated slighting of Tibetan Buddhism. The convent and the church were both razed to the ground, and the rubble taken to the river to reinforce its banks. Then the church bell was carried to the Jokhang Temple. The monks considered pursuing Orazio and punishing him, but this fortunately came to nothing." The High Lama paused and then asked, "Do you know why they wanted to hang a Christian bell in the Jokhang Temple?"

"A traveller explained that this was due to the respect that Tibetan Buddhism holds for other religions, but I am not convinced," I said.

"This explanation does not seem very plausible. The Buddhist monks were incensed. They destroyed the church and they hunted the missionaries. They certainly would not have had an attitude towards it of respect."

"I agree," I said. "What was the reason behind it then?"

"It's certainly an interesting question," he said. "I asked some of my seniors about it. Most of them thought that the bell was a symbol of a religious victory. Tibetan Buddhism and Christianity had been in confrontation in Lhasa for thirty-eight years, and eventually Tibetan Buddhism had won. The missionaries were accused of insulting Tibetan Buddhism by trampling on the scriptures, and the Buddhist priests retaliated. They hung the Christian bell in the Jokhang Temple as a trophy. Do you know where it was hung?" he asked me.

"From the beam in the corridor leading to the main hall; this is precisely stated in the books. Yet I have been twice to the Jokhang Temple, and have looked everywhere for it, but have seen no trace of it."

"Yes, Padma has told me. The bell there now is a Tibetan bell." He seemed saddened. "Did you notice a big iron chain hanging from the beam there?"

"Yes, I did!" I exclaimed. "It looked very old."

"It is said that they hung the heads of heathens from it; have you read about that?"

The High Lama stopped. He gently savoured the tea. I took a sip too. The tea in my mouth slowly slipped down my throat. He could be right: Joseph Rock told of an incident in 1905 in the Mekong Valley where all the priests were killed by the lamas, and Father Dubernard's head was hung at the gate of Atunzi lamasery. I have also seen an old photograph of a lama sitting inside a temple, and from the beam above him hung human heads and animal corpses. Lamas certainly cut off and displayed heads, probably as a trophy.

"Was the lamasery in Shangri-La based upon the Jokhang Temple?"

His kind face showed a little smile. "When James Hilton created Shangri-La, I believe that this was his intention."

"Shangri-La is not found on any map. Why did he use the name 'Shangri-La'?"

"This makes the story all the more mysterious. It's really just a beautiful name."

"Has it any meaning?" I asked.

"I don't think it does." He added, "It's simply an English name. I suppose Hilton didn't know Tibetan."

"But I do feel that Hilton cannot have simply made the name up himself," I said.

The High Lama paused. "I have found a little clue in a book called *The Land of the Lamas*. Perhaps that is where it comes from."

I felt that Shangri-La was slowly coming into focus.

CHAPTER 7

THE VALLEY WITHOUT A NAME

"Shangri-La has remained a mystery since it was revealed by James Hilton in 1933. No one seems to know where exactly it is. You surely want to know what happened to Shangri-La now? and those heroes?" High Lama Dazhi said.

I nodded and listened intently.

"You will remember the story of Shangri-La," he said. "1930 was the critical year I would say."

"Why was that?"

"When Perrault died, Conway, Mallinson and Lo Tsen left Shangri-La together with the porters. Since there were no other candidates, Chang was elected to succeed Perrault as the High Lama. With his enthusiasm and hard work, he soon got the situation under control and things were back to normal."

"Was Shangri-La a paradise as people say?" I asked.

"Shangri-La was simply a peaceful and harmonious community, not very different from other districts in Tibet, but James Hilton's skilful writing and the glamour of Hollywood made it a place of mystery that people aspired to go to. Since the publication of *The Lost Horizon*, there was a steady stream of visitors to Tibet looking for Shangri-La. To avoid interruption, the inhabitants of Shangri-La decided to move away."

"When was this?"

"If I remember correctly, it was in 1934 when they began moving out, and I'm sure you can guess where they went."

"Here! There's so much that is like Shangri-La here," I said.

IMMIGRANTS

The High Lama was looking at me smiling. "This isn't Shangri-La, but as a matter of fact we are Shangri-La immigrants."

"How did they find this place?"

"It was found accidentally by our caravan."

"It takes great courage to adapt to new surroundings," I said.

"It's not easy at all. We worked hard to adjust to new surroundings like those missionaries did before."

"Did all the people move here?"

"No, many stayed behind or left us because prospects were uncertain."

"How many arrived here in the first place?"

"About three hundred," he said. "It took us over five years of toil for the land to be established. The scenes of Shangri-La were recreated here; slowly, people who had once left began to join us again."

"Can't blame them, people are speculators," I said. "Was it uninhabited when they came?"

"There were already about ten families of Monbas and Lobas living here; they were indigenous people, having lived here for at least four generations. They were independent, and lived a primitive life of farming. I heard that they once lived in Lhasa, but moved here in 1894 to escape the *ula*."

"*Ula?*"

"Yes, *ula*!" he said. "It was a form of feudal serfdom in Tibet. To ensure manpower for the lamas and nobles, farmers were required to perform work for them as a form of taxation. They built roads, bridges and houses without any payment. Life was very hard and they had to borrow loans which they were never able to pay off and which went down to their children. That's why many people left for remote mountain areas to escape."

"How did they treat your people?"

"They were hostile towards us at first, and made many attempts to poison us."

"Poison!" I exclaimed.

"Yes, poisoning is a tradition with the Monbas. They think that if a lucky person is poisoned, the victim's good luck will be transferred to their own families. They have all sorts of tricks, and it is difficult to elude them. Before we came, we already knew about the Monbas and the Lopas, and we were wary."

"Was there any incidents?" I asked.

"Very fortunately, no one was poisoned. Though we outnumbered them, we didn't take advantage of them, and treated them with courtesy and respect. Their ill will slowly disappeared, and they became part of this community."

"Social inclusion! That was very good," I said. "Did you grow up here?"

"Yes, I did. I was born here the second year after we came."

"You must have enjoyed your childhood?"

"Indeed!" he said. "This reminds me of Laga, a good friend of mine. He was the son of the Monba leader. We grew up together." The High Lama smiled as he went on, "I remember on one occasion when we were fifteen, he stared at my gold ring and he told me to follow him. We walked for about twenty miles, and he led me through a twisting river valley coming eventually to a secluded stream. Laga signed to me to look into the water. It was flowing fast, but was clear and I could see the bottom. It seemed ordinary. Then, to my astonishment, when a ray of sunlight fell on the surface, it all lit up; the river bed was a seam of gold. When the sunlight was gone, the bed was dark again. It was not easily spotted unless you were looking for it.

"When I told Chang this, he at once went to see it for himself. He was jubilant, and carefully began to plan how to extract the gold and the mining work was to be entirely controlled by the lamasery. We made all kinds of gold ornaments and distributed them to all the cities. Our valley was also rich in wild medicinal plants. There was great demand for these. These are our main sources of income."

"Have you tried to increase the output?" I asked.

"We keep to the principle of moderation that we had in Shangri-La, in our use of resources and in our distribution. The lamasery remains the centre of administration. People supply their own needs, and anything more that may be required is allocated through our administration. In this way everyone has plenty with some to spare."

THE FORGOTTEN HEROES

Henry Barnard

When the High Lama spoke of gold, I thought of Barnard in Shangri-La, and I asked if there was news of him.

"Poor Barnard, there's not been news of him for a long time."

"What happened? Didn't he receive permission to mine gold?"

"He did." The High Lama tried to recollect. "That year, Shangri-La was determined to make an exception for Barnard by allowing him to stay to mine gold in the valley. The reason was that they wanted to encourage Conway to succeed Perrault. But they had not realized that Conway was in two minds, and in the end he was persuaded by Mallinson to leave with him and Lo Tsen.

"In fact, there is a traditional ruling in Tibet that no one may dig for gold. They may only pan for gold on the river bank. Lamas have always considered that gold beneath the surface is like the roots of plants and that loose gold is like the flowers. If gold is dug out, the loose gold in the rivers will disappear and the vitality of the ground will be damaged.

"I heard that after we had left, Barnard continued to be courteously received by the lamas. But he had never been interested in anything but gold, and he did not respect Tibetan Buddhism and its rules. He realized that he would not be staying much longer in Shangri-La, and he was mining gold in large quantities, hoping that he could soon leave with a fortune. The lamas began to be suspicious of his behaviour, and they discovered that he was travelling under a false identity and that he was not a professional mining engineer at all. Soon they expelled him from the Valley of the Blue Moon. Six months later, someone saw a ragged man who looked like him begging along Koko-nor, in a pitiable condition. We at once sent men to look for him, but they could not find him anywhere.

"Poor Barnard, he should have left with us. The gold deposits here are even richer."

"I have read that travellers to Tibet have always been struck by the abundance of gold deposits everywhere, and their travel accounts all speak of finding gold," I said.

"There is much gold in the mountains and rivers of Tibet. Have you heard the story of the gold digging ants? It is often told in early writings." He went on, "Long ago, there were fierce giant ants living on the northern slopes of the Himalayas and in the Altai Range. The ants spent all their time mining gold, and had accumulated a whole mountain of it. This was guarded by ferocious griffins. Even so, there were often men stealing the gold, and they would be slaughtered if they were caught by the beasts. These stories have been in circulation for two thousand years. They may be one of the reasons why western explorers have been drawn to Tibet."

Roberta Brinklow

"I am sure that you will want to know what happened to Miss Brinklow," he said. "Barnard was so attached to the gold mine. Miss Brinklow's aspirations were great, and she decided to leave with us and that she would continue preaching. It was her hope that one day this valley would become a Christian base in Tibet. Nevertheless, her work ended in failure despite all her efforts."

"Why was that?" I asked.

"Buddhism is deeply rooted in the Tibetan culture and this will not easily change."

"I can imagine so."

"But she had made a mistake," he said.

"What was it?"

"In all her activity she denounced Tibetan Buddhism as an immoral and false religion. This antagonized people," he said. "You have probably heard about an unusual form of marriage in

Tibet. A wife would often have more than one husband."

"This reminds me of Danji's family." I looked at Padma. She nodded with a smile.

"I have often heard of one man having several wives. In fact, both my grandfathers had several wives. But for a wife to have more than one husband seems strange nowadays. What is the reason behind this?"

"This is an old institution among Tibetan people. In the past, living standards were low and means of production weak, so the strength of the men and their property were concentrated under one roof. With fewer women together, squabbling was reduced. It was also a good way of protecting the home and warding off attack, especially for people living in a remote place.

"Miss Brinklow passionately opposed it as wicked and incompatible with Christian principles. She pressed Chang to forbid it, and exhorted the husbands in these menages to establish their own homes with their own wives, and to convert. The results can be imagined. She gradually became excluded; but her situation was not as dreadful as that of Francesco Orazio. In less than a year, fewer and fewer people were befriending her, and finally she gave up and left us."

"Where did she go to?"

"She told us that she was going to the border town of Tatsien-lu to preach, as there was a large church there with many members. After that, we lost contact with her."

"Tatsien-lu!" The name caught my attention. "I remember that when Conway, Mallinson and Lo Tsen left Shangri-La, they went with the porters 1,100 miles east to Tatsien-fu. James Hilton described Tatsien-fu as a place by the Chinese border, an important gateway to Tibet and a trading post for tea and all sorts of other goods."

"That's it!" he said. "Miss Brinklow was hoping to go there to meet up with Conway and Mallinson. James Hilton wrote

Tatsien-lu as 'Tatsien-fu'. It was probably a slip, though it could have been to mystify the reader. Do you know where Tatsien-lu is?"

"When I first saw this name, it took me a long time to find it. It is today's Kangding in Sichuan. It was indeed an important gateway town at the border of Tibet described by many travellers."

"Quite right! The Qing Government changed its name in 1908. Up till the middle of the last century, western writers were still using the old name 'Tatsien-lu'. James Hilton set 'Tatsien-fu' 1,100 miles to the east of Shangri-La. I think you could figure out the place 1,100 miles to the west of Tatsien-lu."

Hugh Conway

"Did they arrive at Tatsien-fu? I mean Conway and those people."

"No one knows," the High Lama said. "The first thing we found out was that Conway was unconscious in a mission hospital in Chung Kiang. We were told that an extremely old lady had taken him there, who died soon after. This was certainly Lo Tsen, though no one knows where she was buried and no one knows what happened to Mallinson."

"That's intriguing," I said. "What happened to Conway then?"

"Amazingly, Conway came back to the Valley of the Blue Moon, but he could find no trace of us. Luckily, in Lhasa, he chanced on our caravan that had gone there to procure our supplies, and they brought him back here. He told us that he had been to many places since he left Bangkok and it was a long time before he arrived at Lhasa.

"When he came here, he declined the appointment to be the High Lama, but he was glad to stay and to assist Chang. He made great contributions to our society. He set up our clinic and treated the sick with his rudimentary medical knowledge. He did not display a religious bias, and with Chang's influence he came to appreciate the importance of people of different religions and races living in harmony together."

"Did he leave the valley again?"

"Conway kept up a sensible connection with the outside. He three times returned to England, and each time he brought back a large amount of western medicines and books. Once, he took two men from the valley with him, to let them have the opportunity to learn about European civilization. One of them is still very much with us."

"That's Padma's father, Dr Tserin!" I exclaimed.

"It is! Tserin was originally a student of Chinese medicine. When he was twenty, he was in the mountains collecting medicinal herbs, and wandered into the valley. He found a profusion of caterpillar fungus, ginseng and other precious herbs growing in a ravine. In his excitement, he lost his footing, fell and was not able to get up. In this emergency, a Tibetan girl happened to pass, and she helped him back to her village. Tserin was deeply impressed by this place, and in the end he decided to stay and to study and practise medicine here. The girl was called Amu, and she became Padma's mother." Padma was listening closely.

"When Tserin met Conway, they became good friends." He went on, "Conway taught Tserin much from the west. Tserin was a tireless student. They studied Chinese and western medicine together, and they quickly realized the importance of the way in which the two complemented each other, and brought much relief to the sick. They trained their own students and taught them English, but English is really not spoken much in the valley and it is less and less known today.

"Chang was enabled by Conway's assistance to concentrate on the administration of the valley. They were both deeply respected. Unfortunately, they were old and weak, and did not live much longer. Chang was one hundred and thirty-three, the oldest resident in the valley."

"So, how long have you been the High Lama?"

"Forty years, exactly. It is time now for a gifted person to take over from me," he said. "We no longer insist on a candidate's experience; it is enough that he should be committed to serving our society, a just person. That is all we ask for the next High Lama." Dazhi was staring at me with his kind smile. "Sam, you are a community worker, aren't you?"

"Yes, I am." This alarmed me. I was not ready to be the second Conway. I was disconcerted for a while.

"Naturally, our first consideration would be someone from the valley."

"Very well!" I felt relieved and we had another cup of tea.

East and West

From within came constant waves of low, deep chanting.

"This is the only lamasery in the valley, I suppose."

"You are right," High Lama Dazhi said. "We have sixty lamas at present."

"The architecture of this building seems very restrained, and different from others."

"Yes, that is so. If you would like, I can show you round." He stood up without waiting for me to reply. "Please come with me."

On the balcony was a row of rooms, each of their windows with an awning and hung with neat white curtains billowing in the wind. There was a Mediterranean feel to the place. "You can see many of these in Lhasa. Those determined missionaries not only introduced a new religion to us, they also gave us a touch of Italian life," Dazhi said.

"What about Christianity? Did they have any impact upon Tibetan Buddhism?"

"It's hard to say, but there are certainly many resemblances between the two, the burning of candles, sprinkling of holy water, continual chanting, the giving of alms, prayers for the dead and so on."

"It seems that the labours of the missionaries were not entirely wasted," I said.

"It is a fact that eastern and western cultures were meeting and interacting. As early as the sixteenth century, many missionaries were arriving in China, quickly mastering the spoken language. They were working away on the Confucian classics; works of Chinese literature were being translated into various languages and creating a sensation in Europe. There was a vogue for Chinese culture and philosophy, ladies were seen at court holding Chinese fans and men wore Chinese clothing. Chinese art was a strong influence too."

"Yes, I suppose so," I said, "When I was in Italy, I saw paintings of horizontal scenes by Italian masters in a style very similar to Chinese handscroll paintings, in which the figures and rocky hills were extremely like those in the hanging scrolls in your room. If I am correct, those Chinese paintings, with their strange perspective, are works of the sixth century or earlier. This drawing technique is also seen in Tibetan painting. There could be a link between the East and West."

"You are quite right," he smiled.

"The art of gardening is another example. Whenever my wife and I go for a Sunday drive, we see gardens and parks full of rhododendrons. I always tell her that they were brought back by the British plant hunters from Yunnan."

The Relics of the Missionaries

"Let me show you something. This way, please." The High Lama took out a bundle of keys from his belt and opened a small room. The darkness was only relieved by a glimmer of light from the window. All sorts of objects had been stored here, covered in dust. It looked as though no one had been in here for a long time. He indicated a heavy piece of machinery. "Do you know what this is?"

I studied the object. Despite its age, it was clearly a printing press. Beside it, in a wooden box, were neatly laid out what looked like Tibetan printing type. I gently wiped away the dust from the surface of the box, and read 'Messrs Fantozzi & Co.'. On the floor, there was a pile of very old pamphlets. "Is this Orazio's printing press?" I exclaimed in astonishment.

"Indeed it is!" he said. "All this belonged to the Capuchin missionaries."

"It's unbelievable. These things have still survived."

There was another machine at the side. The High Lama told me that this was a sausage machine. The product label was still there

– 'Made in Birmingham'. There was a bicycle, too, with a wooden frame. It was a simple design, and though the wheels were now broken, one could see that it was in principle the same as a modern bicycle.

"Did these belong to the Capuchins as well?"

"That cannot be proved, but it is very likely. These objects were found when the British army was in Lhasa in 1904. Before then, the Capuchin missionaries were the only people from the west who had lived in Lhasa for many years; everyone else was only there briefly, and would have not had any need of them."

"In that case, if they really did belong to the Capuchins, this bicycle is probably the earliest known bicycle in the world," I added, "and it could be the invention of Leonardo da Vinci."

"That could be so. They were all Italians."

"I suppose that they were not altogether assimilated to Tibetan food," I said, looking at the little machine.

"You are certainly imaginative!" the High Lama said smiling. But these objects were evocative. After we had seen them, we walked out of the room and the High Lama carefully locked the door behind us.

The Phallus Symbol

The distant ranges shone white against the azure sky. From the balcony, one could clearly see the festivities on the plain, the flags fluttering, the crowd as big as ever, and one could still hear the faint rise and fall of the cheering. By the lake, many people were still clustering around the caravan of horses.

When I looked up, I noticed a remarkable wooden carving attached to the wall and protruding out for about thirty centimetres. The High Lama saw me staring at it. "That's a phallic symbol. Do you think it strange?"

"Not really!" I said, "I saw one like that in the Jokhang Temple."

"You are most observant," he said. "Do you know where it came from?"

"I asked several lamas about it, but they all shook their heads and walked away without a reply. Perhaps they had not understood me, or just didn't bother with a passer-by. I felt that they were cold and suspicious."

"They may have misunderstood your intentions."

"Is there a special significance?" I asked.

"You must have read the story of Princess Wen Cheng."

"Oh, yes! She always reminds me of Lo Tsen who went far to the west to marry, lost her way, and was eventually rescued to Shangri-La."

"Yes, indeed. But it was more than 1,300 years ago that Princess Wen Cheng travelled for more than two years till she arrived in Lhasa. How she built the Ramoche and the Jokhang Temple, I think I hardly need tell you. But there was something that many people have overlooked.

"When the Jokhang Temple was under construction, the princess found that there was an evil sign to the east of Lhasa. This was extremely unlucky. So on the top of the Temple, a phallic symbol was placed, and in this way the spell was countered."

"So it faces east. But here it faces west, is that not so?" I ventured.

"Yes, it's because that sign is to our west. Sam, I think that you are working out where we are," the High Lama said laughing.

I felt a little embarrassed when I heard this. "I trust that you do not mind!" I said. "In Shangri-La, Miss Brinklow saw some phallic objects in a Buddhist temple. She must have been meaning the Jokhang Temple?"

High Lama Dazhi did not answer me. He just smiled and gestured to me to follow him.

The Library

It was all becoming clear to me, and I felt satisfied as I followed the High Lama down the stairs. We passed a classroom with a dozen lamas sitting on mats with a stack of broad, thick scriptures in front of them. Their heads were buried in their tomes as they turned the pages and chanted, and they took no notice of us. The adjacent room was a library, a spacious room with a large piano in the centre. It looked an old one. All round the room were shelves filled with books and many of them were Buddhist scriptures in Tibetan.

"Are they printed here?"

"There's no need! There are many publishers in Tibet, and books are easy to come by. There is a large printing house not far from here. Apart from Buddhist scriptures, books on other subjects are being purchased by us all the time from many sources," he said.

"Where is the printing house?"

"Only two days away," he said. "We have also many books in Chinese, on a wide range of subjects. They are over here." He beckoned to us to come forward. On the shelves, we saw many Chinese classics including the Analects of Confucius, the Great Learning, the Doctrine of the Mean, Mencius and the Tao Te Ching. There was much other literature and many novels. The best-selling martial arts novel *The Magical Swords* by Jin Yung was there too.

He carefully opened a cabinet. "Come! Have a look at these." Inside were some very old books. These included the *Water Margin* by Shi Nai-an, *Journey to the West* by Wu Cheng-en, *Romance of the Three Kingdoms* by Luo Guan-zhong and *Dream of the Red Chamber* by Cao Xue-qin.

"These books were Chang's favourites. He was an expert on Cao's work. When he was rescued to Shangri-La, he was carrying this set of books with him." He pointed at it. "Chang told me that they were eighteenth century handwritten copies. They are very rare."

On the bottom shelves were some western books. When I looked closely at these, I nearly cried out. There were some volumes that I was familiar with, including:

Antonio de Andrada,

Novo Descubriment de grao catayo ou dos Regos de Tibet

Athanasius Kircher, *China Illustrata*

Thevenot, *Voyage a la Chine des Peres Grueber et d'Orville*

Beligatte, *Relazione Inedita di un Viaggio al Tibet*

I could not have imagined that these books would still be sitting there neatly on the shelves. They seemed to have been untouched for a long time. As I looked slowly along the titles, I longed to open them.

"These books were Conway's great love. Sadly, when he died, there was no one who could understand them any longer; why not take pleasure in them?" He was encouraging me.

"They are too precious!" I replied, but still felt hesitant.

"However precious they are, if they are locked away for a thousand years with no one to appreciate them, that would just be a waste." He went on, "Many of these books were bought in England by Conway. They are very rare."

I browsed for a little, and saw many early twentieth century books, some of which I knew well.

"These are all very good books, especially for the early missions to Tibet," he said. "But I must add that, in some of these books, not all the historical facts are completely accurate." He took down *Tibet, the Mysterious* by Thomas Holdich, and said, "This book is helpful for understanding the background of the story of Shangri-La."

He passed the book to me, and I turned some of the pages and returned it cautiously to him. "Besides reading his beloved books,

Conway would often play the piano here for pleasure," he said. "When he played Mozart, he would become a little agitated, and a sadness came over his face. Everyone knew that he was thinking of Lo Tsen."

"Did he try to find her?"

"He twice went to the mission hospital in Chung Kiang, and looked everywhere for her, but he never found where she was."

Suddenly, a question came to me. "How did they bring this piano here?"

"In Shangri-La, Mallinson and Barnard asked this question, too. It can only have been carried on people's backs."

"But this must weigh at least three hundred pounds! Is that possible?"

"Of course! Do not underestimate the strength of the porters. Once a man carried a four hundred pound iron safe over the mountains to Tatsien-lu." He was reaching for a book and handed it to me. It was *The People of Tibet* by Sir Charles Bell. "There is a story here that people in Darjeeling have been telling for many years, about a Tibetan woman who carried a piano up the mountain on her back. I imagine that this is where Hilton's idea came from."

THE SECRET OF THE BACK GARDEN

A Japanese Garden

At the back of the lamasery was a spacious garden. From the moment I entered the garden, I felt a sense of peace and serenity. It was delicate, elegant and majestic. Every stone, tree and flower was carefully placed. There was a pavilion, reached by a narrow bridge, in the centre of a pond fed by a stream from a cascade and with lotuses and carp. Nothing was overstated. Colours were restrained, and everything was in harmony.

"Well! How do you feel?"

"How peaceful and quiet, it's beautiful!" I looked round. "I have the feeling, please do not mind if I am wrong, that this lamasery and its garden carry a touch of Japanese style."

"There is in fact a Japanese element."

"Was it built by Japanese craftsmen?"

"No, it's all our own architecture." He went on, "In 1914, Chang met a Japanese monk, Kawaguchi Ekai who was living then in Lhasa, and there were three other Japanese, too. They told him much about Japan and Kawaguchi drew some architectural sketches for Chang. That was how it was."

There were many bonsais, very varied, fresh and vigorous, and evidently tended with much skill. I saw a gardener holding an old root head. He rapidly cut away most of the root and the sprouts and leaves.

"Will it still grow?"

"Yes, indeed. He's helping it grow!" he said. "If the dried up root is not removed the new root will not be able to grow through, it will not be able to take in nutrients properly; decayed shoots and old leaves will hinder growth and easily induce disease."

"No wonder growing bonsai is an art."

"It's a philosophy!" He looked at me with a knowing smile.

By the cliff was a bell and drum tower. In it was hanging an enormous brass bell about three metres high, and there was a big drum on a wooden stand.

"This bell weighs over five tonnes," he said. "The bell tolls clear and loud, the sound carrying for tens of kilometres. It can be used, too, to rally people. At New Year and on festivals, people all come here in celebration to strike the bell and the drum, praying for good fortune. Each spring and autumn, there is a tea gathering here. While enjoying the garden, we can challenge each other's knowledge and study the art of brewing and tasting tea; it all promotes friendship. Sam, you must come and join us."

"I do hope that I have the opportunity."

"It's up to you, not up to fate! Come, and see our tea garden." He signed that we should proceed. The tea garden was fresh and luxuriant, planted against the mountain side. About twenty men and women were at work. They all put their hands together and bowed to the High Lama, and gave us cheery waves. He went on, "It's a small planting, only ten acres or so, but the tea is of the finest quality. This is one of our sources of income."

We went along a cobbled path into a small wood. An immense red cypress stood there, its ancient trunk soaring into the air, the ground beneath in deep shade. Its girth must have been ten metres or more, and it must have been over a thousand years old. Coloured ribbons were attached to the branches, and at the base were many offerings. This must be a wishing tree for the valley people.

As we went on, there was a sudden clamour of voices. We came upon thirty lamas locked in a debate. Some were standing, some sitting on the floor. The standing lamas were lifting their feet, bending their waists, raising their hands, prayer beads round their arms, bringing them down, exclaiming loudly, slapping their palms in threatening gestures, as they put questions to the seated lamas. They must be answered immediately. Sometimes they were glaring at each other, sometimes laughing. There was excitement in the air, but harmony too.

"This is the traditional way in which the scriptures are debated. Through debate and the citing of proofs, the real meaning of Buddhism is understood." He went on, "It is a way of assessing each lama's progress and a standard form of testing to determine their grading. Outstanding lamas will go on to Lhasa to debate in public at the great *dharma* gathering where they may be awarded the highest honour of Gexi-laranba."

"What is that?"

"Gexi means 'good knowledge'. It is Tibetan Buddhism's highest doctoral degree. Holders of this degree may be chosen to be high lamas of large monasteries."

The Rose Cemetery

The scent of roses drifted across. I took deep gulps of air.

"Are you fond of roses?"

"Oh yes! I love the scent!" I replied.

"Conway especially loved roses."

"Did he?"

We came to a flower garden planted with roses of a great variety of colours. It was exclusively a rose garden in a formal and unique setting. "These were all roses that Conway brought back from England. When he had a little time, he would cultivate roses here. Books and gardening were his interests."

On a lawn in the garden, and in the centre, were set three stone tablets. About ten metres beyond was a wooden frame standing about two metres tall, and in the middle of it hung a bell. My gaze had been drawn to it from the start. I could not see it clearly, but its shape was familiar to me. "Padma, do you see that bell?" I asked quietly.

"Of course, I do. Don't get excited yet!" she whispered back.

We went over to the tablets. On the first was written, "In

Memory of High Lama Perrault, British, born in Germany, 1681 – 1930, aged 249.”

“In theory, Perrault … I mean Orazio had died in 1745, but Perrault …?” I was puzzled.

“I understand what you are saying. ‘Perrault’ in fact was a general name, and it stood for Francesco Orazio and his successors. After 1745, Perrault was no longer Orazio, do you understand?”

“Was there a successor to Orazio?”

“Yes, it was a Tibetan who had been baptized by Orazio.”

“What was his name?”

“Anthony,” he said. “At that time, the lamas detested the Christians, and the church had no choice but to go underground, and for some time there was no news of it.”

“Was it finished then?”

“Not quite,” he said. “In 1838, a new leader of the church appeared, a British man of German birth, who was brought up in England and went to study in Italy. He was an adventurous man and had been drawn towards mysterious Tibet. He pretended to be a Moslem and lived for twelve years in Lhasa. He spread a rumour of his own decease to evade being killed by the lamas and he finally became the leader of the underground church.”

“Were there any Tibetan converts?”

“There were about forty Christians at that time. They decided to conceal their names and to keep no records so that they would not be persecuted by the lamas,” he said. “He was not bigoted, and believed that different religions could coexist and that their strengths and weaknesses could complement each other. Apart from his secret evangelism, he was a serious student of Tibetan Buddhism, and he obtained a degree in Buddhist studies and eventually became a high lama.”

“Then he was High Lama Perrault?”

"He was one of them, the last one," he said. "That is why Perrault lived from 1681 to 1930. It was a master stroke of James Hilton to give him an age of two hundred and forty-nine."

"What about Chang? Was it a general name as well?"

"It was his own name! He came to Shangri-La when he was twenty-two."

"Was he a Buddhist?"

He nodded. "He was a Christian, too."

The inscription on the middle tablet read: High Lama Chang, Han Chinese, 1833 – 1966, aged 133 years. When I looked closely at the tablet, I saw a little cross in gold paint and there was one also on Perrault's.

"Are there still Christians in the valley?" I asked.

"Er…, only one." The High Lama paused. He seemed to avoid my question and continued, "After Miss Brinklow left the valley, no more missionaries arrived here. The last Christian family has also left."

"Was that Baibuqi's family?"

"Yes."

"It was Miss Brinklow who baptised Baibuqi's father. Padma, remember?" I looked at her and she nodded.

"Sam, do you have religious belief?" the High Lama suddenly asked me.

"It's a bit illogical; between 'yes' and 'no'," I said. "When I was a little boy, I would usually go with my mother to the temple to pray. I would follow my mum, burn incense and kneel before the Buddha. This influence stayed with me all through my childhood, and I have always felt affection for temples and the feeling of dark solemnity. But I normally tell people that I have no religious belief. I enjoy being in a temple and I don't object to go into a church, when I happen to be nearby, and pray for spiritual comfort! But I do not believe that religious belief can solve human problems, and I do not agree with practices of confession and remission for wrongdoing."

"Do you accept the term 'superstition'?"

"My interpretation is that an excessive belief in any religion could be regarded as superstitious," I said. "I believe that the object of most religions is to lead people to goodness, and that they all have their merits and accumulated riches of content. Through many centuries of challenge and refinement, they must have truth and value to have gained their profound hold over us. Many preachers believe their own religion to be supreme and quickly reject the others as false without a proper knowledge or understanding of them. They dismiss as 'superstition' what warrants careful consideration. The world is immense, and there are many religions, each with its own characteristics. Must we hold that because one religion is true, all others are bound to be false?"

"That is what Chang said," he said. "The world is at its best only if it is harmonious. Respect and tolerance are essential for harmony among human beings."

The third tablet read: Hugh Conway, British, 1893 – 1997, aged 104.

"Conway's birth wasn't given in the book."

"The book didn't tell us that he liked roses either, did it?" he said. "Conway told me that and much about Britain. He told me the Queen of England lives in Buckingham Palace, and that the Houses of Parliament have a bell called 'Big Ben' ...."

"All right!"

The Church and the Bell

Beside Perrault's tablet was a small and delicate wooden plaque with an inscription in Tibetan གར་ཆུད་ན་ཁ .

"What is this about?"

"It says, 'Shachen Naga'. That's where the church was built." He went on, "Two hundred and sixty years after it was torn down, people are still looking for the church site, but without any success."

"Do you know where it was?"

"Not for sure," he paused. "But I believe that Chang knew the secret."

"How do you mean?"

"He and I would often go to Lhasa to visit the Jokhang Temple. Every time, he would always take me to a waste piece of ground in the East District where he would look and linger. I once asked him why he did so, and he was going to say but never did. He never told me the reason.

"Three years ago, I was looking through a book when I came upon a note that Chang had made: 'Shachen Naga Bana-shol'. I then realized that it had something to do with the church. I went at once to Lhasa to see, but sadly the whole city had changed. Everywhere had been replaced by new housing, and I could make nothing out. It was my mistake, not having recorded the place carefully."

"Not altogether. Chang must have had a reason for not telling the secret."

"It may have been to do with property entitlements!" he said.

"When I went back to Lhasa, I didn't see the bell either."

We stood in silence for a while, and before we left, I bowed in respect before the tablets.

'Dang, dang, dang', rang out a clear bell. Lama Wangdui was now standing by the bell frame, pulling the clapper. We moved slowly towards it. My eyes were fixed on the bell and I knew it so well. I had often had a photograph of it in my pocket and had looked at it so many times. I could have shut my eyes and described it in detail. On the upper part were inscribed the Latin words: *TE DEVM LAVDAMVS*.

"That's the Capuchins' bell!" I cried out.

"It's a copy," he said.

"Oh, really?" I felt disconsolate.

"When we were leaving Shangri-La, we wanted to bring the original church bell with us, but some of the lamas who opted to stay objected. We finally decided that we should cast a replica. The original bell must be still in the Jokhang Temple. I don't know when the clapper was lost."

"It's a Tibetan bell now hanging in the Jokhang Temple, and it doesn't have a clapper either," I said.

"It may be that people were often looking for the bell, and they substituted another one like it, and removed the clapper."

"And that's why Padma went to Lhasa, to look for the original bell?"

"That's true."

"When did you last see the bell?" I asked.

"I cannot remember now. It was the last time that Chang took me to Lhasa." He thought for a while. "It would have been in 1955! The bell was still hanging in its old place, from the beam in the corridor. When Chang died, I didn't return to Lhasa for many years. Then I went three years ago, but the bell was no longer there."

"Did you make enquiries?"

"It got me nowhere. They do not readily disclose any information. As you said, they are very wary."

I took the photograph out of my pocket, and showed him. He was astonished. "Yes, that's it. When was this taken?"

"1954."

He pored over the photograph, as though looking beyond its surface. He must have been thinking of the Capuchins' exploits. After a long pause, I heard him say gently, *'Te Deum Laudamus.'* Then he handed it back to me.

"Is this the bell of Shangri-La?' I said quietly.

"I'm sorry, what did you say?'

"The bell of Shangri-La." I went on, "The Tibetan scholar, Hugh Richardson, described the bell as 'Ye-shui chen-po' -- the great bell of Jesus; Father Vannini called it 'the bell of Lhasa,' but I think that 'the bell of Shangri-La' is more appropriate."

"'The bell of Shangri-La'! It's a good name," he exclaimed

"I hope 'The bell of Shangri-La' will once again be there in its beauty for all to see."

"And now you know the truth of Shangri-La!"

I nodded in assent. "Are you anxious about my disclosing this secret?"

"It doesn't really matter. This is just an ordinary place, much the same as others. What is distinctive is our harmonious and moderate society; we are satisfied and happy.

"Are visitors allowed here?"

"If they can make it over the difficult approach, perhaps with a bit of luck too, we welcome anyone here. Of course, our visitors must respect our customs and behave well, otherwise we will take measures ..." He spoke with deliberation. "In fact, in recent years, there have been tourists passing through, especially westerners. But no one has yet found anything out of the ordinary here. Perhaps I may quote the famous Su Dongpo's words: *Unaware of the appearance of Mount Lu, you just find yourself lucky to be there!"*

"Why not keep it as a secret forever?"

"I hope people will stop making wild guesses, like 'the blind men describing the elephant', each with his own opinion. Some people, for commercial reasons, make strange claims. Every time that the 'real' Shangri-La is announced, there is a stampede, and traditional cultures and the natural environment are severely damaged."

"Why choose me? I mean why bring me here?" I asked.

"It might be coincidence! But it may be your luck and merit, too. Lao Tzu said:

> *Scholars of the highest class, when they hear about the Tao,*
> *earnestly carry it into practice.*
> *Scholars of the middle class, when they have heard about it,*
> *seem now to keep it and now to lose it..*
> *Scholars of the lowest class, when they have heard about it,*
> *laugh greatly at it..*
> *If it were not laughed at, it would not be fit to be the Tao."*

And the High Lama laughed loudly himself.

"What is the name of this valley?"

"A name is good, but no name is better still."

"You mean the 'Nameless Valley'!" I said.

"No, not the 'Nameless Valley'. We just don't have a name, like Shangri-La itself, a place that you will not find on the map. Do you understand what I am saying? " he explained. "Do please come back here, whenever you wish."

"I most certainly will." I looked at Padma and she smiled.

Finally, he shook my hand in parting and he muttered: *"Te Deum Laudamus!"*

I took for granted that the High Lama was saying this in good will, and I replied respectfully: *"Om Mani Padme Hum."*

Later, Padma told me that High Lama Dazhi often recited these words. He must indeed be the valley's last …

THE VALLEY WITHOUT A NAME

When we left the lamasery, the sun was slowly setting behind the mountain tops. The pilgrims were beginning to go downhill on their way home. Looking back at the lamasery on the mountain side, it looked like a little fort steeped in history, alone against the cliffs.

It was at sunset that the charm of this wonderful valley was displayed at its best, for having dropped behind the western range, the sun still sent shafts of golden light pulsing down the valley, touching the great expanse of ricefields. The golden spikes, full and ripe, bent heavily in the breeze. Along the paths between the fields plodded the farmers in their straw hats, carrying their hoes, leading their oxen home. Padma waved and called out a friendly greeting to them all.

The mountain forests, the weeping willows along the river banks, everywhere there was peace. On the deep green lake, its surface like a mirror, were several boats at anchor. The fishermen were sitting in the stern, smoking their water pipes. Along the gunwales like rows of soldiers stood dark grey cormorants. Suddenly, at a command from the fisherman, the troops plopped into the water, creating clear circles of little ripples on which the sunlight danced and flashed.

Soon, up they came one after another. The fisherman put out a pole and gently scooped them up. They clung to the end of the pole and fluttered back onto the boat. Fish tails were sticking out from their bills. The fisherman quickly removed the fish. He gave the order again, and back they went, and again and again, and he rewarded them each with a little fish until he was satisfied, and took the oar and rowed to the shore. Behind the boat stretched a clear wake on the quiet surface; the birds stood to attention along the sides. This was a tranquil picture full of life, a scene that many artists have sought to capture.

The lake was quiet again, the caravan on the shore had packed up and gone; the festival was over, and people were taking down the tents. Villagers were starting to go home carrying their bundles. Cooking smoke was drifting up from the houses; it would soon be supper time.

Butter Tea

When we were back to the house, Amu was making butter tea. I had drunk it often, but had not seen how it was made, so I watched carefully. She tore off some leaves from a tea brick and put them in boiling water to infuse. Then she poured the tea into a wooden cylinder, adding butter and some salt, pounding it with a wooden plunger until it was fully mixed, and then she poured it into a pot to heat it up. This made the butter tea beloved by the Tibetan people.

When it was ready, Amu at once poured us two bowls of piping hot butter tea. I took mine, drank two mouthfuls and set it down. She immediately topped it up again. This happened several times. I gestured that that was enough for me. Amu was smiling.

"This is our rule to fill up our guest's bowl constantly. If you feel you have had enough, leave the bowl until the end and then drain it in one," Padma explained.

"Why do Tibetans drink butter tea?"

"We drink it all the time. On the high plateau with its dry cold climate, high fat butter is good for our bodies, but it's very rich. According to Chinese medicine, tea helps to break down fat, and a balance is maintained if they are drunk together." Padma's explanation sounded plausible.

The Source of Wealth

Meanwhile, Dr Tserin and his assistant were busy packing herbal medicines and tea leaves. Many bundles and boxes were laid out on the floor. Soon, some young men came in. I recognised them as members of the caravan. Dr Tserin and the leader Gesang counted and made calculations. All was carefully recorded.

"This brings in income for the whole valley. *Apa* is in charge of the valley's resources and the caravan is responsible for selling these goods in the cities, and they buy what we need and bring it home. We have a cooperative system run centrally, with fair distribution," Padma said quietly.

I watched Tserin carefully taking out from the cupboard a beautiful wooden box which was full of splendid gold and silver ornaments. He noted the items one by one and then handed them to Gesang. At an order from him, they all promptly picked the goods up and carried them out, strapping them onto the horses' backs, and prepared for the next journey.

As he saw the caravan depart, Tserin breathed a sigh of relief. "Every time the caravan comes, we're too busy even for a cup of tea."

His wife was very attentive and at once brought before him a bowl of butter tea. "It's just fine to drink. Dinner will soon be ready." The temperature was just right. Tserin drank his bowl in one.

At Dinner

Some simple light dishes, fresh eggs collected from the henhouse, soft green vegetables and chilli peppers picked from the garden, potatoes given by the old farmer we had met on our walk, and of course fish.

"Dr Tserin, may I come in?" a woman called at the door.

"Oh, it's Zhamei from next door. Do come in!" said Tserin.

Zhamei brought in a cooked dish. "Come, try my cooking! I've just made some stewed chicken with mushrooms. I hope you will like it." She set the dish on the table and left before she could be thanked. Next a middle-aged man appeared holding a bottle. "A meal without wine is incomplete. This is a secret family recipe, for your guest from afar." He put the bottle on the table.

"Sangba, sit down and drink with us," Tserin called.

"No, thank you very much. If Mr Chau is free tomorrow, please come to my house and be my guest," he said to me.

I hesitated and looked at Padma, but her head was down. "Maybe I can, thank you very much." Sangba was satisfied and left.

This place was filled with the simple kindness of country people. They provided for themselves and lived sufficiently. They adapted to circumstances without fuss, seemingly without upset or anxiety or fear, placid and with an optimistic and devout confidence in the future. I was conscious that I was only a passing guest. Why was I so fortunate to be treated like this, with such generosity and kindness? I wondered what I could give in return. For a little, I was overwhelmed, and there were tears in my eyes.

They saw that I wasn't eating. "Eat, eat, it's getting cold! This evening Padma is going to a *Guozhuang* dance." Tserin filled my cup.

A Jiarong Beauty

After supper, Padma put on traditional Tibetan costume. Her appearance was completely changed and was fascinating. She had untied her plaits, and her long hair was tied back with a pink scarf. On her head were agate, coral, gold and silver ornaments. Over her pink dress she wore a lovely cloak with black and white stripes. Her restrained make-up complemented her rich costume perfectly. She was a real Tibetan beauty, and it was hard to realize that she was half Han. I was entranced.

"How do I look, Uncle Sam?" she said shyly.

"You look super. What costume is this that you are wearing?"

"Can you not see that our lovely Padma is a product of the Valley of the Beauties?" Tserin cut in, delighted.

"Do you mean the Danpa Valley?"

"That's it! Amu is a Jiarong Tibetan from the Danpa Valley."

Amu helped her daughter adjust her costume. When they heard our conversation, they smiled with satisfaction.

"Would you like to go to the *guozhuang* party? Uncle Sam, we all hope you can come!"

"No, this is for young people. I'm a bit old!" I said.

"You still look young to me," said Tserin.

"Thank you all the same. But I feel a little tired."

"Very well! We'll see you in the morning!" and Padma walked out in high spirits.

As they watched her go, Tserin and his wife smiled with delight; but then they would sit in silence too, lost in their thoughts. After a while, Tserin asked. "Are your children all grown up?"

"Yes, they are."

"Then you can enjoy life."

"What should I say?" I said. "It's certainly not easy being a parent. When the parents could be enjoying a comfortable life, their children are already enjoying one. Don't you agree?"

Tserin smiled and nodded and raised his cup, "Come, let's drink some more."

"No! I won't be able to stand!"

"Then we'll have some tea." Amu kindly brought a pot of green tea with two cups.

We drank the cups, and fell silent for a while.

Perrault's Secret

"When did you come to the valley?"

"It was 1960, just after my second year at university, during the summer vacation; I was going everywhere collecting medicinal herbs, and I came here. You must know the story after that. The time has passed so quickly and in no time my daughter has grown up. How satisfying and happy it is to see a child growing up!"

"Yes, indeed!" I nodded.

"Whenever I see Padma, I am reminded of something that happened." Tserin slowly lifted his cup and drank some tea. "It was in summer 1965, Chang asked to see me and he told me a secret. Perrault as a young man had met a Tibetan girl who had looked after him in a difficult time. Perrault thought of her as a soul mate, but he was inhibited by his standing as a missionary, and could only see her in private. Later, they were in love, and had a daughter, though sadly the mother died in childbirth. Fortunately, Chang was very helpful and arranged for the child to live in a noble's family. Perrault could only look on in silence as his daughter grew up. He did not dare reveal what had happened. The girl grew up beautiful, with fair, clear skin. People said that she was like a European. On one occasion when she was in Shigatze, she met a British man who was on an official visit. They quickly became very fond of each other, and decided to spend their lives together. They eloped to India, and had two little girls. Later, they all went to the father's home in Scotland.

"Perrault was always trying to find out where the granddaughters were, but he died without being able to realize his wish. He passed his hopes on to Chang. Later, Chang asked Conway to look for them, but on two visits home to Britain he was not successful. So this time, he specially sent me with Conway to Britain, to see if I could be lucky in Scotland."

"And did you find the girls?"

"No. It was all so long ago, I didn't think the chances were high. Maybe you could help."

"Was this your main reason for going to Scotland?"

He nodded.

Reminiscing about Scotland

"I think that Scotland is a splendid place, with hills, lochs and sea; blessed by nature," Tserin said.

"I do, too. Scotland has been the parent of many great people. There was Adam Smith the famous economist, Watt the pioneer of steam engines, George Bogle, George Forrest, all known throughout the world."

"I found the Scots kind," he said. "Once, I was lost in Glasgow and met a local man on a bicycle. To my amazement, he spoke Chinese, and after a few sentences we had become firm friends. He invited me to his home on a little hill, and cooked traditional Scottish sausage for me. It was black in colour. What do you call that?"

"Haggis!" I said.

"Yes! Haggis. It tasted odd but delicious. I asked what was inside. He just laughed and never told me."

"What was his name?"

"His name was Tom, and he told me he had studied Chinese at Oxford. He took me to many places sightseeing. We visited Bogle's birthplace at Daldowie, some five miles to the east of Glasgow, but we found that the home had passed out of the family. Ten years before, it had become a crematorium. Most sad. Tom took me to the cemetery behind Glasgow Cathedral and we found George Bogle's grave. But we found out later that it was actually his grandfather's who had the same name."

"Are you still in touch with Tom?"

"To begin with he would often send postcards, but then that stopped. The last one must have been thirty years ago."

"He could still be in Glasgow. Let me ask for you when I go home."

We raised our cups. Tserin had a notion, "I heard that on the Scottish border, there is a little town that lovers elope to."

"Ah, right! I think it's the town called Gretna Green that you're talking about."

"What was the story?" he asked.

"In the middle of the eighteenth century, a new law came out in England that no one under the age of twenty-one could marry legally without the parents' permission. This led to many young lovers running away to Scotland and marrying in the first town that they came to, Gretna Green. There was a blacksmith there who used to witness these marriages, and they were right away legally married. Today, the blacksmith's forge is a tourist destination, but many couples still go there to get married, and the old memories are kept alive."

"Did the blacksmith leave any record of the marriages?"

"I am not sure, but it's possible," I said.

"It's splendid that lovers finally got together. They must be happy people there. If I have a chance, I will go and see for myself." Tserin had evidently not given up his search for Perrault's descendants.

"Will you visit Scotland again?"

"I do hope I can."

"Do let me know. I'm an 'old Scotland hand'. I will take you all round Scotland, and we'll go and look for Nessie."

"Good, that's settled."

"Do you believe that everyone is happy in this valley?" I asked.

"People have their griefs and joys, their togetherness and separation. The moon has its dark and bright times, its waxings and wanings. It is hard to find completeness in one's life. Happiness and otherwise have many aspects. I feel that one cannot find happiness unless one has satisfaction, and that satisfaction only comes with giving; if one is only taking, one will never have satisfaction. Giving more than taking is the source of happiness."

Night Noises

Darkness fell, a gleaming moon hung high in the sky against a background that seemed punctured with myriads of star holes. In the distance on the plain the *guozhuang* fires still burned brightly.

I leant at the window, quietly listening to the sounds of the valley. I could hear indistinct laughter and shouts mixed with intermittent barking of dogs, the constant buzzing of cicadas, owls hooting, crickets in the grass, frogs in the ponds, one or two ill-timed cock crows and some noises I didn't recognise, rising here falling away there, blending in a chorus as though orchestrated by a musician. All these sounds were so delightful that one would keep guessing what would come next, and felt that the pleasure they gave could never fade.

Lights were flickering far on the horizon, it was uncertain whether they were torches or stars, moving here and there, the whole valley and the sky merging together. In surroundings like these I felt wistfulness as I wondered what we look for in life.

Life rises and falls, as though drifting with the tide for a few ten years and quickly passing away. When I see all the activity on every side, people fighting to survive, to fulfil their desires, to pursue pleasure and joy, to struggle for power and prestige, I feel sick and tired. I am more and more losing interest in city life and material pleasure. I want to get away from bustle and stir and live in solitude, to be closer to nature, to gain an understanding through contact and intuition of how everything in nature interrelates, to look for harmony in life. To find delight in the song of birds and the scent of flowers, to look for consolation in dawn and sunset, this is what helps us to understand life and cleanses our spirits.

There was a squall of rain, and the stream became noisy. It was hard to sleep as my mind was racing. Sometimes when there was a strange noise, I would jump out of bed to investigate.

LEAVING THE VALLEY

Morning Songs

Very early, at about half past five, I ran up alone to a hilltop from where almost the whole valley could be seen: the tidy houses, the broad grassy plains, the rich farmland; the awe inspiring mountains, the tranquil lakes and the running river nurturing this magical place. In the mist the village was concealed and indistinct, like an old black and white photograph. In this secluded mountain valley, time seemed to have been arrested, the past strangely alive within the present.

The colour of the heavens was changing by the second. From black, it turned to deep blue, and then to grey. Suddenly a pool of yellow light appeared on the summits to the east, and the clouds around were fringed with gold. A little red dot emerged slowly from behind the mountain rim, in no time almost half, and then more than half, and when I looked at it again, there was the sun's disc over the summits. The angry red light was like a phantom city ablaze, tainting the whole sky red and yellow. Now light streamed through the clouds and lit up the entire valley, with rippling flashes of gold from the lake. I involuntarily put both hands up to my face and enjoyed the magnificent spectacle from between my fingers. The grey mists in the valley slowly dispersed, and the sky turned to a light blue. By half past six, the whole valley had awoken.

Another day had begun. From each house smoke was rising. Farmers were going to the fields, children were going to school; women were washing clothes in the streams; snatches of song came across from every corner of the valley. Everything here was serene and relaxing, there were no crowds jostling or shifts of workers. There were no money complications, bills to pay or tax problems, and there was no political struggle or fear of nuclear war, and there wasn't any …..

I sat on the grass quietly watching what was going on about me. One or two cuckoo calls echoed across the stillness of the valley. In the morning sunshine, bamboo leaves were fluttering like feathers, and the dull green leaves of the rhododendrons were gleaming. In clefts of the rock tough ferns and creepers were beginning to shed their beads of morning dew. Between the twigs, little spiders were laboriously mending their homes, spreading out their silver webs one after the other.

About twenty metres away, a small dappled deer came out suddenly from the bushes, it stared at me for a while and then started to graze. Then a little wild pig appeared scurrying here and there. Two exotic pheasants trailing long tails chased each other. None of these creatures seemed to take much notice of me.

Even more surprising was a tiny yellow finch that suddenly flew over and landed on my shoe. Before I knew what was happening, it had hopped onto my leg. I kept still and watched. It chirped and pecked away at my trousers. I carefully took out of my bag a small piece of biscuit, broke it up and held out the crumbs on my hand. It responded to my invitation, and sleekly flew onto my palm. It was so delicate, affectionate and calm. When finished, I gently raised my hand and it flew up to a twig where it chirruped away. I felt very happy, as I had never felt so at one with nature before.

It was an intoxicating sight before me. The air was fresh. I closed my eyes, thought back to the quiet night filled with flickering stars and a silver moon, relished the dazzling glow of the rising sun at dawn. I enjoyed the fitful breeze on my face, breathing in the heady smell of flowers, listening to the singing of the birds and the rustling of the bamboo grove. It was like a symphony. I felt myself, from deep in my heart, in harmony with nature.

I gazed at this wonderful place, where I had been received with such courtesy and hospitality. My experiences had been like the fisherman of Wuling, who, many years ago, stumbled upon the peach blossom garden that seemed like fairyland, with kind people inviting him to their homes, offering meals and presenting wine, and asking about the world beyond. Once he left, he could never find his way back. I would soon be departing myself, and I wondered whether I would ever be able to come again.

The Old Shepherd

'Ding-ling! Ding-ling!' a crisp sound of bells distracted me. An old Tibetan appeared driving a herd of yaks towards me. As he walked, he was blowing on a leaf and making a weird, unpleasant noise, but he seemed to be enjoying very much.

His hair was turning white, his wrinkled face deeply lined, but he was sprightly and strong. His mouth broke open in a grin, an empty mouth but for two front teeth. He wore a pair of big hoop earrings, they were actually gold when I looked carefully. His earlobes had evidently been pulled down by the weight of the rings which swayed and sparkled as he walked, making him the more imposing. He strolled across and greeted me, "Zhaxi-dele! You must be Mr Chau?"

"How do you know me?"

"How could I not know you? The whole village is talking about you. I know everyone here."

"You've lived here a long time?" I asked.

"Seventy years ago, my father carried me on his shoulders when we all came here, and I've been here ever since." The old man smiled as he looked down on the village, and he seemed proud of himself. "You've come from Mr Con's place, have you?"

I realised that he meant Conway. "Yes, from Britain," I said.

"Where's Britain?"

I pointed to the north-west. "Behind that mountain, far, far away … a far away place," I said with emphasis.

He thought for a while. "Did you fly here on an iron eagle?" he asked, "Yes, you must have! I remember when we were in Shangri-La, our hero Talu used an iron eagle to take Mr. Con and others to the Blue Moon Valley. It was a pity that he died when his job was done."

"Is that so?" I was astonished, though I understood what he was talking about. I pretended to be serious, looked up at the sky, and searched for traces of the great eagle, hoping to find a change of subject. He reminded me of Joseph Rock. When he went on an expedition, he looked at the great mountains and gorges in front of them and he said to a nomad in his party, "If we flew in an aeroplane we could reach Amnyi Machen in the time it takes to drink a bowl of tea." To which the nomad replied, "I heard that people in the west can fly inside an eagle." Rock explained that a machine was used for flying, but the nomad insisted that the machine was made from eagle feathers.

All at once, I heard faint rumbling in the far distance. The old man looked puzzled as he said, "I've heard that people outside use metal to surface roads, but aren't metal roads too slippery and too hard? They would be uncomfortable to walk on, and I am sure my yak wouldn't like it."

For this old man, aeroplanes and railways were meaningless concepts, and to try to explain them would confuse him. Better to let him be! Time was moving on, and I briskly shook his hand and said goodbye, with a final 'Zhaxi-dele'.

Meeting with the High Lama yesterday had more or less clarified my uncertainties about Shangri-La, and I thought it was time to leave the valley today.

Yet I felt uncertain about disclosing the secrets of this valley to the outside. I feared that enterprising businessmen would be quick to come here to develop tourism, build bridges and roads, hotels, cafeterias and places of entertainments. Very soon a tranquil fairyland would become a turbid dye vat. Then the people would move again. However, the last few words of the High Lama had certainly reassured me.

It was hard to leave; I still felt a little undecided. A strange sensation of loneliness came over me. I told Padma my plans. She was startled at first and then said calmly, "Very well, it's four days now since you left Lhasa."

Saying Goodbye

At noon, the villagers had gathered, and just as when I arrived, they were all wearing beautiful costume. They were standing in a line to see me on my way.

Padma did not say anything, with only a reluctant smile on her face. Then she took a white *khatag* and put it round my neck. "Goodbye, Uncle Sam," she said softly, "and good luck!"

I smiled too, nodded and murmured goodbye. "This is for you, as a keepsake, it belongs to the valley!" I put the stone that Dorje had given me into her hand.

"I will remember you." Padma clutched the stone in her hand, and did not say more. She motioned with her hand, and two Mosuo girls wearing formal costume offered me three cups of wine. Then two sturdy Yao men picked up the sedan chair for me to sit in.

"When you have drunk the *sulima* wine, you will remember your time with us here," said Padma. "We will send you on your way! And don't worry, you'll be on time."

I was feeling confused and for a little while was losing my composure as I tried to keep back tears. I drank the wine in one draught and sat in the chair, and waved goodbye to the villagers. At this point, the Mosuo girls broke into song, '*My friend, do not hurry on your way. The journey is far, and the time is long. When you see the green mountains, rivers and lakes, do not forget your time with us here, madami* ...' Just then, the bell began to toll, from the lamasery on the mountainside. I think that this was the kind thoughtfulness of High Lama Dazhi. I listened to the lovely singing and the toll of 'the Bell of Shangri-La' as the sedan chair went swaying on its way up towards the pass.

I suddenly realized that Padma was no longer beside me, and as I looked all about me, I saw Tserin and his wife in the crowd and Padma, head down, close behind her mother. Tserin was wearing a leather hat very like my own. He was smiling broadly, and raised his hat and waved it to me, "See you in Scotland," he called out.

I at once raised my hat and said, "Yes, bring Padma with you!"

Now Padma waved too, "Bye, Uncle Sam. You take care!"

"You take care too. Padma. Bye!" Amidst these happy sounds, the view of the village was gradually receding. I was feeling very tired, just as I had done when I arrived. I wanted to go to sleep, and I did.

Return to Lijiang

"Wake up! Up you get!"

Still three quarters asleep, there seemed to be someone shaking my shoulder, and I opened an eye a crack. "Where am I?"

"You're in our guesthouse!"

"Where?"

"In Lijiang," the girl said.

"What? Lijiang?" I did not know what was happening.

"What's the matter? Are you all right?"

I sat up slowly, rubbed my face with both hands, and composed myself. "I'm fine. When did I come here?"

"Last night, about twelve o'clock. A Tibetan girl brought you here, and there were two young men."

"Where is she?"

"She didn't stay, she went away."

"Did she leave a name?"

"No ... but she was beautiful." The girl smiled and left the room.

At once, I thought of Padma. It must have been her. I sat in thought for a while on the bed, and felt a slight headache. I lay down again and closed my eyes. I hoped to let my dreams take me back once more to the valley, that magical place.

The girl was back. "Sir, you must get up! She said I must wake you this morning, as you have a plane to catch, isn't that right?"

I opened my eyes at once, sat up and took my ticket out of my bag, Lijiang to Shenzhen, 29 September, 11.30, that was today. I looked at my watch, it was just after seven. There was still time. I dressed quickly, and went out for a wander.

It was still early morning. The shops were closed and the tourists were not yet up. On the stone flagged streets were only a few elderly Naxi people quietly going their way, slowly as ever. Lijiang was back to its old simplicity. I went here and there without much attention to my surroundings, thinking only about what had happened in the valley. In Lhasa, I had had altitude sickness, but when I met Padma and then Tserin and the High Lama, I had found the dream. How had I come to Lijiang? Was it, after all, a dream or my imagination, or was it real?

Not many people were in the street, but I had a feeling that I was being followed. I looked back, but saw no one. When I came back to the guesthouse, the girl said to me, "The girl who brought you here last night has just been and left a packet for you. She said you left it in her car."

"Which way did she go?" I questioned.

The girl pointed to the left of the front door. I at once ran off in excitement carrying the parcel, down streets and lanes, over stone bridges, now here, now there through the alley ways, but I saw no sign of her. I sat down sadly at the side of the street and opened the parcel. It was my digital camera, and there was a note in English which said, "Hope you enjoyed your trip. Sorry about the camera." I at once looked through the photographs on the screen, and found that the last had been taken in the Jokhang Temple. All the time in the streets, I had felt that someone was nearby watching.

At nine o'clock, with my pack on my back, I paid at the reception. The attendant gave me a card, and courteously said, "Thank you for your custom. We hope that you will return. Did you realize that Dr Rock once stayed in your room?"

"Goodness, did he?" I said, "I'll be back."

As I walked out of the guesthouse, I looked all around me. I felt a sense of loss. I took a taxi to Lijiang airport. The plane left on time for Shenzhen, and I continued by bus to Hong Kong. A week later, I was back home in Scotland.

CHAPTER 8

REFERENCES

REVIEW

After I came home, I went around for several weeks in a distracted state. Was it jet lag? Was it the effects of altitude sickness? For some time, I could not get myself back into focus, and my wife often told me that I was daydreaming. Whenever I closed my eyes, those beautiful memories came back to me, scene by scene. I picked up my worn copy of *The Lost Horizon*, 1960 reprint, and looked at the story once more.

The story was set in 1930. At that time there was rioting in an Indian city, Baskul. Four westerners, the British consul Hugh Conway, the deputy consul Charles Mallinson, an American Henry Barnard and a missionary Roberta Brinklow were to be evacuated in a small plane to Peshawar. But the plane did not take the route it should have done, but flew along the Himalayas heading north-east before making an emergency landing in a mountain valley. The four passengers were unhurt, but the pilot, Talu, died of his injuries. Talu managed to tell them that they had come down on the Tibetan plateau, and that not far away was Shangri-La.

In their great distress, a group of men approached from far off, led by an old Chinese. He gave them juicy mangoes and wine. He told them that they were in the Valley of the Blue Moon and he could take them to Shangri-La. They had little choice, and followed him.

Dominating the valley was a beautiful mountain, a perfect cone of ice and snow, called Karakal, rising to over 28,000 feet. There was a lamasery in the valley, the administrative centre of Shangri-La. Most of the people were Tibetan and Chinese, and they were of various religions, Confucianism, Buddhism, Taoism and Christianity, living together in harmony. Shangri-La adhered to the principle of moderation, and its people lived in freedom, peaceful and satisfied, without crime and with no need for a police force.

The lamasery had a modern system of central heating and baths. There was a grand piano and the library held famous seventeenth century travel accounts, and musical scores of Chopin and Mozart. There were Chinese art treasures including early ceramics, lacquer ware and ink paintings.

Perrault was the high lama of the lamasery. He had been a Capuchin missionary who had come to Shangri-La by chance and he had later become its leader. He had built a church and had baptised a few converts, blessing them with the words of *Te Deum Laudamus*. He had discovered gold in the valley, but was interested in particular in herbal medicines. He deprecated polygamy. He studied Buddhist classics, translated western literature, and wrote a polemic against Buddhism. Later, he practised yoga. He lived to an immense age, and it was said that he possessed the power of clairvoyance and levitation.

Chang was the second man in Shangri-La. He had been a troop commander fighting the brigands. He had lost his way deep in the mountains and had been brought to Shangri-La.

A Manchu princess, Lo Tsen, was betrothed to a prince of Turkestan. On her journey to Kashgar, she had lost her way and was eventually rescued to Shangri-La.

Conway thought that Shangri-La was the most settled and harmonious society that he had come across. He was received on several occasions by Perrault who wished him to be his successor. This was why they had been brought to Shangri-La.

Barnard had been miserable with altitude sickness. He found that Shangri-La was full of gold. He decided to stay to help the lamas to increase production. But he was found to be travelling under a false name.

Miss Brinklow had discovered much immoral practice in Shangri-La. She had seen phallic ritual objects in a temple, and she thought that these were signs of pagan degradation. She decided to stay and to preach. She hoped that all the pagans would convert.

Only the obdurate Mallinson was always wanting to go. But he did not dare risk it alone and he implored Conway to go with him. When the High Lama died, Lo Tsen and the porters were waiting at the snowy pass. Conway was confused and finally agreed to go with them. They left for Tatsien-fu, 1,100 miles to the east.

Conway was next found in a mission hospital in Chung Kiang, and had lost his memory. The hospital staff said that he was brought in by a very old lady who died just after. They knew nothing of Mallinson. Conway gradually got better and was returning to England. Aboard the ship, he heard Chopin being played, and this brought back part of his memory. That night they were at Honolulu, and Conway calmly went ashore; no one knew where he was going. Three months later, a friend received a letter from him telling that he was setting off from Bangkok, north-westwards with a long journey ahead of him.

EARLIER WRITERS

The Lost Horizon was published in 1933. James Hilton, the author, said in the book that the story was set on the Tibetan plateau, but there is no record that he ever went to Tibet himself, and his material was almost certainly taken from earlier writers.

In 1904, Graham Sandberg and Thomas Holdich brought out books *The Exploration of Tibet* and *Tibet, The Mysterious*. Both give similar accounts of missionaries in Tibet and state that there was a Christian mission in Lhasa for 38 years, but there is a vagueness over the date when the Capuchins arrived in Lhasa and over their numbers, and it is not clear where the writers took their figures from. James Hilton in his book also gave 38 years. Very likely, Hilton had got this idea from Thomas Holdich. These two sentences may be compared:

> *Tibet, The Mysterious*　　　　　　　　　　　P. 75
> *"It seems strange now to recall the fact that for thirty-eight years a Christian mission existed in the very capital itself ..."*

> *The Lost Horizon*　　　　　　　　　　　　P.133
> *"... it is a remarkable fact, not realized by many Europeans today, that for thirty-eight years there existed a Christian mission in Lhasa itself."*

I was again amazed to find in the bibliography to Holdich's book four of the titles that Conway had read in Shangri-La. This is not likely to have been a coincidence. Another little detail was that they both transcribed the word in the six syllable mantra as 'Mane,' whereas it is generally written 'Mani'.

It would not have just been Holdich's book that Hilton would have read. There were other writers before 1933 that he may have used, such as Clements Markham, William Rockhill, Joseph Rock and Alexandra David-Neel.

In 1876, Markham's *Mission of George Bogle to Tibet and the Journey of Thomas Manning to Lhasa* gave a graphic account of Bogle's journey and his audience with the Panchen Lama at the Tashilhunpo Monastery, and he told how Manning in 1811 had reached Lhasa and been received by the eighth Dalai Lama.

It would be interesting to point out that Markham, as well as Edmund Candler, in their books, wrongly gave 1719 as the year when Francesco Orazio first came to Lhasa. This is the year that Hilton gave for the arrival of the Capuchins in Shangri-La.

William Rockhill

William Rockhill (1854-1914), an American diplomat and orientalist, published his book *The Land of the Lamas* in 1891, in which he gave a detailed account of his journey through from Hsi-ning to Tatsien-lu. He had seen much gold washing activity along the river; he met a fortune-teller who looked like a European in disguise and said that he was practising clairvoyance; he wrote about Buddhist temples and Taoism; he described the tea porters on their way to Tatsien-lu; and he wrote that smoking is indulged in moderately by the people in Kanze. All these materials could also be found in Hilton's story. And it was the marriage customs that Rockhill described which I find most interesting.

Polyandry

Polyandrous marriage was practised in Tibet and was mentioned by many early writers. Rockhill wrote at length about polyandry in Kham region. Brothers would share the same wife, and the mother would tell the children who their father was. He cited Antonio de Andrade and Francesco Orazio's opinions. Both considered that polyandry was an improper practice associated mainly with the poor, and one of which the upper class people disapproved.

Rockhill pointed out that temporary marriages were recognized throughout Tibet, and these unions were not held to be immoral. As regards their marriage relations, these people were little removed from promiscuity, which was but indefinite polyandry joined with indefinite polygamy.

James Hilton wrote that there was inbreeding in Shangri-La. He touched on Perrault's opposition to polygamy, but only alluded to polyandry in *The Lost Horizon*:

> *"...people in Shangri-La are 'moderately chaste."*   P.74

> *"... the women of the valley have happily applied the principle of moderation to their own chastity....."*   P.155

Rockhill cited an explanation given by Samuel Turner, the British envoy to Tibet, for polyandry, a custom he thought had not been unfavourable on the manners of the people.

Conway asked if there were never disputes about women. Chang: "Only very rarely, because it would not be considered good manners to take a woman that another man wanted," Conway: "Supposing somebody wanted her so badly that he didn't care a damn whether it was good manners or not?" Chang: "Then, my dear sir, it would be good manners on the part of the other man to let him have her, and also on the part of the woman to be equally agreeable."   P.114

Last year I passed by Yanjin in the northwest of Yunnan. When I was eating a bowl of minced beef fried rice in a little shop buzzing with flies, a bulky untidy Tibetan came in carrying a large pot. He asked the shop lady for some water, but she shouted at him to leave.

Outside the shop, I saw him and his family sitting under the wall having a rest. There were eight of them, of various ages, looking pitiful. I went over and asked what the matter was. They told me that they were three brothers with their father, their three children, and the wife. They had walked from their home at Shiqu to Deqin and were going to circumambulate Mount Meili. The short second brother was forthcoming and introduced everyone, "This is my wife and my children, this is my older brother and my younger brother, and my father." The older brother's hand was on the woman's shoulder, and he smiled and said, "She's mine too." The younger brother was nodding to me too and smiling, and looked a bit bashful.

I had not been to Shiqu, which is near the border of Sichuan and Tibet, but had read about it. Many men there, of all ages, share the same wife. Even today, there are many counties in the west of Kham where polyandry continues, so when they told me that they came from Shiqu I realized who they all were.

In 1909, Chao Er-feng, the Viceroy for Sichuan border affairs of the Qing government, was promoting agricultural improvements in Shiqu. He convened a meeting with the villagers and recommended ending the custom of polyandry.

Chao said: "There are too few households here, and the reason is that too many of you are becoming lamas or are in polyandrous marriages. From now on, you should follow the Han practice: however many brothers there may be in a family, each should have his own wife."

To which the villagers replied: "If each brother has his own wife, too many children will be born, and it will be hard to provide for everyone. We will have to become beggars to get our food and clothing."

Chao: "There is land to plough and mountains for pasture. Why should you be worried about clothes and food?"

Villagers: "We have heard that Han people are very numerous, and that they find it hard to clothe and feed themselves, so they join the army and come here for sheepskins and *tsamba*. Too many people results in great hardship. We would rather be few than many."

Polyandrous family

Chao: "Brothers sharing the same wife is a perversion and should be punished with the death penalty."

Villagers: "We are simple people and do not understand such proprieties. Brothers have been married to the one wife for many generations. Living in harmony helps to increase production and to avoid famine."

(Fu Songmu, Xi Kang jianshengji 1988, P.74-76)

Before leaving, I asked the family if I could take a photograph to remember them by, and they were delighted to agree. They gave me their address, and after I returned to Scotland, I sent them a copy, and do hope that it reached them. From their body language and the way they stood, the subtlety of their family relationships can be imagined.

The Name 'Shangri-La'

Most likely, William Rockhill gave James Hilton inspiration for his book, and he probably gave him a beautiful name too.

When Rockhill reached Baron in Tsaidam, he was told that there was a small village called Shang where the rivers flowed with milk and butter. It was situated in a broad valley surrounded by high mountains. There were some three hundred families, administered by the head lama who insisted on one wife one husband and strongly opposed polyandry which was widely practised in Tsaidam region.

The map illustrated in Rockhill's book shows his route from Hsi-ning (Xining) in Qinghai Province to Tatsien-lu in Sichuan. It passes the village of 'Shang' or 'Shang Chia' on the east side of the Tsaidam Basin. This is today's town of Xiangride. Rockhill described this village at length, and its position was written in capital letters 'SHANG' in his map. When I saw the explanatory notes, I felt that I had found the answer. The notes give: 'ri = mountain' and 'la = mountain pass'. I believe that this is where the name 'Shangri-La' comes from.

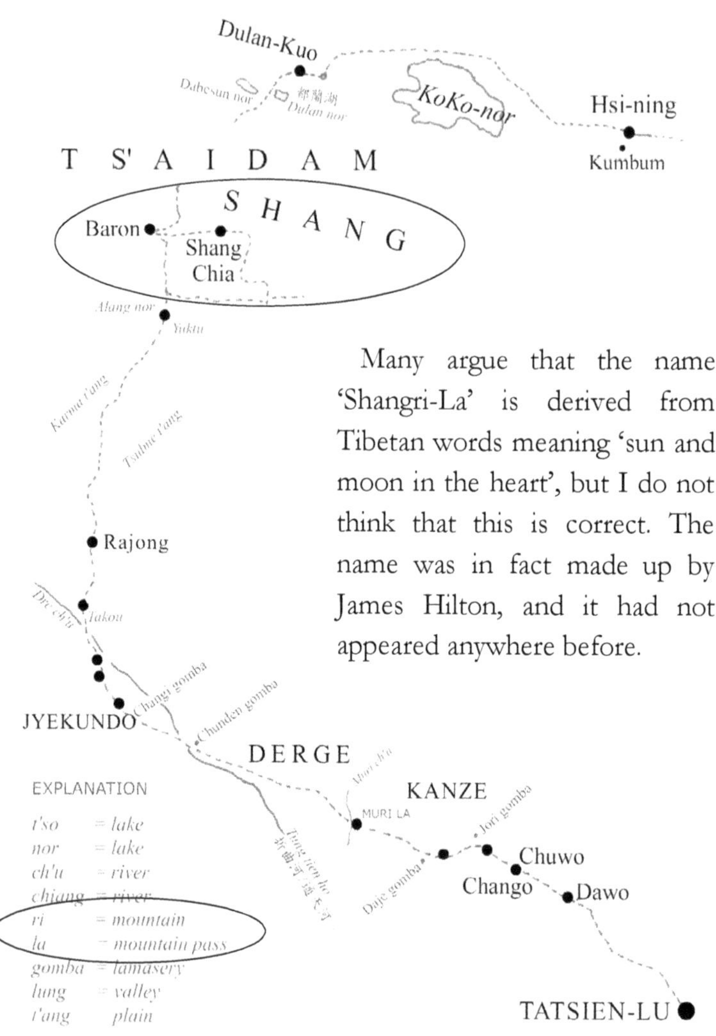

Many argue that the name 'Shangri-La' is derived from Tibetan words meaning 'sun and moon in the heart', but I do not think that this is correct. The name was in fact made up by James Hilton, and it had not appeared anywhere before.

----- *William Rockhill's route of exploration 1888*

Recognition

In his expedition, Rockhill was following a route taken by the Indian explorer Pundit A-K Krishna Singh who spent four years travelling all over Tibet and finally in 1882 arrived in Tatsien-lu.

He gathered much valuable geographical information about Tibet for the British Government. After him came two other distinguished Indian explorers of Tibet, Nain Singh and Sarat Chandra Das. William Rockhill wrote, "If any British explorer had done one third of what Nain Singh, Sarat Chandra Das, or A-K accomplished, medals and decorations, lucrative offices and professional promotion, freedom of cities, and every form of lionizing would have been his; as for those native explorers a small pecuniary reward and obscurity are all to which they can look forward." In fact, since the beginning of the twentieth century, most British diplomats and explorers have received knighthoods and public recognition.

James Hilton portrayed Conway as a shrewd and able diplomat. When there were riots in Baskul, he performed courageous rescues which well deserved a reward. Maybe, with the right connections and introductions and plenty of reports written, there could have been a New Year's honour ahead for him. Perhaps James Hilton was writing of his own dreams.

Joseph Rock

Joseph Rock (1884-1962), revered by the people of Lijiang, lived among them on and off for twenty-seven years. If James Hilton was influenced by Joseph Rock, that could only have been through the eight articles that were published before 1933 in the American National Geographic Magazine:

> November 1924: Banishing the Devil of Disease among Nashi
> April 1925: The Land of the Yellow Lama
> September 1925: Experience of a Lone Geographer
> August 1926: Through the Great River Trenches of Asia
> November 1928: Life among the Lama of Choni
> February 1930: Seeking the Mountain of Mystery
> October 1930: The Glories of Minya Konka
> July 1931: Konka Risumgongba

Many readers in the west were amazed by Rock's illustrated articles. He described a weird ritual performed by a Dongba priest to cure sickness; he introduced the unknown kingdom of Muli in the far west of Sichuan; he crossed mountain ranges, followed the Yangtze River, the Mekong and the Salween north to Atunzi, and admired the magnificent Kaakerpu snow range; above all he loved the beauty of the mountains, and he went far north to Qinghai to look for the mysterious Mt Amnyi Machen; he explored the brigand-infested Konkaling region and Mt Minya Konka, 'the king of mountains' in Sichuan.

Of all Rock's articles, I find the way he described the mountain sceneries most fascinating.

In January 1924, Joseph Rock went on a pioneering expedition to the kingdom of Muli. One evening at Baiyiwua when he looked south to the Lijiang plain, he wrote, "After the sun disappeared, magnificent rays streamed forth above the mountain battlements. The (Likiang) snow range assumed the aspect of an icy dragon floating in mid-air, for the deep valley was filled with smoke-blue mist, and only the peaks and the ice fields reflected the silvery light of the full moon." And again, "Long before sunrise, I stood on the platform before the temple gate to watch the snow peaks turn from gray to pink. Soon the range was blood-red, while the blue smoke which rose from the houses at our feet lay over the valley like a veil, pierced here and there by the dark tops of the fir trees."

Before the snow range in Deqin, he exclaimed, "*Peerless* Mt Miyetzimu, monarch of the Kaakerpu Range... is the most glorious peak my eyes were ever privileged to see... It is like a castle of a dream, an ice palace of a fairy tale, or an enormous mausoleum with gigantic steps and buttresses ... At dawn... Mt Miyetzimu looked deathlike in the cold, gray morning sky, but turned to a rich pink when the sun's rays were reflected from its steep snowfields."

When he visited Konkaling, he wrote: "In a cloudless sky before me rose the peerless pyramid of Jambeyang, the finest mountain my eyes ever beheld. The sky was greenish black. The snowy pyramid was gray, but the apexes of both it and Shenrezig suddenly turned a golden yellow as the sun's ray kissed them."

Rock seemed to like to emphasize the majesty of mountains with the word *'peerless'*, and he wrote again, "… *peerless* Minya Konka rose high above its sister peaks into a turquoise-blue sky. A truncated pyramid with immense lateral buttresses flanked by an enormous glacier many miles in length."

James Hilton has a similar description of Mt Karakal:

> *"…it was to the head of the deep valley that his eyes were led irresistibly, for there, soaring into the gap, and magnificent in the full shimmer of moonlight, appeared what he took to be the loveliest mountain on earth. It was an almost perfect cone of snow."* P.50

> *"Framed in the pale triangle ahead, the mountain showed again, gray at first, then silver, then pink as the earliest sun rays caught the summit,"* P.52

> *"the summit of Karakal, peerless above the blue tiled roofs."* P.97

In 1923, Joseph Rock met the British traveller General George Pereira at Tengyueh in Yunnan. He told Joseph Rock that on his expedition, he had seen the spectacular Amnyi Machen range, a hundred miles away. Pereira reckoned that if it were accurately surveyed, it might prove higher than Mt Everest.

Joseph Rock wrote of his own approach to Amnyi Machen, "I shouted for joy as I beheld the majestic peaks of one of the grandest mountain ranges of all Asia. … Not being supplied with a theodolite, I could not take the actual height; but from other observations I came to a conclusion that the Amnyi Machen towers more than 28,000 feet." Later, when its height was proved to be only 20,610 feet, Rock's estimate became rather a joke. But this was not his only mistake. He once claimed that Minya Konka was the highest mountain in the world with an elevation of 30,250 feet, over a thousand feet higher than Mt Everest (29,028 feet), and it was later found to be below 25,000 feet.

James Hilton wrote:

> *Chang : "It is called Karakal ... over 28,000 feet."*
> *Conway: "Indeed? I didn't realize there would be anything on that scale outside the Himalayas. Has it been properly surveyed? Whose are the measurements?"* P. 59

At the end of the story, he wrote:

> *"I had the luck to meet an American traveller, ... I asked if he had ever heard of a cone-shaped mountain almost as high as the highest of the Himalayas, and his answer to this was rather intriguing. ... There were even rumours about mountains actually higher than Everest, but he didn't himself give credit to them. ... he admitted that they had never been properly surveyed. ...He had been travelling then for some American geographical society, with several colleagues, porters, and so on − in fact, a pukka expedition."* P. 222-225

It is quite certain that the American traveller described by James Hilton was Joseph Rock. There would have been few others who travelled in such style. Every time he went out on expedition, there was a large entourage of men and horses and he took armed bodyguards with him. These are often described in his articles.

From all this information, one cannot say that James Hilton wrote his book without reading Rock's articles. Above all, Rock wrote that the brother-in-law of the king of Muli had the Chinese name of 'Chang'. He was the army commander, and had made a fortune earlier as a bandit. Chang in Shangri-La was also commander of the troops used against bandits. This cannot be a coincidence.

Alexandra David-Neel

The gifted Alexandra David-Neel (1868-1969) was the first western woman to enter Lhasa and she was called 'the most astonishing woman' of her time. In 1912, David-Neel had an audience in Sikkim with the thirteenth Dalai Lama who encouraged her to study Tibetan. David-Neel travelled all over Tibet for fourteen years, studying Tibetan in monasteries and translating Buddhist scriptures into English and French. She also practised the lama's feat of out-of-body travel and *thumo reskiang* -- self-generation of heat. She wrote in her book, *My Journey to Lhasa*: "I saw some hermits seated night after night, motionless on the snow, entirely naked, sunk in meditation, while the terrible winter blizzard whirled and hissed around them! I saw under the bright full moon the test given to their disciples who, on the shore of a lake or a river in the heart of the winter, dried on their bodies, as on a stove, a number of sheets dipped in the icy water!" This story was quoted by James Hilton en bloc:

> *"The lama appeared to have odd powers of body control. I have watched them ... sitting by the edge of a frozen lake, stark naked, with a temperature below zero and in a tearing wind, while their servants break the ice and wrap sheets around them that have been dipped in the water. They do this a dozen times or more, and the lamas dry the sheets on their own bodies."*   P.224

David-Neel was a devout Buddhist and she was also a believer in Shambhala. She told of a strange encounter: One evening while they were preparing supper, a curiously dressed lama appeared noiselessly in front of them, as though sprung from out of the ground. The lama told her that he had many faces which he could change at will, and that he could go unrecognized by anyone. He discussed Tibetan philosophy and mysticism with her. Finally, he stood up, and strode away silently like a ghost into the forest. She believed that he was a messenger from Shambhala.

Nicolas Roerich

Nicolas Roerich (1874-1947) is perhaps one of the most prominent figures of the early twentieth century. He was an artist, philosopher, theosophist, explorer and ethnographer. Roerich was the founder of the Agni Yoga Society and he was nominated for the Nobel Peace Prize by the University of Paris in 1929.

In 1924, he set off on an expedition from Bombay, going north to Xinjiang, then over to the Gobi Desert, continuing into the Altai Mountains and on to Mongolia, before turning south and returning through Tibet into India. He had crossed thirty-five mountain passes, and his journey lasted four years. All this time, he was looking for traces of Shambhala.

In 1928, Roerich published *Altai-Himalaya* in which he recounted reports and his own experiences of Shambhala. He wrote: "When approaching Khotan, the hooves of our horses sounded hollow as though we rode above caves. Our caravan people said that long ago people lived there; now they have gone inside; they have found a subterranean passage to that subterranean kingdom." A Buryat lama told of how he had been led by an underground passage to Shambhala. Roerich also quoted from an account in an Indian newspaper that an army officer, while camping in the region of the Himalayas, saw a tall man almost naked, standing. The man suddenly leaped from the rocks and disappeared. Local people said that he had seen a snowman who was a guard of the sacred land.

Roerich claimed in his book that individual lamas possessed powers to produce low forms of materialization, levitation, manifestations of will, clairvoyance and clairaudience. His paintings, writings and lectures on the cult of Shambhala aroused wide interest in the West.

I think it is of interest to mention the introduction to his book written by Claude Bragdon in which he described Roerich as being deeply Oriental in temperament, sympathies and point of view, like a reincarnated Eastern sage. He also described Roerich's vision, as a prophet and a pioneer, clearly foreseeing and quietly planning a better order in a world still in the grip of its so recent terrible nightmare. Could his prophecies come true, and could his dreams of binding humanity into a brotherhood through beauty materialize?

James Hilton has very similar descriptions in the conversation between Perrault and Conway about dream and vision, foreseeing the chaos of the future world and that his vision will come true.

To some extend, I believe that James Hilton has made use of Roerich's character to describe High Lama Perrault.

Shambhala

When I asked lamas and people in Tibet about Shangri-La, many gave vague replies and didn't know what it was, but when I asked about Shambhala, they all told me that Shambhala was paradise. Some then said that Shangri-La and Shambhala were the same. Tibetans think of Shambhala as a world of bliss where the immortals live.

It is said that Shambhala is hidden between the Himalayas and the Gobi Desert, to the west of Mt Kang Tise. It is also said to be in Metok County in eastern Tibet; northern Kashmir is also discussed as a possibility.

Shambhala is said to be surrounded by tier upon tier of mountains. It is made up of eight districts, like the eight petals of a lotus flower. Each district teems with villages, and at the centre are the capital and the palace. Everywhere are inexhaustible treasures of gold and silver and precious stones. The inhabitants live to an immense age. They have magical, supernatural powers, and they have marvellous technology and powerful weapons.

The Buddhist scripture, *Kalachakra Tantra* - Wheel of Time Teaching, is said to contain a clear record of the history of Shambhala with the names of each king and the date of his accession, and prophecies about future happenings in other countries. The world will become a lurid place of rampant material desire. Peoples will attack each other, and an evil ruler will come to universal power. Then it will be that Shambhala is manifested, and the thirty-second king of Shambhala will lead a great army and overthrow him. This is profoundly believed by the Tibetans, and maintained throughout their lives by the Buddhist lamas who hope that they will finally reach Shambhala. The way is very difficult, and one cannot enter Shambhala without the permission of its guardians.

Present Writers

There are still people looking for Shambhala today. One well-known instance is Charles Allen, whose *In Search of Shangri-La* came out in 1999. Charles Allen went with a BBC film crew far up the Sutlej Valley to Kyunglung in western Tibet. He saw a wide area of ruins to the east of the village, with the remains of small temples and of many stupas among the ravines. Along the cliffs were rows of little caves. He was convinced that these ruins were the site of Kyunglung Ngulkar, the Silver Castle of the Garuda Valley, which he claims to be the capital of the ancient kingdom of Shang-Shung, James Hilton's Shangri-La. He concluded that the name 'Shangri-La' came from 'Shambhala'.

Michael Wood, an acclaimed historian and broadcaster, has presented numerous television documentary series. In his book *In Search of Myths and Heroes*, he ventures in search of four of the world's most popular myths: Shangri-La, the Golden Fleece, the Queen of Sheba, and the Holy Grail. Seemingly, he concentrates on the Tibetan myth of Shambhala and traces the footsteps of Antonio Andrade in the seventeenth century to western Tibet, where he believes the origin of Shangri-La to be. His search was documented and broadcast worldwide. Another successful writer, James Redfield, has the same kind of publication, *The Secret of Shambhala*. His story is set in the mountains of Tibet in search of the mythical Shambhala which, he claims, is also known as Shangri-La.

There are also books in similar titles by Bernard Jensen, Michael McRae, Laurence Brahm and many others, each telling their own accounts of finding Shangri-La.

The Mysterious Symbol

When I visited the Jokhang Temple, I saw a huge phallic symbol inset high on the east wall of the upper floor. When I asked lamas in the temple how it came to be there, they were evasive, and did not tell me anything. I wondered whether the symbol related to what was mentioned by James Hilton.

William Rockhill, Austine Waddell and Perceval Landon wrote special reports[1] on the Jokhang Temple, but nowhere was this symbol mentioned. Where did James Hilton's idea come from?

Hugh Richardson, the Scottish diplomat, was twice posted to Lhasa between 1936 and 1950 and lived there for eight years. In 1972, he published an article, *Phallic Symbols in Tibet*[2], in which he revealed that there was a phallic symbol on the upper floor of the Jokhang Temple, noted and explained in many books of Tibetan history. These books included the fourteenth century *The Clear Mirror of Royal Genealogies* by Sonam rgyal mtshan and the seventeenth century *Chronicle of the Fifth Dalai Lama*.

These ancient texts record how the Jokhang Temple was built: It tells that Princess Wen Cheng was skilled in the art of

---

[1] W. Rockhill, Tibet: a geographical, ethnological and historical sketch derived from Chinese sources. J.R.A.S. 1891 pp. 70-76, 263;
A Waddell: Description of Lhasa Cathedral, translated from Tibetan, 1895;
Perceval Landon: The Jokang in Lhasa, The Times 24th September 1904

[2] Hugh Richardson: Phallic Symbols in Tibet, Bulletin of Tibetology Vol IX No. 2 14th July 1972

divination. She found out that the topography of Tibet was in appearance similar to a female demon lying on her back, and that she recommended that the Temple be built on Lake O-Ma-Thang, which was the position of the demoness's heart, in order to keep her in subjugation. The Princess also found that to the east of Lhasa there was a cave which resembled the private parts of the demoness, emanating evil omen, and had the phallus installed to counteract it.

In Richardson's article, phallus is written as *dbang phyug chen po* in Tibetan. Its Chinese name is 'Da Zi Zai Tian'[1] which refers to Mahesvara or Shiva, the Hindu lord of the universe. Hindus worship Mahesvara as the god of creation and destruction. His symbol is the linga, Sanskrit for phallus, an object of worship.

Apart from the Jokhang Temple, Hugh Richardson also revealed that there was a phallic symbol on the east facing wall of the Dalai Lama's summer palace, the Norbulingka, not obvious but clearly seen nonetheless. Perceval Landon, in his book *Lhasa*, wrote of a symbol that was alien to Tibetan Buddhism on the south-east outer wall of the Norbulingka. This was presumably the same symbol that Richardson described. There is another example on the outside wall of the Gandan Monastery in Lhasa, but I have not found any written mention of it.

In his book *The Riddle of the Tsangpo Gorges*, Kingdon-Ward mentioned that there were many signs of phallic worship in south-east Tibet. On ground outside the villages, wooden phalluses were frequently set up. Beside hunter's cabins in the forest, there were often tree-stumps carved to resemble them. He said that in parts of Bhutan almost every house had a carving of a phallus inside suspended from the roof ridge.

---

[1]   Soothill, Dictionary of Chinese Buddhist Terms, P. 94 and
       Dr. E. J. Eitel, Handbook of Chinese Buddhism, P. 91

I have found that the phallic worship mentioned in Roerich's *Altai-Himalaya* was the closest example to Hilton's description. When Roerich visited the cave temple of Elephanta in India, he found a phallic cult – Lingam, and at the sanctuaries he saw the traces of fresh offerings. Roerich claimed that, in Hinduism, the linga was once 'the vessel of knowledge', but the ancient wisdom had been forgotten, and the basis of this worship had degraded into superstition.

James Hilton wrote:

"Miss Brinklow had been watching for symptoms of pagan degradation. She discovered abundant immoral evidence … and her most imaginative scrutiny of a Buddhist temple revealed only a few items that could be regarded as somewhat doubtfully phallic."

P. 107

In conclusion, the materials for Shangri-La were largely drawn, sometimes obviously sometimes discreetly, sometimes in bulk and sometimes in minor detail, from earlier writers.

The Phallic Symbol of Jokhang Temple

CHAPTER 9

IN SEARCH OF THE BELL

The quest for the Capuchins' bell has become the main focus of my study of Shangri-La. The Latin words of praise, *Te Deum Laudamus*, which were heard in Shangri-La, kept me doggedly searching.

On August 4, 1904, Colonel Younghusband marched with his troops into Lhasa. With him was the Tibetan scholar Colonel Austine Waddell, the Daily Mail correspondent Edmund Candler, the Times correspondent Perceval Landon, the geographer Sir Henry Hayden, and several other adventurers with a good knowledge of Tibet. When they were in Lhasa, they looked everywhere for traces of the church site, but found nothing. However, they found a church bell with a Latin inscription in the Jokhang Temple. They were all sure that this had come from the eighteenth century Capuchin church, but they provided no supporting evidence. After that, western scholars kept reporting that they had found the bell.

When Edmund Candler was in Lhasa, he sought in vain for any trace of the chapel and the hospices built by the Capuchin Mission. In his book *The Unveiling of Lhasa*, he wrote: "The most enlightened Tibetans are ignorant, or pretend to be so, that Christian missionaries have resided in the city. In the Cathedral, however, we found a bell with the inscription *Te Deum Laudamus*, which is probably a relic of the Capuchins." Perceval Landon and Sir Henry Hayden also claimed to have seen the bell in the Jokhang Temple.

240

Sixteen years later, the bell was still there. Sir Charles Bell, a British political officer serving in Lhasa in 1920, claimed that nothing remained of the convent and church. However, he had found a small trace. He wrote in *The Religion of Tibet*: "I used invariably to go into the Holy of Holies, the chapel in which the image of the Buddha – brought to Lhasa in the 7th century – is enshrined. A little passage leads to it. Suspended from the ceiling at the entrance to this passage was a large bell, and on the bell were inscribed the words *Te Deum Laudamus*."

Since then, there have been persistent reports from European travellers of seeing this bell. They include Spencer Chapman, Hugh Richardson and Heinrich Harrer before the middle of the century.

In 1954, two Czechoslovaks, Vladimir Sis and Josef Vanis, visited the Jokhang Temple. When they made their way to a narrow passage leading from the courtyard, they were surprised to see a cast-iron bell hanging over the entrance to the mysterious sanctum and its shape was an unusual one for a Tibetan temple. They wrote: "The faint light at the entrance to the corridor threw into relief the unusual inscription standing out on the rim of the bell … we could easily read the Latin inscription *Te Deum Laudamus*." Astonishingly, the guide told them that the bell had been presented to the Temple by Marco Polo on the occasion of its third rebuilding, and had been hanging there since the late thirteenth century. This must just be a story without foundation. It is widely known that Marco Polo skirted the northern edge of Tibet on his way to China, but there is no evidence that he ever went to Lhasa, and I doubt he had even heard of the Jokhang Temple!

In these accounts, the church bell was hanging in the Jokhang Temple and had been in the same place for a long time. It seems to me that the two Czechoslovaks were probably the last foreigners to see and report the church bell hanging in the little passage. No one seems to know when it was taken down.

In 1976, Father Fulgentius Vannini published *The Bell of Lhasa*, in which the courageous lives of the Capuchin missionaries working in Lhasa in the eighteenth century were carefully recounted. He concluded that the missionaries left the uplands of Tibet a long time ago and nothing now remained to remind a casual traveller of the great missionaries who penetrated the very depths of the forbidden city to preach the good news, and of their toil and sufferings there, except a lonely bell. He wrote: "If it could speak, it would reveal the fate of those poor Christians who were left behind. It is the one solitary witness, over the years, to see the rise and fall of Tibet. It is still there, like a forlorn child, waiting for the return of the loved ones. It will be a serious omission if we forget that bell and all that it exemplifies."

I read with great interest the scholar of Tibet, Professor Wu Kunming's book *Zaoqi Chuanjiaoshi jin Zang Huodongshi 1992* on the history of early missionaries in Tibet. Professor Wu told of their achievements and he provided and translated much supporting historical material. He told in particular the story of their work in Lhasa for thirty-eight years until its conclusion in 1745, how the church was destroyed, with only a bell with a Latin inscription, hung in the Jokhang Temple, surviving.

Professor Wu was seemingly inspired by Vannini's book. He was probably the only Chinese scholar who mentioned the bell, but he had never seen the bell nor the photograph of it. He had tried hard to find out where the bell was, but without any real results. When he was writing his book, he had always wanted to include a photograph of the bell in it. When one of his colleagues was going to Tibet in 1990, he asked him to find the bell in the Jokhang Temple, but he came back without success. In 1991, again, he asked his friends, directors of the Tibetan Research Institution, if they would look for the bell and take photographs of it. They were keen to trace the bell. A research team was organized and a journalist photographer was there. With help from the staff of the Jokhang, they searched exhaustively at the Temple, in the main chamber, on the roofs and everywhere else, but were unable to find the bell. The Chairman of the Management Committee, Lama Tudan told them that westerners had come for a time to look for the ancient bell, but without any success, and it had probably been lost during the Cultural Revolution.

Father Vannini and Professor Wu never saw the bell themselves, and Father Vannini had probably made a mistake when he claimed that the Latin words *Te Deum Laudamus* were around the base of the bell. But neither of them realized that Vladimir Sis and Josef Vanis in 1954 had taken pictures of the bell and published them. The bell was then lost until 1994, when an Italian found it again in the Jokhang Temple. I am not sure whether Professor Wu knew this before he died in 2006.

RETURN TO THE JOKHANG TEMPLE

"'Finished your dreams yet?" Lin asked.

"I'm awake now!"

"Then you won't need to go to Tibet again?"

"I want to go back."

"What? You are nuts!" she said.

"It's that church bell."

"I thought you had found it."

"I want to find the real one." I was determined.

"I see you're too late for help!"

What could I say?

Preparing for the Visit

On 9 October 2006, I was in Lhasa again. Before I set off on my journey, I had requested assistance from the Chinese Consulate in Edinburgh, and through the help of the Department of Foreign Affairs in Beijing it had been arranged for someone to meet me at the Jokhang Temple.

All went to plan, and I arrived punctually at the Temple entrance. An official from the Division of Local Foreign Affairs and the head guide at the Jokhang Temple met me, and after we had exchanged greetings, they took me round the Temple on a standard tour. This was certainly not what I wanted to see. When we came to the familiar dark corridor which led to the main sanctum, I saw the Tibetan bell still hanging from the beam as I had seen it before. I was beginning to run out of hope. I was anxious not to lose time, and asked the guide without delay about the church bell. He was puzzled at first, and I took out photographs of it for him to see. He thought for a little, wrinkled his brow, and then said a bit vaguely, "Yes! I have seen this bell. It belonged to missionaries, didn't it?"

When he spoke like that, I had hope again, and felt pleased that I had found the right way forward. He seemed well-informed about the objects in the Temple. "That's right!" he went on, "that bell used to hang here."

"Where is it now?"

"I don't know."

I explained to him that the reason for my coming all this way to Lhasa was to look for this bell. I would be very grateful if he could help to locate it. When I continued to press my request, he reluctantly reached for his mobile, dialled and spoke for a few minutes in Tibetan. Then he said, "I was speaking to the High Lama, and he confirmed that that bell is now kept in the storeroom for cultural property."

"Is that definite?" I still felt a little sceptical.

"Yes, it is. The High Lama says that that bell has a European inscription. It must be the one."

"Could I just have a quick look?" I asked. "A glimpse would be good enough for me."

"No, you cannot! Absolutely not!" he answered. "The storeroom requires three keys to open it, each held by a high lama. Visitors may only visit with the permission of the Cultural Property Bureau."

I could only accept this. I had phoned the director of the Division of Local Foreign Affairs to ask for his help, but his answer was the same. I had also made several calls back to the Edinburgh Consulate, but they were not able to help me at such short notice. I lost hope and was very disappointed. They were very sympathetic, but there was nothing that they could do to help.

I stood hesitant and paced about outside the Administrative office of the Temple on the upper floor. There were very few tourists. It was drizzling and the air was cold, and loneliness was welling up inside me. I felt a little abstracted. Suddenly, it was so quiet around me. I didn't seem to hear any noise at all, neither the sounds of visitors, nor the chanting of scriptures by the faithful.

But I seemed to have heard the muffled sound of the bell. It was calling me, appealing to me. I could sense that it was there, and the sense grew stronger and stronger, my instinct telling me that the bell was only feet away, waiting mute in a dark corner. I looked at the locked office door, and felt that that abandoned child was in there behind it. I told myself that the day would come when I would rescue the little child from the darkness and let it see the light and tell its story again, so that everyone could see its splendour and remember the hard endeavours of those fathers.

At this moment, however, I could really do nothing, but could only look to the future, and hope that a miracle might happen. Slowly my eyes became warm and moist, and rain mingled with tears ran down off my nose. Daylight was fading, and with great reluctance I left the Jokhang Temple.

IN SEARCH OF THE CHURCH

During the three days that I was in Lhasa, I rushed here and there trying to find traces of the Capuchin church, with the outcome that one might imagine.

The first person to reveal the location of the Capuchin church was probably Father Graham Sandberg in his book *The Exploration of Tibet* published in 1904. He based his enquiry on the diaries of the Capuchin Father Cassiano Beligatti, a contemporary of Father Francesco Orazio, who described in detail the purchase of the piece of land and the building of the church. This was at a place called Sha-chen Na-ga, near Meru Temple, but unfortunately Father Beligatti did not give the precise location.

Austine Waddell also mentioned Sha-chen Na-ga. He claimed that the church was built near the Ramoche Temple which is in the north of Lhasa. This does not seem to fit the records left by Father Beligatti.

Sha-chen Na-ga is translated from the Tibetan ཤར་ཆུད་ན་ཁ. I have consulted many Tibetans about this and I was given the same answer. Sha-chen ཤར means 'east,' and Na-ga ཆུད་ན་ཁ means 'wet grassland'. It is a piece of wet grassland in the east. This may not be the specific name of a place.

When Perceval Landon was in Lhasa, he found that to the north of the Jokhang Temple was an immense area of swamp and ruin, and beyond this was the location of the Meru Temple. Landon asserted that the temple had been built over the site of the old Christian chapel. Unfortunately, no vestige remained.

Landon's claim was supported by Sir Henry Hayden. I think this is very unlikely. Father Beligatti in his notes stated clearly that the Meru Temple already existed before the church was built.

According to the information that the Capuchins left, the church was built on a piece of land which was a square of 12 *colonen* each side, worked out to be just over 4,000 square metres. If Sandberg is correct in giving this figure, it was a sizable piece of ground, and if still intact would be easy to find. However, modern east Lhasa is crammed with housing, new and old, and it is hard to find any empty space. The streets are narrow, and sometimes far from sanitary. I explored through streets and lanes, and carefully examined several old buildings, their appearance and structure, but without finding any trace of church or convent.

There is very little information indeed about what Lhasa looked like before the twentieth century. Perhaps the earliest surviving photograph of Lhasa was taken by Tsybikoff in 1900, showing the Pargo Kaling stupa at the western gate of the city.

Following the British expedition to Lhasa in 1904, many books were published and photographs taken over the next fifty years. One can see, in half a century, that there was little change in the appearance of Lhasa. From the descriptions of Thomas Manning in 1811 and of Edmund Candler in 1904, Lhasa and probably the whole of Tibet appear to have developed extremely slowly, if at all, and I suppose that Lhasa looked much the same in the middle of the eighteenth century.

In 1878, the Indian explorer Krishna Singh drew what must be one of the earliest maps of Lhasa, and then Sandberg, Waddell and Landon all included maps in their books. Waddell's is probably the clearest and most detailed.

If the Jokhang Temple is taken as the heart of the city, to the north were lakes and water channels and marshland extending to the north-east corner where the Meru Temple stands. Near Lingkor Road, there was a saddlery and harness bazaar; to the south-east, a sky burial ground and an area where beggars and ragyabas lived; to the east, the residential Bana-shol district, with a horse and grass market, a tannery, meat market, Chinese herbal shop and many restaurants. Sandberg said that there was a famous establishment called '*Ani Sa-khang*' or the 'nuns' eating house' which could accommodate two hundred people. Poorer people and monks, locals and visitors, would congregate there every day for meals and social activities, but today it has disappeared. Could that be on the site of the church, or near it? It is hard to judge.

Over busy Beijing East Road is the ancient Meru Temple. At the front are two wooden pillars, their paint almost worn away. It does not seem to have had any repairs done in years, and looks sadly run down. I was surprised to find no lama in the courtyard and I saw many of its rooms were occupied by ordinary citizens. It looked squalid and untidy. Tourists were not seen here, and the prospects for the temple did not seem bright.

If the Capuchin church was built on marshy ground in east Lhasa, and if it was near the Meru Temple, then I would suggest that the site of today's Bana-shol Hostel is a likely place. Waddell's map shows that this was previously a big grassy expanse where a stupa stood. Many traders from Naqu used to put up tents here and hold a market. Their tents were made of

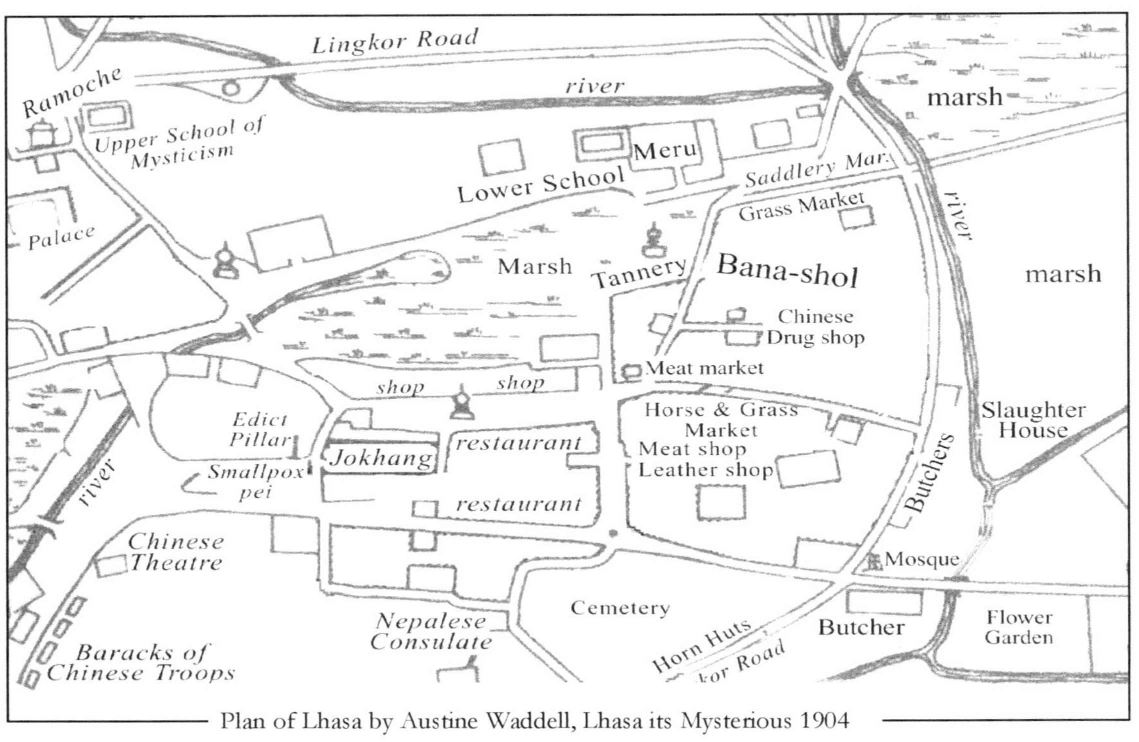

Lingkor Road
river
marsh
Ramoche
Upper School of Mysticism
Meru
marsh
Lower School
Saddlery Mar:
Grass Market
Palace
Marsh
Tannery
Bana-shol
Chinese Drug shop
marsh
Meat market
Slaughter House
shop
shop
Edict Pillar
Jokhang
restaurant
Horse & Grass Market
Meat shop
Leather shop
Butchers
river
Smallpox pei
restaurant
Mosque
Chinese Theatre
Nepalese Consulate
Cemetery
Hom Huts
kor Road
Butcher
Flower Garden
Baracks of Chinese Troops
Plan of Lhasa by Austine Waddell, Lhasa its Mysterious 1904

black yak-hide, and the place was known as *Bana* in Tibetan, meaning 'black tents'. When the hostel was built, it was called the *Bana-shol*.

I have studied carefully the location of Bana-shol Hostel and its surroundings, but there was no trace of the Capuchin church at all. The search for the church site has been attempted by many western explorers, but there is too little information to go by, and they have not been successful. It is almost certain that the site is at the east side near the Meru Temple. Perhaps with further research undertaken by Tibetan scholars, the truth will be forthcoming.

A Memorable Shadow

On the last day in Lhasa, I was sitting in my usual place outside the entrance of Jokhang under the high wall behind which were the old tablets and the poplar tree, watching the pilgrims incessantly prostrating themselves up and down, and people streaming along in front of me.

This time in Lhasa, I had not forgotten Padma. I was always watching out for her. I tended to pay more attention to girls with veiled faces, watching their movements and appearance, but there was no sign of her. I stared blankly at the light flashing from the golden wheel on the Temple roof, and when I felt tired, I simply closed my eyes and listened to the sounds round about. At this moment, I seemed to hear the friendly summons again, 'dang … dang … dang!'

Suddenly, I heard someone say, "Excuse me, sir, I've hurt my finger. Could you give me a plaster?"

I started. My first thought was that it was Padma. When I looked up, I saw a veiled Tibetan girl standing in front of me, but as her back was to the light, I could not see her face clearly. "Of course I will! But you are …?" I wondered, and questioned.

"I'm sorry for disturbing you. Are you alright?"

"No, no, not at all, sorry I was miles away." I asked her to sit down, and took a plaster out of my bag. Her finger was bleeding, and I did not ask her what had happened, but tore open the wrapping and put it on the cut. It seemed that I was repeating the same thing once more. I was observing her all the time. But she kept her head down and seemed to be avoiding my gaze.

"Where have you come from?"

"Somewhere far, far away.'

"What is it called?"

"A little valley, it doesn't have a name."

"Really!" Her words really struck in my heart. 'A little valley' recalled my memory of Tserin, Amu, and of course Padma. I gazed at her, but no more than a pair of eyes could I see. "Do you know Padma or High Lama Dazhi?" I asked.

Our eyes locked for an instant and then she turned away. She did not answer me and just shook her head.

"May I take a photo of you?"

She did not answer my request either. I supposed that she had no objection. Then I held up my camera at her, but she slightly turned her face away. I noticed in her eyes how strangely dull her expression was.

"Thank you, sir, I must be going. You take care, Zhaxi-dele!" She placed her hands together.

"You take care too, goodbye, Zhaxi-dele." I kept my eyes fixed on her as she slowly receded. I longed for her to look back and say 'goodbye' again. I was waiting, hoping. A cold gust of wind struck my face as it passed, and I shivered. When I was composed again, she had already disappeared in the crowds.

At half past six, the golden roofs of the Jokhang Temple were especially brilliant in the low sun. Black smoke was pouring from the incense stoves in front of the temple and the air was rich with the smell of juniper leaves. It was slowly getting dark, the pilgrims and visitors were leaving and the traders were packing up. Barkor

Street was gradually quietening down, and it was with heavy steps that I walked slowly back to the hostel.

Tomorrow, I would be leaving Lhasa, and did not know when I would return. I could only wish the 'Bell of Shangri-La' safe keeping in the Jokhang Temple, and hope that someday very soon it would be seen again, for all to admire; and wish Padma and the people of the valley happiness for ever.

> *"Lost in reveries about this mysterious land,*
> *ridiculously sentimental,*
> *I find my temples turning grey too soon.*
> *Oh life is just like a dream,*
> *I sang quietly to the moon."*

PURSUING THE BELL IN ITALY

"Did you find your bell?" Lin asked.

"No, I didn't!" I couldn't really say anything else.

"I found a bell."

"What bell?" I didn't take it seriously.

"One with the Latin words, *Te Deum Laudamus.*"

"What? Where?" I asked eagerly.

"In Italy."

"Ha ha!" I didn't give it a thought. She must be teasing.

"I really did, in a little town called Pennabilli."

"What? Pennabilli! That's where the Capuchin Father Orazio was born. How did you find that out?" I was suddenly full of excitement.

"There was a news report that on 30 July 2005 the Dalai Lama went to a little town in Italy to inaugurate the Bell of Lhasa," she said.

"Really!" I exclaimed.

"Not quite, it's only a copy, but it was cast from a mould of the original. It's its twin!"

I could not take it in. "What is the news all about?"

My wife quietly handed me a printout that she had made of a news report from Italy. It started with the introduction of Father Vannini's book which gave a brief account of the story of the Capuchin missionaries in Lhasa and of the church bell that they had left there. In 1994, an Italian had gone to Lhasa to look for the bell, and he had found it in a storeroom in the Jokhang Temple. He took photographs of it, and he also recorded its chime. Ten years passed, and in August 2004, a professor of the University of Bologna went to the Jokhang Temple, and once again the bell was brought out from storage. He took many photographs of it and recorded its detailed dimensions, and when he came back to Italy, a mould was made and a bell was cast. He installed it on a little hill behind Francesco Orazio's birthplace. What is more, the 14th Dalai Lama was invited there to inaugurate the bell. This was big news in the local press.

When I had read this, I thought for a while, and then said to Lin with a smile, "Next week I have a four day Easter break."

"You're not saying that you want to go to look for that bell, are you?" she asked.

"Wouldn't you like a trip to Italy?"

"Okay!" In making decisions, Lin is more forceful than I am. She at once sat down at the computer to book air tickets; Holly was busily looking for accommodation and car hire for us both, and she found us a map of the road to Pennabilli. It was certainly a remote place, with no public transport, let alone an airport.

On April 4, we flew from Glasgow to Pisa, then by bus to Florence. It was a chance to see this wonderful city which is famous as the birthplace of the great genius Leonardo da Vinci. He appeared to be the emblem of Florence, and everyone seemed to be talking about him.

The atmosphere of Florence is saturated in art, with museums, galleries, monasteries, old buildings and statues all over the place. Tourism is the cornerstone of the economy of Florence. Hotel, restaurant and pub businesses have flourished in every corner of the city. There seemed to be more tourists than Florentines in the streets. It is a thriving city.

In Florence, the Uffizi Gallery is a must for any tourist who wants to make the most of their visit. We did not want to miss our chance. The Gallery opens at eight-thirty, and we were there half an hour early. There was already a queue of around two hundred people, and fifteen minutes later, there were another three hundred behind us. The staff say that every day is the same. After touring round the Gallery, we thought though that the visit was worthwhile, as we saw paintings by Michelangelo and Leonardo da Vinci, and many other great artists.

Pennabilli is about a hundred and fifty kilometres to the east of Florence. After making an enquiry at the tourist information office, we found that there was no public transport from Florence to the little town. With no alternative, we decided to hire a small car to make our journey there. It was quite expensive at one hundred and thirty euros for a day.

The weather was good, and the scenery radiant. Apart from one stretch of motorway, most of the way was on twisting mountain roads. Used to a driving seat on the right-hand side and suddenly sitting on the left, I did not find the driving easy and had to go far slower than usual for safety. It was not very far, but it took us four hours, with a short break halfway, and we finally arrived in Pennabilli at half past twelve. For the Easter holiday weekend, Pennabilli seemed very quiet. Other than ourselves, there seemed to be no other visitors, and just a few local people ambling down the street. In Florence, I had not found many English speakers, and here none at all.

Pennabilli

We only had a street map downloaded from the internet to go by. It was said that the bell was hung on a hilltop, and we could only start to climb, past a garden behind a big old farm house, and following a path up a small hill. There was a great cross at the summit, and remains of some decayed buildings, but not the church bell that we were looking for.

From the top of the hill, there were wide views in every direction, and in the distance on the mountains there were still some white patches of snow. On the fresh green slopes were many new houses, and round the small hill were traditional buildings. About eight hundred metres away from us, on another hilltop, I could make out two tall poles, with different coloured pennants fluttering in the wind. As I looked carefully, it did not take me long to recognize that these were what I had seen many times, the colourful Tibetan prayer flags.

"It's over there!" I cried out confidently.

Pennabilli

She looked where I was pointing, and understood. She took some quick photographs of the flags in the distance, and at once followed me down the hill towards the next. We made our way through little alleys among the houses. It was strange that we saw nobody, and just heard some dogs barking. Slowly the flags were coming into sight, closer and closer. At the top of a flight of steps, there was a stone inscribed in Italian, '*La Campana di Lhasa*' meaning 'The Bell of Lhasa'. In front of us was a carpet of green grass freckled with yellow flowers, and the two poles, and between them was the church bell. I felt nervous, and went forward slowly with my eyes fixed on the bell, camera clutched in my hand, with Lin behind me continually taking photographs.

I stood there in front of the bell frame, looking up and down at it, and taking many photographs from different angles. Looking at the bell, I thought of the Capuchins, who had gone to such immense pains to take such an object to Lhasa. Though it was a copy, it could still be seen as the true appearance of the Bell of Lhasa. On it were the clear Latin words '*TE DEVM LAVDAMVS TE DOMINVM*'. It was stupid of me to forget to bring a tape measure, and I found a dry grass stalk to do instead. I took down the details to allow me to work it out again when I got home: the diameter at the mouth was 43 centimetres and the height was about 32 centimetres; I estimated the weight at around 40 kilograms.

The church bell and three Tibetan *mani* wheels were in a row fixed to an iron frame. Two poles rose high into the air, and on their tops were bundles of bamboo leaves, dried out and yellow but still in place. The pennants with five colours swayed in the wind, subtly, corresponding to the cross on the other hilltop. It looked a little incongruous, but I felt that there was a sense of tolerance and mutual respect between different religions.

Lin asked many questions about the history of the bell, and I gladly told her everything I knew.

"What is the connection for you between this church bell and Shangri-La?"

"It was these words *Te Deum Laudamus*." I pointed to the Latin inscription. "They could be heard in Shangri-la."

There was nobody else around. I could not resist pulling the bell's clapper, Dang ...! I quietly listened to the clear sound reverberating in the calm air. My heart seemed to be carried away with it, and I thought of its older brother, still patiently waiting in a dark corner, waiting to be rescued and to see the light again. Then, it would be so wonderful for the two bells to ring out together at different sides of the world.

We sat together on the grass for a long while gazing. Our goal had been realized. Slowly we gathered everything together and started to go home. Before we left, we stopped for a little rest in a café. With a little difficulty, we managed to order the two cups of cappuccino we wanted. We tried to ask about the Capuchin Father Orazio, but because of the language barrier we did not have any success. All the same, our journey had not been in vain. It was more than four hours to Florence, and we could not dawdle any longer. We had a quick look round and left.

The Easter holiday was quickly over. Back home, I sat again on the sofa writing, thinking all the time about our wonderful journey, and still feeling a bit of excitement. When I thought of the happy moment I saw the bell, the exhilaration returned.

"How is your book coming on?" Lin asked.

"It's time now for the conclusion."

"Do you need to go anywhere else for your research?"

"No, it's enough! I feel tired, really." I drew out the words slowly. At this point, I knew that it was now enough.

EPILOGUE

'The Lost Horizon' came out in 1933, a pocket sized novel of just over two hundred and thirty pages. It was not beautifully printed, but quickly became a best seller. It was subsequently adapted for the stage and made into a film. 'Shangri-La' attracted much attention and became known all over the world. James Hilton must have been surprised himself. He made up the attractive name which is generally regarded as a 'paradise', and for the Chinese it is the early scholar, Tao Yuanming's, *Peach Blossom Garden*, a utopia untouched by civilization. Shangri-La has become a place of universal aspiration.

James Hilton was born in 1900 in Lancashire into a family with a good educational background. His father was a headmaster and his mother a teacher. In 1921, he graduated from Christ's College Cambridge, the same college as Frank Kingdon-Ward. He worked as a writer, and was a theatre critic for the Daily Mail; his ambition was to be a successful novelist. When he was fourteen, the First World War broke out. Industry in Great Britain suffered terrible losses for at least the next two decades. The whole economy declined with persistent high unemployment, and the standard of living was low. In the worst of times, Hilton created a mystery, a paradise in the East. It became a good topic for readers to enjoy and reminisce about. It was intriguing that Hilton had never revealed the secret of Shangri-La before he died in 1955.

Ever since the story appeared, the searching for Shangri-La has gone on and on. Many have braved hardship to look for it in Central Asia, Kashmir, Nepal and India, and it was only from 1993 when Tibet was opened for travellers that more and more people began to explore the Tibetan Plateau that Hilton mentioned in his book on several occasions. By the end of last century, many claimed to have found the paradise, writing books to establish their case and competing to reveal their secrets. The presentation may be attractive, but the accounts conflict.

While I was writing the book, I was always aware of news about Shangri-La. I would feel nervous whenever I noticed a new book or article appearing. But when I read that they were preoccupied with beautiful scenery and lamaseries, I immediately felt great relief. Recently there was a report, 'The Great Riddle: Shangri-La not in China', by a Chinese explorer who had spent ten years to prove that Shangri-La is in Ladakh. I regret that I have still not yet had the chance to read his arguments, but I am not sure if it would be necessary.

My interest was caught by an article ten years ago, and I began my long journey to search for Shangri-La. In my understanding from reading the story of *The Lost Horizon*, I find that Shangri-La is by no means a paradise, but a place with a peaceful and harmonious society. There seems to be some degree of exaggeration of this heavenly place. However, the mystery of its location could well inspire those indomitable dream searchers to go after it.

In 1997, Yunnan Provincial Government announced that Shangri-La was in Diqing Autonomous Region, and in December 2001 Zhongdian County changed its name to 'Shangri-La County'. The authority has greatly developed tourism, building an airport, new roads, hotels, and of course places of entertainment, and more and more visitors are being drawn there by the name. In the year 2006, there were well over three million visitors to Diqing, three hundred thousand of them from abroad. No one would disagree that tourism on this scale is an impressive result. Lijiang and Yading in Sichuan did not wish to be left out, and they both claimed to have found evidence of Shangri-La.

Then suddenly there came a designation of 'The Greater Shangri-La' district, apparently comprising parts of Yunnan, Sichuan and Tibet, an area extending from western Kham in the east to Linzhi in Tibet in the west, Lijiang in the south to Shiqu in the north. This large area may not be correct, but hopefully it should not be too far away, and there will be an equitable share in the returns. The claimant for this is being considerate and it is certainly imaginative. Other countries bordering Tibet are also laying out their claims, and hoping for their part in the Shangri-La feast. James Hilton could not have imagined that his Shangri-La could become multinational territory.

It seems strange that among all the voices being raised for Shangri-La, that of Lhasa is not much heard. No one has yet put in a word for Lhasa, perhaps a case of the most obvious being the hardest to spot. If someone asks me, I will confidently reply: "Shangri-La is no doubt in Tibet, and it is centred on Lhasa. James Hilton fused the history of the valiant Capuchin missionaries in Lhasa with the culture and the geography of Tibet, and added much material taken from nineteenth and twentieth century explorers' writings, together with his own imagination, to create the story of Shangri-La."

Though my discovery of the mystery may not please or satisfy everybody, and might even have a negative effect on some tourism development projects in China or in the other countries, yet it may play a part in disclosing the story, and reduce reckless and poorly managed development with its heavy toll on the environment. Since Lijiang was brought to people's attention, it has been reported that so many tourists have been riding the new cable car up Mt Yulong that the glacier is being damaged and part of it is now starting to melt; the vegetation is being badly trampled; wild animals gradually disappearing; and the ecology seriously affected. But it is not just Lijiang! We are intimately linked to nature, and if our natural surroundings are damaged, we ourselves will suffer eventually.

Through the promotion of the tourism industry, many people believe that they have been to Shangri-La, and many others are still looking for it. Friends of mine have purchased a little house in a remote village. Every day they can enjoy fresh milk, eggs and green vegetables available from their own farm. They pursue their own interests, and lead a full and happy life. At their gate is a sign 'Shangri-La'. I have not yet found my Shangri-La, but it will not be somewhere that you can reach sitting in a comfortable coach. It will be somewhere away from obtrusive noise; without the nuisance of red tape; somewhere without conflict or cheating; with honest, friendly faces around me; a place of mutual tolerance and respect. The location of Shangri-La itself is unimportant, what matters is the spirit of it, 'Tian Di Ren He : Heaven Earth People in Harmony'. Without these it is just a name.

In 1955, the Russian traveller Peter Goullart wrote in his book *Forgotten Kingdom*: "To me Lijiang was paradise. Here there were no hotels, no cinemas, few bodily comforts, no funicular to the top of Mount Satseto and no natives to perform for a tourist's fee, just the friendship and trust of the simple and honest people among whom I lived."

Goullart concluded: *I had always dreamed of finding, and living in that beautiful place, shut off from the world by its great mountains, which years later James Hilton conceived in his novel 'The Lost Horizon'. His hero found 'Shangri-La' by accident. I found mine, by design and perseverance, in Lijiang.*

For me, it was both: for it was by accident and by design and perseverance that I unveiled the secret of Shangri-La.

亂假成真真亦假
形虛作實實則虛

*"When the false passes for true, the true is false.
When nothing has a place, the place is nowhere."*

Milton Keynes UK
Ingram Content Group UK Ltd.
UKHW022002300823
427775UK00012B/1178